SECRETS

An Instruction In Esoteric Rune Wisdom

ᚠ ᚢ ᚦ ᚨ ᚱ ᚲ ᚷ ᚹ
ᚺ ᚾ ᛁ ᛋ ᛃ ᛈ ᛇ ᛉ
ᛏ ᛒ ᛗ ᛖ ᛚ ᛜ ᛞ ᛝ

Vincent Ongkowidjojo

Published by
Mandrake of Oxford
PO Box 250
OXFORD
OX1 1AP (UK)

Acknowledgements

Jonas Jatidjan for the illustrations and
Wouter Lismont for author photograph.

Contents

```
            A
   A        S        A
            A
```

ODIN

Your horse I ride, High One of Asgard

You bring me the flower of your blooming wisdom

I listen to your songs of lingering might

My gift to you, Odin, is this garden of words

My gift to you, Odin, is the oath that you bound me with

Seekers of wisdom, sit down and drink

Sail together the waves of Wish-granter's son

The rocks of Bragi are brightly stained

Valkyries and heroes will hallow the lore-stead

Valkyries and heroes will harness the truth

Deep in the well the warder is hid

Loud though is heard his harkening speech

Mimir awakens the warriors to rise

Dive all in the well

Rise all as you will

Foreword
by Freya Aswynn

It is with great pleasure that I introduce this extraordinary book. A work of scholarship and intuition Vincent digs deep in the Well. The first part of the book is taken up with a discussion about the origins of Runes and the Celtic connection, very interesting.

Secrets of Asgard is aptly named as in this book Vincent forges new connections with Runes to reveal a multidimensional web of correspondences between other schools of thought partaking of the perennial Wisdom Tradition. Expanding the Runic meanings and offering a deeper layer of Rune might than ever before.

Like me, this author's native language is Flemish/Dutch and so plugging into the unconscious more linguistic aspects are uncovered and discussed proving fascinating new insights into the Runes: lots and lots of new stuff, subtle seemingly little things so small that no one me included actually took the time to look at!

Vincent brings in a lot more of the natural world, as in his section on Berkana. It is clear that this monumental Work contains a wealth of scholarship as well as insights especially in the practical applications of Runes.

Vincent interprets the 3 aettir in a sociological context according to Dumezil, however he allows for evolution from thrall to Jarl within an initiatic concept; he also recognized a correspondence with the astrological crosses, something I had overlooked, I can honestly say that Vincent has taken the whole kit and caboodle to a new level.

Correlations with the writings of Alice Bailey are discovered and discussed. This book will appeal to Runesters and Heathens who cultivate an open mind and wish to go beyond religion into the Initiatic Mysteries of the Runes and the Gods.

About the Gods as well as their Runes, Vincent offers some very interesting differing and sometime radically opposing views to my own, solidly backed up by an alternative look, lore and his own intuition. Invocations and instructions for successful Rune magick are a large and rich resource. This book has something for everyone, sound lore and deep magick. This excellent work shows a deep and powerful occult current as well as keeping true to the tradition. Fine scholarship and impeccable integrity breathe through this work.

May it open many doors in the minds of those who wish to explore beneath and beyond exoteric heathenry.

Freya Aswynn

Preface by David Beth

Northern Gnosis and the Pathway of the Soul

Mistral wind, chaser of clouds,

Killer of gloom, sweeper of the skies,

Raging storm-wind, how I love thee!

Are we not both the first-fruits

Of the same womb, forever predestined

To the same fate?

Friedrich Nietzsche

When great German philosopher Friedrich Nietzsche announced the Death of God he was not, as has often been falsely believed, supporting a bleak nihilism but on the contrary pointing towards an alternative to this threatening void. Nietzsche's vision of a counter current against the degeneration of times was personified in his majestic and terrifying *Uebermensch*. This 'overman' has been largely characterized as 'Dionysian' in nature, representing the principle of darkness, irrationality, the collapse of order and transgression of boundaries. While Nietzsche understands the place and value of the 'Apollonian', the principle of light, rationality, order and clear boundaries, it is the resurrection of the Dionysian elements buried for too long in Western man that will allow the *Uebermensch* to rise above the herd mentality; to see oneself as part of a whole versus the notion of an individual as separate from other realities, passion and dynamics versus reason, rational and dispassion.

The realization of his Dionysian nature and its proper use are a key to the manifestation of the awesome powers of this God-Man. What Nietzsche calls Dionysian however can also easily be called Wotanic or Odinic. It was, amongst others, Carl Jung in his essay 'Wotan'[1] who has pointed out the close resemblance of the figures of Zarathustra and Dionysus in Nietzsche's work with the wild huntsman Wotan.[2] It is thus the identification of the initiate with the God Wotan | Odin and his principles which ultimately defines the *Uebermensch* as the perfected cosmic ideal.

With this in mind, the introductory quote taken from Friedrich Nietzsche´s haunting poem 'An den Mistral'[3] can be easily appreciated as an invocational adoration to Wotan. Understanding it this way reveals important secrets that may point the seeker of knowledge to some of the most fundamental mysteries of Northern and Rune Gnosis. A deep, Gnostic embrace and symbiosis with the Gods of the Germanic world and the awesome powers behind the Runes is only possible for a practitioner who feels a distinct vocational calling from the pleromic center of the divine realms.

This unmistakable voice of the Gods to a true shamanic priesthood however can only be heard by the kosmic Man. The kosmic man possesses a distinctive and rare quality of the soul necessary to make contact on the inner planes with the spiritual energies of the Northern Gnosis. His soul will be able to function as an Instrumentum Magicum making it possible for the initiate to experience the mystery of the *Rausch*, the ecstatic rush and trance. Only through this *extasis* of the soul and the subsequent freedom from the tyranny of the rational, mechanical and analyzing spirit are the gateways opened which lead to the daemonic, esoteric reality of the Germanic universe. Everything that exists in the kosmos is *beseelt*, has a soul, and together forms the soul of the world. The spiritually prepared soul of a magical practitioner can connect with every living, daemonic aspect of the universe, become empowered by it and receive its secrets.

Equating Wotan with the 'raging storm wind', the 'chaser of clouds' and the 'killer of gloom' leads us towards the true nature of not only *Allvater* Wotan but of all the Gods of the Northern pantheon: They are deeply chthonic Beings who draw parts of their might from the living essence of the kosmos. They impact on us as powerful rays from depths of the World-All, their most intense forms coming from the Plutonian and trans-Plutonian regions of space. To unleash their true potentials however, these God-rays must connect and unite with symbiotic poles within the esoteric organism of the initiate. Through the soul as activated magical instrument, the shaman is able to undertake magical journeys into the darkest and most primordial spaces of the inner universe. Within this shadow universe we find an unlimited number of Gods, spirits, daemons and esoteric vampires. They become fully alive when the outer God rays unite with these dark Gods of the inner cosmos in a magical Hieros Gamos creating a Gnostic syzygy.

The Fraternitas Borealis, working within a Northern Gnostic framework, teaches that the soul essence is to be found mainly in the blood. The aim of the Northern sorcerer must be the activation of the soul essence within the blood, the manifestation of the *Blutleuchte,* the blood lamp or blood glow. It is the practical work with the runic mysteries that greatly aides in the empowering of the soul and the subsequent ignition of the blood-lamp resulting in the ecstatic union of initiatic Man and God in the Nietzschean ideal of the *Uebermensch.*

'How I love thee' proclaims Nietzsche in the climax of invocational, erotic passion for the Wild Hunter. The love he embraces however is not profane passion or eros but the mystical Cosmogonic Eros which explodes within the initiate when God and Man become One in a moment of supreme Gnosis. What results is not only the spiritual empowerment by God-energy but a deifying realization that Nietzsche carved into a rhetorical question: 'Are we not both the first-fruits of the same womb, forever predestined to the same fate?' The awakened initiate suddenly knows and understands with the 'mind of his heart' that he and his God(s) are divine twins, both the first fruits of the same womb. The soul-womb gave birth to the Gods as well as the true divine nature of Man and through the magical Hieros Gamos they have been joined again manifesting in supreme deified identity. Man and God, who are now one, are indeed 'predestined to the same fate' as the body of the initiate has been spiritually turned into the supreme body of the genius of Wotan of whom all other Gods are but aspects. Resurrected in his Wotanic body the

Northern Gnostic now becomes the true master of his path and exists outside the Fate of Norns.

David Beth

Author of *Voudon Gnosis*

Head of the *Fraternitas Borealis*

Hierophant of the *Société Voudon Gnostique*

1. Carl Gustav Jung, Wotan, Neue Schweizer Rundschau (Zurich). n.s., III (March, 1936), p. 657-69
2. Wotan, Woden, Wodan, Odin are different names for the same God depending on language area
3. Transl. 'To the Mistral'

Introduction

Since the revival of the Old Religion many seekers have felt their way into the bygone traditions of their ancestors. Ancient mysteries again open their gates and we now live in an era of growing spiritual awareness and liberation. Never has the Bond been broken. Through the collective consciousness and the gene pool we are still connected with the traditions of our forebears. Through our very souls we are always in touch with reality behind the veils. The Old Gods call upon us. And many of us hear their prayers.

Yet, belief in the Old Gods is still frowned upon in our society, because the schism between the material and the spiritual way of life has become so pronounced. Even so, mankind as a whole has much evolved on a level of consciousness; so much so that I have confidence that the existence of deities will be generally accepted within a few generations. Until then we might consider them as psychological concepts. They are the living Archetypes of the collective subconscious that binds us all.

The Runes reflect those archetypal energies that stand behind the mechanisms of daily life. They are expressions of spiritual living – and as principles of unseen forces are sensed and recognized by many. As such, they form an integral part of the Path of the North, or the Northern tradition. It is a path equal to any other, such as Yoga and Taiji of the East, and Wicca and Kabbalah of the West. Each individual resonates more with one tradition than another, but all of them lead to self-realization and an expansion of consciousness.

The Runic system offers such an opportunity to anyone who feels connected to the Germanic group soul. Although this tradition has sprung in Northern Europe, this path is open to all races and temperaments. How many Westerners do not engage in Yoga? How many non-Jews do not study the Kabbalah? To all those who sincerely intend to take up the Runes this book opens the way to Asgard and the Well of Mimir.

1

THROUGH NIFLHEIM'S MISTS PERCEIVED

The Runes have been passed on as a system of writing. But the Rune alphabet is also a magical alphabet. The idea to create a native alphabet was built on an indigenous mystery tradition although it may have sparked from relations with the Greco-Roman world.

The oldest Rune find dates from the early second half of the second century: a bone comb carries the inscription **harja** 'warrior'. A possible older find dates from the first century. We therefore assume that the Rune alphabet already existed in its entirety at that time. It is termed Futhark, after the first six characters of the Rune row. The language represented is Ancient Germanic.

Pax Mundi

We believe the first Runes to be designed by Germanic people, but the historical origin of the Futhark remains uncertain, aptly veiled in the mists of antiquity. Most likely the Runes took form in the area of the Roman *limes*. At the time, the Roman Empire was at its height and dangerously expanding. Gaul had been invaded and occupied. The Roman Empire stretched as far as the earlier Celtic borders. Moreover, Roman annals tell us that the army attempts further expansion northwards and east across the Rhine. Simultaneously the so-called Migration Period begins. The Ancient Germanic peoples wander farther south in search of new land and are pushed against the Rhine consequently forced to take more eastern routes. From this historical context the Runes emerge.

The area along the Rhine is a melting pot of Roman, Celtic and Germanic habits and customs. That is why it is uncertain whether the Runes were originally designed for the Germanic people in the first place. Possibly Druids first designed the alphabet and only later the Germanic people adopted it. The Celtic Ogham alphabet stems from roughly the same period, and exactly when the Ancient Germanic Futhark flourishes, at about the fifth to sixth century, we notice an increase of Ogham inscriptions among the Celts as well. On top of that, the Futhark contains at least one redundant Rune that suits the Ogham, and likewise the Ogham alphabet contains at least two superfluous characters that fit the Germanic alphabet sound values. All of this, and more, hints at a common school of magic or regular communication between initiates of both mystery schools in the least.

Contact of the Germanic priesthood with Celtic and North Italic mystery schools is confirmed by the so-called Negau-B helmet find. This helmet has been found at the area of Negau, Slovenia, and bears a second century BCE inscription set in North Italic characters – but is written in Ancient Germanic. The area is known as a Celtic cult place. The helmets themselves were fashioned two centuries earlier and ritually deposited at the site in 50 BCE.

Let us not forget that the Celtic tradition was firmly associated with the Ancient Greek one. Druids are known to have travelled to Greece on a regular basis. Contacts between Northern European, Western European and Mediterranean magicians must have been a reality. For the Northern tradition specifically, we have to keep in mind that the Scandinavian Germanic peoples were heavily influenced by Saami and Central European shamanism.

Ek Runoz Writu

The earliest runic finds stem from the Continent, where the different cultures met. Scholars agree that a foreign alphabet was taken as a model to design the Runes. Some researchers like to see elements of the North Italic alphabet; others recognize Greek or Latin characters. As with every alphabet, in this early period, letter shapes still held many variants. At that time, inscriptions most often occur on war gear and were obviously ritualistic in nature. Later on, towards the sixth century, Runes also appear on stone monuments and became more standardized. From then on, the Runes are spread throughout the whole of Northern Europe having its centre in Denmark and Gotland.

The Ancient Germanic runic alphabet is termed the Elder Futhark. Later on, a new version in Scandinavia developed, known as the Viking or Younger Futhark (Futhork). This alphabet was made of sixteen Runes. On the continent the number increased. This Rune row is known as the Anglo-Saxon or Old English Futhark (Futhorc). The Angles and Saxons took this alphabet with them from the Frisian districts to Britain. The most elaborate version of this Futhark housed 33 Runes.

However, the very first inscriptions must have been in wood. This is suggested by the shape of the signs. Of course, these early examples have been lost as this medium of writing easily perishes. Also, Runes are called staves, pointing to wood as an original medium. The Ancient Germanic word *staba* 'stave' has been attested carrying this meaning in a Migration Period stone monument inscription. Evidently, Runes are older than the first archaeological pieces of evidence.

Continuous into the Past

Every one of the Runes embodies a cultic concept prevalent at the time of their inception. All of them involve the Ancient Germanic mystery tradition and specifically allude to the Sun cult of their religion. We have to remind ourselves that the Ancient Germanic peoples had a living belief system of their own before they adopted any outlandish writing system. Their ceremonies and cultic practices are recorded in archaeological data. Scandinavian Bronze Age rock engravings, known as the Hällristningar, show that these people had a well developed arsenal of symbols, insomuch that we can speak of a symbolic language. Their myths and mysteries are the backdrop against which the creation of the Runic alphabet must be set.

These rock carvings from the Scandinavian Bronze Age (1800-600 BCE) undoubtedly helped fashion certain Runes, like Pertho, Algiz, Sowulo, Teiwaz and Inguz and those Runes found later in the Younger Futhark, such as Hagall, Sol, Madr and Yr. Again, other Runes definitively correspond to Latin letters, like B, C, F, H, I, R, S and T, or Greek, like Gebo and Pertho. The s- and t-Runes seem to have been drawn from both, as do other Runes.

Hints to Magic

The Bronze Age story gives a first clue as to the magical nature of the Rune alphabet. A further hint we find in the very word itself.

'Rune' means secret and goes back to a root meaning to whisper. Personally, this reminds me of the wind that rustles the oak leaves at Dodona when a priest of Zeus wishes to learn the words of the Gods. The word also refers to secret meetings. In his Gothic translation of the Bible, Wulfila uses the word *runa* to denote both the Greek concepts of *boule/symboulion* and *mysterion*. Both *boule* and *symboulion* refer to an assembly. In Old English, the alliterative phrase *ræd and run* is glossed *consilium* in Latin. These moots reflect the Germanic folk assembly. On a spiritual level, the Runes are naught but the dictates of the Aesir and Nornir assembled at the oracle of Urd. Through ceremony the will of the Gods is divined – the secret revealed. Curiously enough, this distinctively Germanic word found its way into the Celtic languages (Welsh *rhyn*, Irish *run*).

The Ancient Germanic initiates went about very carefully constructing a model that would hold as good as all of their esoteric teachings. That is why the configuration of the Elder Futhark is what it is and why we can explain it to be a magical alphabet. Every Rune has a name. It refers to an idea that represents a part of the mystery teachings. Every Rune has a position. The order in which the Runes are arranged is native to the Germanic people only. It is different from any other alphabet. There are twenty four Runes. And the alphabet is divided into three equal parts.

The name of each Rune refers to a concept prevalent at Ancient Germanic times. But where do these names come from? They are known from later sources, such as the Old English and the Viking Rune alphabets. The names have mostly come down to us through the Rune Poems. A third source, akin to the runic alphabet but independent of it, is the Gothic Alphabet. It was developed by bishop Wulfila to translate the Holy Bible in a language his people could actually understand. His alphabet is mainly inspired on the Greek one, but has Germanic names assigned to each letter. Not surprisingly, they correspond to those of the Runes – as do some of the shapes. The alphabet was designed in the fourth century, making it a pre-runner of the Old English Futhark. The attestation of Rune names in both these alphabets makes one realize that a well established school of mystery was operating among the Germanic tribes in late Roman times.

Based on this information, the Ancient Germanic Rune names of the Elder Futhark are reconstructed. Usually, the Old English names are favoured, as the Old English alphabet preserves each of the twenty four letters. The Gothic alphabet and the Younger Runes of the Viking Futhark corroborate the reconstruction. However, we must bear in mind that the English Futhark was only able to survive because of the role it played in the English manuscript tradition, which was overtly Christian. The Younger Futhark would have preserved the pagan naming more accurately, but did not keep all of the twenty four Elder Runes.

Sá váru Rúnar Vatni Ausinn

The Rune names refer to twenty four concepts that were of great magnitude to the Ancient Germanic cultures. As Polomé puts it "it seems reasonable to look for the motivation (of naming the Runes) in the actual use of the Runes in the socio-cultural context of the contemporary Germanic community". In concluding, he states that the Rune names are "imbedded in the Germanic concepts about the world of the Gods, nature and man". He also stresses their relevance to the life of the farmer.

In my opinion, the Runes embody twenty four cultic concepts and were relevant to the life of the priest. At least a third of the Runes refer to divine or supernatural forces: Thurisaz, Ansuz, Algiz, Sowulo, Teiwaz, Berkana, Inguz and Dagaz. Most of the Runes can be linked with solar worship. All of the Runes are associated with myths and/or rites. Some of the Runes specifically point to Ancient Germanic ritual. Uruz (rite of passage), Gebo (wedding), Nauthiz (need fire) and Berkana (May tree) are good examples of this; as also Fehu, Raido, Kenaz, Wunjo and Laguz, although Fehu was more frequently the object of rites.

We have to remind ourselves that the creators of the Futhark were well aware of any figurative meaning beyond the evident naming. In the Viking Age, poets take on an important role in their society. And poetry evolved from the mystery tradition. We can see how the skalds use the myths to create metaphors. It was no different in earlier times. The concepts of the Runes seem to refer to aspects of everyday life, but their metaphoric meaning was more important. Every Rune name stands for a teaching that was enacted in a rite and expressed in a myth. It was at last reflected in the concept the name refers to. Psychologically, the Runes are nothing else than archetypes, symbols. Esoterically, they are energies, clothed in sound, shape and structure. Runic letter shapes either confirm or complement the abstract meanings of the concepts.

Last but not least, the arrangement and number of the Runes seem to underlie magical thought. Therefore, I believe that the Runes refer to religious concepts and that they were used by initiates to pass on their mysteries. The peculiar arrangement of the Futhark contains an esoteric background and can be explained mythologically.

Rune	Sound	Name	Meaning	Number
ᚠ	f	**Fehu**	cattle	1
ᚢ	u	**Uruz**	aurochs	2
ᚦ	þ	**Thurisaz**	giant	3
ᚨ	a	**Ansuz**	Áss	4
ᚱ	r	**Raido**	to ride	5
ᚲ	k	**Kenaz**	torch	6
ᚷ	g	**Gebo**	to give	7
ᚹ	w	**Wunjo**	joy	8
				9
ᚺ	h	**Hagalaz**	hail	10
ᚾ	n	**Nauthiz**	need	20
ᛁ	i	**Isa**	ice	30
ᛃ	j	**Jera**	year	40
ᛇ	i	**Eihwaz**	yew	50
ᛈ	p	**Pertho**	apple	60
ᛉ	z	**Algiz**	protection	70
ᛋ	s	**Sowulo**	Sun	80
				90
ᛏ	t	**Teiwaz**	Tyr	100
ᛒ	b	**Berkana**	birch	200
ᛖ	e	**Ehwaz**	horse	300
ᛗ	m	**Mannaz**	man	400
ᛚ	l	**Laguz**	sea	500
ᛜ	ng	**Inguz**	Ingi-Frey	600
ᛟ	o	**Othila**	estate	700
ᛞ	d	**Dagaz**	day	800
				900

There are twenty four Runes. This is significant, since there were undoubtedly more concepts of cultic importance. Esoterically, 24 is the number of time. It represents the hours in a day, but it also refers to the combination of the so-called involutionary and evolutionary arcs. The involutionary arc is also known as the Wheel of Matter, whereas the evolutionary arc is known as the Wheel of Mind. Both follow the twelve signs of the Zodiac, albeit in opposite directions. The involutionary arc covers the first half of the Futhark and the evolutionary the second half. The twelfth Rune, Jera, marks the reorientation towards the spiritual, as Freya Aswynn earlier has pointed out.

As an alphabet, all of these Runes represent a sound, but this is only partly true. The Futhark was designed as an alphabet so that every Germanic sound was represented, but two Runes fail to suit the system – emphasizing the magicality of the Futhark. These are Eihwaz and Pertho. Not accidentally, they appear next to each other.

The sound value of Eihwaz has not been assessed with certainty, although it seems to replace the i-Rune in certain inscriptions. This means that Eihwaz has nothing to offer except on a symbolic level. Pertho, on the other hand, although apparently representing a useful sound is well nigh never found in inscriptions. It is only attested in alphabetic magic. Whenever a p-sound was needed in an inscription, the b-Rune was used. In my opinion, Pertho did not have a phonetic value at all. Therefore, it had only a symbolic meaning. Pertho proves the melting pot of Celtic and Germanic influences to be the basis of materializing a Germanic alphabet. *Perþo* is not a Germanic but a Celtic word. Conversely, the Ogham letters Uath and Straif represent Germanic sounds, otherwise unattested in the Celtic languages.

Eihwaz and Pertho are an interesting pair for another reason. They switch places. Going through the Ancient Germanic attestations of Runic alphabets, we see that sometimes Eihwaz comes first and sometimes Pertho. Their position had not yet crystallised in early times. The same is true for the pair Othila and Dagaz. And this is still a point of debate.

However, position seems to have been significant from an early stage onwards. This is mainly deduced from the Gothic alphabet. The Gothic alphabet nicely follows its Greek example, but cannot maintain it when it comes to the letters Q, J and NG, which have no Greek counterpart.

Gothic Alphabet		Greek Alphabet	
Λ	a	A	a
B	b	B	b
Γ	g	Γ	g
Δ	d	Δ	d
Є	e	E	e
Ц	q		
Ζ	z	Z	z
h	h	H	e
Θ	þ	Θ	th
Ι	i	I	i
Κ	k	Κ	k
Λ	l	Λ	l
Μ	m	M	m
Ν	n	N	n
Ϭ	j	Ξ	x
∏	u	O	o
∏	p	∏	p
Ρ	r	P	r
S	s	Σ	s
T	t	T	t
Υ	w	Υ	y
F	f	Φ	ph
ц	ng	X	ch

| **X** | hw | | **Ψ** | ps |
| **Ϙ** | o | | **Ω** | oo |

Gothic Q has been allotted a position in the first Gothic *aett*. It occupies the sixth position in that *aett* and precedes the letter Z. The Gothic letter Q (Qairthra) is peculiar in that it mirrors the letter P (Pairthra). Its shape is an inverted Gothic P. In addition, the elder Rune p-sound is represented by a tilted Gothic P, which ultimately derives from a Greek Pi. Gothic Q is a double of the p-sound, reminding us of the p-/q-split within the Celtic languages. It is interesting to see how the combination of QZ corresponds to PZ in the Elder Futhark. Pertho being a Celtic word, it could just as well have stood for Q. And it is in the sixth position, followed by Z, where it appears in the second *aett*.

Considering the Gothic letters J and NG, we notice they have been both inserted in the sixth position as well. Again, their positions correspond to the Elder Futhark. Gothic J (Jer) is preceded by N and is found in the Futhark as the complex NIJY; I, J and Y all being variants of the i-sound. Gothic NG (Igguz) is followed by Hwair and Othal. Hwair is a letter alien to the Futhark, but Othal corresponds to Othila. This pair, too, is kept; NG is in the sixth position of the third *aett*, neatly under the p-Rune, followed by the o-Rune. These pairs show that letters were not randomly added.

All this is of historical and mystical importance, because it gives us a clue of the earliest Germanic magical thinking.

Happy Together

The alphabet was divided into three groups of eight Runes. These groups are known as *aettir*. The first *aett*, headed by Fehu, is dedicated to Frey. The second is the *aett* of Hagal and the third belongs to Tyr. This division makes the Futhark particularly magical, since the number 8 stands for the horizontal plane of existence and the number 3 for the vertical plane. Therefore, the numbers 3 and 8 integrate the qualities of Heaven and Earth. The number 8 refers to the cardinal points. The number 3 refers to the Underworld, Middle

World and Upper World.

The *aettir*-system appears as early as the fourth century CE on runic bracteates and stone monuments. The same division is also found in the Gothic alphabet in which it is associated with number magic. These numbers correspond to the Greek and Hebrew systems of alphabetic numerology as these alphabets uphold a tripartite division as well. Wulfila thus accounted for the deep-seated desire nowadays to create a Runic numerology.

The Gothic system corresponds to the Kabbalistic system of Gematria by assigning units to the first row, tens to the second and hundreds to the third. Wulfila's alphabet does not have sufficient letters to provide for every number, so that he decides to create two extra symbols. The Gothic numbers 90 and 900 occur at the end of their respective *aettir*. They properly show the threefold *aettir*-division, which must consequently have been a well established fact in Wulfila's time. I would dare say that the *aettir*-system has been part of the runic system from when it was first designed.

It is characteristic of magical alphabets to assign names and numbers to the letters, to have them arranged in a particular order and to divide them in three separate families. In this respect, the Runic alphabet corresponds well to the Celtic and the Hebrew – Ogham being associated with Druidism and the Hebrew alphabet with Kabbalah resounding in the Greater Arcana of the Tarot – *arcanum* meaning secret.

Despite the fact that the Futhark was used as a writing alphabet it is unavoidably also a set of symbols. It can only be set against the background of earlier Scandinavian mystery and religion, its words of power brimming with the ancient mythology it is related to. Infused with life energy and intention, they become the very expression of magic. Even their literal meaning reveals the hidden operative potential of the Runes as living symbols.

We are therefore faced with twenty four secrets, mysteries, esoteric concepts, cosmic laws. These twenty four secrets were stored in the alphabetic model that lies before us. A riddle to be solved. A pathway into the mysteries of life and death and everything beyond. Hot points, sacred places in mind and myth to guide us from initiation to initiation. Twenty four doors.

And a lifetime of opportunities.

2
A SHARE
OF
THE
MEAD

FEHU   ᚠ

Fehu means cattle. Since Neolithic times sheep and cattle have been a source of food, but the concept quickly turned into a measure of personal wealth. In our modern day society, Fehu stands for money. From a magico-religious standpoint, cattle were a fertility symbol associated with the Vanir deities. Hence energy is essentially the keyword of this Rune.

In antiquity, farmers held cattle not for their financial worth. Their original worth lay in their production of milk and secondarily of meat and wool or leather. Soon enough, livestock was considered a status symbol and was associated with material wealth. As in many cultures, the Ancient Germanic people too used livestock as a means of payment. The Latin word for money *pecunia* is derived from their word for cattle and is cognate with Ancient Germanic *Fehu*. Nowadays, money still seems the cornerstone of our society, much like Fehu's role as the foundation Rune of this first *aett*.

In the evolutionary history of mankind, both sheep (11000 BCE) and cow (8000 BCE) rank among the first species to be domesticated – explaining the compliant energy of this Rune. About the same time, wheat (Jera) was domesticated (9000 BCE). These innovations initiated a new era, that of sedentary civilization. Therefore, Fehu markedly symbolizes the pretend dominion of man over Nature. It also symbolizes the energy of the masses and herd instinct.

On a more positive note, the cow is a symbol of fecundity and of life itself the world over. The cow personifies Mother Earth and accordingly Fehu is ruled by the Vanir. Both Njord and Frey are called *fé-gjafa*. They bestow riches. The epithet translates as a bind Rune of Fehu and Gebo. Later on, costly materials such as gold and amber partially took over the cattle's role as a means of payment. The Goddess of gold is Freyja, presiding over treasures, jewels and everything precious.

On a subtle level, Fehu represents energy. Cattle, gold and money are only the tangible expressions of our life's energy. In accordance with our system of modern civilization, we are compensated with money for our labour expense. With this money, we sustain ourselves. When we are exhausted, we save our strengths, but when vigorous we work even harder spending our energy. Fundamentally, energy rules our life's quality. Money is only a reflection of it, and only one possible manifestation.

There is a rather spontaneous feel about this symbol. This may be due to the unrefined instinctual nature of domesticated animals. On the subtle scale, Fehu would be unrefined life energy. The energy of Fehu prompts impulsive decisions. By means of this energy you can excite yourself or find that power within yourself to venture on an arduous project. It is the spark that ignites a chain of events.

If the Vanir allow, Fehu helps you acquire riches of a material, etheric and/or spiritual nature. The energy of Fehu is rather fickle and often works only for a short while. Sometimes the Rune indicates a once in a lifetime opportunity. This Rune represents a person who radiates power but is blind to the needs of others. This is someone who draws riches towards himself.

While the stanzas on the first Rune are generally kennings for gold, they also harbour an esoteric meaning. The 'fire of the flood' of the Icelandic Rune Poem occultly signifies holy inspiration expressed through brilliant ideas. Such an overload of brilliant ideas would be termed *óðr* in the Northern

tradition. However, it can unbalance the mind. There are too many initiatives that need your attention. You will have your hands full and not be able to dedicate yourself to one project at a time. That is why Fehu may easily create an imbalance. And it takes about six Runes to find your balance again! In spite of that, Fehu does not care. Its only job is to infuse you with new ideas and incentives. Luckily for us, Gebo is not too distant a relative of Fehu. In the end, the glint Fehu sparks off is meant to have grown fully in Wunjo. The last Rune of this *aett* is what Fehu ultimately aims at.

A negative Fehu denotes greed and quarrels. Money and gold have the power to cause discord and separation. Greed and desire are attributes of the wolf archetype. In particular, the F of Fehu refers to the big bad wolf Fenrir. He bides his time and strikes when people are off guard, then being most susceptible to the wolf's influence. As the saying goes, hunger drives the wolf out of the woods...

The wolf mentioned in the Norwegian Rune Poem can be considered the enemy of the wood, referring to fire as either a destructive force or a potential burst of energy. The fire of creation is the same fire that eventually destructs. Fehu is the life spark that initiates evolution.

URUZ   ᚢ

Uruz means aurochs. The animal (*Bos Primigenius*) was an indigenous not-domesticated bovine species inhabiting Europe until the end of the middle ages when it became extinct by overhunting. Already by the Iron Age, Denmark was as good as devoid of aurochs. It was a fierce looking beast with a pair of impressive horns on its head. The aurochs' imposing look evoked danger, initiative, boldness, challenge and confidence. As the opposite of tame cattle, Uruz symbolizes the wild power of Nature.

Caesar mentions a Germanic tradition that involved hunting the aurochs but was especially designed as a rite of passage. It involved single-handedly killing an aurochs. A similar tradition still survives today in the Andalusian bullfighting, which may originally have been a Vandal custom. In Jungian psychology, the offering of a bull represents the triumph of the mind over the animal aspect of man. The motif is found in a Greek myth and much resembles Caesar's account. In order to win the Golden Fleece the hero Jason has to yoke a team of fire-breathing bulls. Those seemingly untameable bulls were magically forged by Hephaistos. From this point of view, the Uruz Rune implies a challenge or trial while also denoting courage and willpower. Stamina is one of the key words of Uruz. The Egyptian bull hieroglyph symbolizes power, virility and dominion. It became later associated with kingship. Among the Celts, the word for bull was a kenning for warrior. Someone who is like the aurochs asserts himself.

In many cultures the bull was a Moon symbol, but in the Minoic tradition and the Mithras cult the bull personified the Sun. Much of the symbolism of Uruz is found in the two latter traditions.

The widespread bull cult must have originated from an earlier aurochs cult. The aurochs hunt is found depicted everywhere in European Neolithic cave paintings. The classical symbolism of the bull known today veils the true mystery of the aurochs. Generally, the energies of the bull symbolize natural instincts. It symbolizes our deep unconscious, the body mind. As an emblem of power, bulls were fecundating agents. Their virile blood and fertile sperm were likened to rain and the might of storms. Bulls are frequently associated with water. Bulls were Poseidon's sacred animals. So were horses. And Paleolithic cave paintings show pairs of aurochs, pairs of horses, or an aurochs and a horse paired up. Both creatures complement each other. Sometimes one is the celestial ruler and the other the chtonian, sometimes the other way around. In Northern lore, the sacredness of the ox is remembered in a *thula*-poem by Thorgrim.

The energy of Uruz is well associated with instinct. Nonetheless, its influence is calming and soothing. It sometimes implies the stillness before the storm; a turning inwards that will soon lead to an explosion. It is the determination of the silent victim and the unpredictability of the drunkard. Uruz denotes an outbreak of unbridled aggression. A lack of Uruz energy shows in abandoning a decision. Uruz is a good Rune to call upon when in need of courage.

Much of the Rune's symbolism concerns the animal's horns. They were adorned and made into either drinking vessels or blowing horns. In the Bronze Age, the famous lurs were fashioned after the original blowing horns. These were made for cultic purposes. Associated with the drinking horn is the Germanic drinking ritual known as *symbel*.

The drinking horn corresponds to the Cornucopia or Horn of Plenty of classical mythology. The Cornucopia is one of Amalthea's horns. The goat is famous for having fed Zeus, in which respect she has much in common with Audumla. Nonetheless, the Northern goat of plenty would rather be Heidrun. She grazes off Yggdrasil's leaves on Valhalla's roof and provides Odin's Einherjar with an everlasting source of mead. Another myth surrounding the Cornucopia says that the horn belongs to a river God, in which case the Cornucopia may be likened to the horn of Mimir or the horn of Heimdal, hidden in the same well. Heimdal's affinity with water manifests in his power to change into a seal.

The association of the Horn of Plenty with the Sacred Mead is also found in the name of one of Frigg's maidens. Fulla means full and refers to a horn

that is ever filled to the brim! In Western Occultism, the drinking horn is likened to the chalice – the outstanding symbol of the element Water. Many of you will already have guessed the horn's association with the Grail mysteries. In the Northern tradition, the Sacred Mead involves a quest, demonstrated by heroes like Odin, Sigurd and Fjolsvin, to find the most beautiful girl of the world. This girl represents the hero's *anima*. She bestows wisdom on the hero by sharing the mead.

Etymologically *Uruz* suggests the proximity of water. In the Younger Futhark this Rune is called Ur, while the cognate Old Norse word *aurr* means mud. This substance is a mixture of water and earth and symbolizes the *prima materia*, incidentally linking the Rune with Taurus. Uruz is the matter out of which the world is created. It is earth from out of the water. In the same way, Uruz is related to Ouranos, whose name is based on the same proto-Indo-European root. The name of this ancient Greek deity refers to rainfall. The same meaning is also attributed to the Ur Rune of the later Younger Futhark. It means drizzle. Assigning Ouranos to this Rune, also ties in on a mythological level, since the Titans are his children. They are a race of giants, alluding to the next Rune, Thurisaz.

The relation between Uruz and *aurr* strongly connects the primordial giant Ymir to this Rune. By his own kind, Ymir was called Aurgelmir. Even more interesting is the mention of Old Norse *úr* in *Gylfaginning* where rain is said to come down from the world of Niflheim.

On an esoteric level, Uruz is connected with the vitality of the etheric body; hence this Rune's association with health and healing. Uruz is the driving power behind the subtle energy structure of the physical body.

In divination, Uruz stands for perseverance, slight resistance or an opposition that scares at first but can nonetheless be easily overcome. In a negative way, Uruz stands for fear of failure and the tendency to disregard oneself. In a positive way this Rune denotes confidence and honouring promises. Sometimes you have to make a leap of faith. Sometimes it stands for clumsiness, imprudence or inelegance.

The God Ull is linked with this Rune, because the bind Rune of his name is used as a seal for healing. In addition, Ull presides over duels; in this case between the warrior and the aurochs. In myth, Njord is associated with oxen, because of his relation to cultivating land.

There is a good deal to say about the relationship between Uruz and Fehu. In relation to Fehu, Uruz represents a cooling force. The pair expresses the polarity found throughout the whole Futhark – and in the whole of Northern mythology. Fehu represents the up-fire of Muspelheim and Uruz represents the down-water of Niflheim.

Fehu is very active but cannot control itself. It is power cut loose like a sudden surge of inspiration or the rage of Odin coming through. Your hands tingle and you need to act. Uruz on the other hand is down to earth. It may reflect a state of depression, whereas a Fehu personality would be manic and shooting rays of force in an uncontrolled way. The colour of Uruz is deep blue connected to the abdomen. It is the howling of wolves.

As a person, Fehu would be interested mainly in material gain, whereas Uruz is a seeker. Fehu represents sedentary life, whereas Uruz represents the nomadic way of life.

The bull symbolism of Uruz matches that of Taurus. Interestingly, Fehu links in with Aries. The sheep associated with Fehu certainly insinuates this. And there is an element of Fire in Fehu. The Rune's impetuosity well fits the sign. And if this is true, maybe it is true for the other signs, too. Thurisaz would be Gemini. Ansuz would be Cancer. Raido would be Leo. Kenaz would be Virgo. Gebo would be Libra. Wunjo would be Scorpio. Hagalaz would be Sagittarius. Nauthiz would be Capricorn. Isa would be Aquarius. And Jera would be Pisces. Food for thought.

THURISAZ ▶

This Rune has had quite a history in ancient times. It is glossed Thurs in Old Norse, but the Anglo-Saxons name it Thorn. To make things even more complicated, the Gothic TH was called Thiuth 'good'. We then have three different Rune names to reconstruct the elder one.

The Thurisaz Rune refers to a mythological class of beings, *þursar*. They are a class of giants inhabiting Jotunheim. As creatures of magic, the Thursar are most akin to trolls. They symbolize the energy of conflict. The race of giants is battled by Thor on a daily basis to keep their undermining forces in rein. The storm God's temperament matches that of the Thursar well and is expressed by the lightning flash, a powerful image of energy release. Etymologically, *þurisaz* means 'strong one', referring to a typical giant quality, shared with Thor.

Thurisaz is a natural phenomenon associated with trolls and witches. In the world of man, trolls appear as lightning flashes or in the shape of bolts. They are regarded as destroyers and evil sorcerers. Magic is termed *trolldom* in Iceland. Thurisaz deals with negative magic. In the *galdrabok*, Thurisaz is always used to spell curses.

The Anglo-Saxon Rune was probably renamed under the pressure of Christianity. Nonetheless, Thorn is known as an alternative name for the primal giant Ymir. Thorn may be a kenning for sword. Battle axes were associated with troll wives.

Lightning symbolizes a troll's destructive nature. But as a natural phenomenon, Thurisaz symbolizes a discharge. In man's experience, this often shows in fury, or more pleasantly in an orgasm. This discharge is a release of built-up energy. You could view Thurisaz as an empowering Rune accumulating, gathering and outwardly directing energy. Occultly speaking, Thurisaz represents the discharge of focussed and directed will power to bring about change.

The very power of Thurisaz is to draw might from the will to achieve. Sometimes it is the frustration that comes with it. This Rune motivates to

physical action. On the level of emotions, a good fight can clear the atmosphere.

The shape of the Thurisaz Rune is fundamentally based on the triangle. This includes the symbolism of Fire as well as the Triangle of Art used in ceremonial magic to summon entities confining them to the limited space of the Rune. The space inside the triangle represents the power of an engine. It is the contained giant rage which can be wielded via the Rune's shape.

Magically, this Rune is used to claim one's space, to apply inner energy externally and to channel forces. Often Thurisaz appears as a Rune of protection. Lightning is the attribute of Thor, the God of Thunder. This Norse deity protects Gods and men alike and battles against the hostile giants. When Thor slings his hammer thunder resounds and lightning flashes. The giant race represents basic instincts, passion, emotion and the subconscious. Thurisaz may symbolize a longing, not seldom sexually.

The giant among the Gods is Loki. He fathered curses in person and spawned monsters as offspring. As an antagonist, he tries the orderliness of the Gods. He symbolizes unpredictability and untrustworthiness; two features he shares with the *þursar*. Thurisaz easily confuses people, or makes them angry. It is a Rune of rebellion. This power can be found in sceptics and criticasters. It is both the veil and the secret to tear it apart.

Thurisaz has an unsettling function. Its influence does at the same time obstruct, thrust forward and discharge. The energy of Thurisaz is not easily controlled. It is explosive, and in a sense it is more an effect than an actual cause. However, its energy can cause your life to be cleared from all the dross accumulated throughout the years hindering you from getting what you really want.

ANSUZ ᚨ

Ansuz refers to the Aesir, a race of war Gods, whose strength lies in the handling of crises. As supernatural beings of good counsel they are invoked for advice through divinatory means. On a psychological level, they represent the power of rational thought and communication.

Originally they were venerated by the Goths as the spirits .of their forebears: *semideos id est anses*. In later Scandinavian mythology, the Aesir were celestial rulers. They met in a daily organized assembly to govern world affairs. Their collective symbolizes orderly consciousness. Etymologists connect this Rune name with Hindu *asura, asu* meaning vital power. The related Old Norse word *önd* means breath and refers to the concept of Spirit.

The realm of the Gods is called Asgard and is ruled by Odin, the father of all the Gods. The myths recount that the Aesir come together at times of great distress and difficulty. They meet at a sacred space symbolic of the centre of the universe and collectively reflect on the problems at hand. That is where the power of this Rune lies: contemplation in order to resolve. According to *Voluspa*, the Aesir call their holy meetings at turning points in the process of creation. At these moments, the Aesir define aspects of the cosmos; they institute time and space and generally create order. Ansuz organizes the chaos of Thurisaz and symbolizes healing on a mental level. These Aesic gatherings are an answer to sudden crises, the concept being analogous to the mind responding to any threat to what it holds as real. The way the Aesir define every aspect of reality inherent in the process of creation recalls the observer effect of quantum mechanics. The Ansuz Rune therefore has a rather rational ring to it, though its magic gives good counsel and offers solutions. The overall power of this Rune lies in the intellect, the ability to reason and contemplate.

There are twelve Aesir. Each of the Aesir embodies a particular mental faculty. Together, they constitute the full capacity of the human mind. Figuratively, when the Gods gather in Thing, the mind focuses. Their meeting symbolizes the mental effort to concentrate. When the act of concentration

is prompted by an intention, it will be in the nature of meditation. Lost memories can be tracked, past lives remembered, and solutions to pressing questions found. The names of the twelve Aesir are Thor, Balder, Njord, Frey, Tyr, Bragi, Heimdal, Hoder, Vidar, Vali, Ull and Forseti. They are headed by Odin.

Ansuz, or Áss, is one of Odin's names. Consequently, many aspects of Odin are found in Ansuz. The Rune stands for communication, inspiration, rage, the spiritual and the divine, though also death. To priests, it represents their vocation. It is the Rune of skalds and poets and madmen alike.

Odin's name literally means rage and this expresses itself in the mind of man as gales of inspiration, possession and drive. Ansuz is a Rune of both berserkers and poets. Before berserkers threw themselves into combat, they invoked Odin, by whom they became possessed. Then, the channelled force compelled them to go straight forward which made them practically invincible.

Ansuz is connected with the mind. The Rune teaches that the mind works in a logical, associative and intuitive way. Through its energy solutions are found. Situations requiring a mental effort are supported by the influence of Ansuz. Invoking the quality of Ansuz in a working or visualization will add mental power to it. Simply recall the Rune's energy.

Consciousness is communication and communication is consciousness. In particular, Ansuz is a God communicating through the mind of a person. Gods, such as Odin, are the medium through which we as incarnate human beings communicate with the cosmos. Between equals, Ansuz promotes mental coherence and consequently telepathic sensitivity.

The energy of this Rune opens and reveals, as if a fresh wind frees your spirit. This Rune opens the mind, enlightened by means of understanding, intuition and inspiration. Enthusiasm can be the result of the Ansuz energy. In meditation Ansuz helps to temporarily ignore the physical to become aware of the qualities of the mind. From another perspective the same experience is initiated by the energy of Gebo.

Ansuz's real power is to find answers and create insight. The Rune petitions the Gods for counsel. Divinatory means can be used to map the subtle impulses from abstract realms or to scry the shady bits of one's own consciousness. Ansuz's energy stimulates our mental skills. If suffering from stress, Ansuz offers at least a provisional relief. Opening the mind welcomes inspiring influences.

In magic, Ansuz is related to the breath of life used in ceremonial workings. This is known in Ancient Egyptian sources as the opening of the mouth ritual, but is referred to in the Scandinavian anthropogenesis as well. Incidentally, the corresponding Anglo-Saxon Rune means mouth. The breath of life has been an expression of the universal life energy in many cultures. The Chinese *qi* also means breath, so do Latin *spiritus*, Greek *pneuma* and Sanskrit *prana*. According to the Ayurvedic texts, the Sun (Sowulo) is the ultimate source of prana (Ansuz). Earlier, Fehu was associated with energy. From this it will be readily deduced that the Runes are nothing but different qualities of the same universal energy.

Ansuz stands for a solution or escape. Sometimes it indicates authority, such as the State or parents or teachers. All kinds of information are headed by Ansuz, including gossip. The Rune stands for communication and advice. Sometimes this involves meddling. Wise persons are associated with Ansuz, as are priests. Those who study fall under the rule of Ansuz.

As a pair, Thurisaz and Ansuz express the mythological polarity of giants and Gods. Thurisaz represents the unknown, feared and instinctive part of the mind. Ansuz stands for the urge to define everything, think logically and have things well planned ahead. They are chaos and order. In physics, Thurisaz corresponds to entropy. According to the second law of thermodynamics, there is an inherent tendency in the universe towards chaos. This is balanced by a principle of order: consciousness. Entropy can only decrease by means of communication.

RAIDO ᚱ

The symbolism of Raido is rather straightforward. The Rune name refers to the activity of horse riding, which is a symbol of control. Navigating an animal stands for dominance, management and decision-making. On a psychological level, it means controlling our animal instincts. The Rune exemplifies the energy of ritual and the associated folk custom is ritual procession.

In ancient times, horse riding was reserved for the Germanic noblemen only. A similar thing happened when the first cars were manufactured in the early 1900s. Both horses and cars were a status symbol. Chieftains and priests rode with their horses to the regularly held folk gatherings. According to Tacitus, these assemblies were held on the new Moon or the full Moon and called Thing. As a God of peace, Njord presided over these. In times of war, too, people gathered, albeit to beseech the favour of the war Gods and prophesize the outcome of battle. In myth, this custom is mirrored by the Thing of the Aesir, held near the world tree Yggdrasil. Twelve Aesir come together at Urd's well, the fountain of destiny. The myth is reflected in the Runic triad Raido-Eihwaz-Laguz. Raido symbolizes the Aesir who ride to Thing. Eihwaz represents Yggdrasil. Laguz represents Urd's Well.

The image of a rider implies an objective, but achieving a goal is never easy. To get there, Raido teaches to pick the most efficient route. It is the path of which we want to wander as little as possible. Raido symbolizes the direction of our intention. Whether a straight line is followed or not depends on the capacity of making a decision. Life is a succession of choices. Life is a chain of decisions eventually establishing an individual's personality. Raido makes us conscious of what we want and who we are. We move towards our goals. At the end of our journey, we may realize we have become a totally different person, with different goals and different wants, because of the choices we make. A Raido personality is self-confident, knowing where he is going and acts according to his objectives. He rarely reconsiders a decision.

Often Raido is associated with travelling, being on the road and moving house. I like to compare people's personalities with how they drive cars.

How do they behave on the road? Do they stay focussed? Are they pressed or rather at leisure? How do they respond and interact with other drivers? On a grander scale, Raido is a person's path in life. Life itself is always on the move.

The combination of Raido and Kenaz offers an interesting insight. The sequence may be reformulated as 'moving towards enlightenment'. Kenaz stands for the skill that a person (Ansuz) trains for. The conscious effort to achieve is expressed by the energy of Raido, the conscious effort being Ansuz (and the effort itself being Thurisaz). The Raido Rune strengthens one's sense of duty and stands for taking responsibilities.

In Ancient Germanic times, the riding of Raido had a ritual meaning. Once a year the Scandinavian fertility Gods were driven around the fields to give their blessings to the land. Most notably, a man representing Frey took place in the wagon and was driven about. According to source material, this festive procession was held in winter. That many of the Northern Gods go about in carts may well be a vestige of this custom. Njord owns a wagon pulled by oxen and is called the God of the Wain, but Frey and Freyja too are driven around. The Sun Goddess rode a wagon, too, reminiscent of Bronze Age rock engravings depicting solar rituals. This explains the winter connection. After Midwinter, the Sun grew in strength and was taken out to have her bestow her life-giving blessings.

Another folk custom associated with Raido is the Wild Hunt. It takes place every fall. The legion of the hunt is made up of those who died in the past year and is commanded by Odin. In Scandinavia, this hunt is known as *oskorei*, the Ride of Oski, the latter being a name of Odin meaning Granter of Wishes. Odin still comes around every year in this regard dressed as either Saint Martin (11 November) or Saint Nicholas (6 December). Both dates allude to the Wild Hunt. The Hunt only signifies that the boundary between the world of the living and the world of the dead is down. As such, Raido is a suitable instrument to get to the Underworld. Again, the triad of Raido-Eihwaz-Laguz comes into play, because Laguz symbolizes the Underworld and Eihwaz serves as a pathway. The triad suggests a technique for travelling to the Underworld. As for its direct connection to the Wild Hunt, Raido stands for the host of the dead, or Einherjar, Eihwaz represents Odin, or either the time of the year, and Laguz stands for the otherworldly aspect, or maybe Odin's power to grant wishes.

Yet another God is firmly linked with this Rune. That is Thor. He drives a vehicle pulled by goats riding the clouds, the cart's wheels thundering and sparking as a blistering storm. It must be remembered that Thor is also firmly associated with the Sun. Bronze Age carvings show the axe as a solar weapon. The axe originally belonged to Thor and only later changed into the hammer. However, the connection remained, since the Swastika is repeatedly called Thor's hammer. Also, the wheel has always been a solar symbol. The cross-quartered circle and variants universally represent the Sun. Undoubtedly, since the dawn of the wheel, this invention has been incorporated in solar worship. Thor's hammer was also said to bestow fertility. The God's connection with solar worship and fertility rites resulted in him driving a chariot. 'Thor's chariot' used to be the Germanic name for the Great Bear (Ursa Major).

Wagons were first introduced in Europe at the onset of the Bronze Age (3000 BCE), with the wheel having been around from about 3500 BCE in the Near East. Since then, it has been regarded as the mother of all technology and has been connected with solar mythology the world over. In Roman lore, it was the attribute of Fortuna, being associated with a person's power to guide his own fate.

Thor stands out among the Gods. When the Aesir go to Thing, he is the only one who travels by foot, because he is the only one strong enough to wade the rivers that part Asgard from Midgard. From the Runes, the same is inferred. From the race of giants (Thurisaz) the Gods descend (Ansuz) and from among the Aesir, Thor arises (Raido). The next Rune (Kenaz) in this case refers to Loki. Thor's decisiveness and power to act are his main traits corresponding to Raido.

Raido is a Rune of control. It tells you to act with determination. However, in itself it does not show you the way, although it helps guiding the energies in the right direction. Therefore, if you want to direct something in a certain direction, you link it to the energy of Raido. In magic, usually, a thought needs direction. You will then not only have to visualize the content of what you will direct, but you will also have to visualize a sense of destination for the combined energy to flow the right way.

In divination Raido proffers sound advice and often points to good advice bestowed by others. Its energy incites to action and is capable of getting something going again. Raido rebalances a broken rhythm. It has an organizing influence. The sequence Thurisaz, Ansuz and Raido symbolizes chaos, order and routine. The pair Ansuz-Raido reminds us that every innovation is preceded by an idea first.

KENAZ ⟨

The k-Rune yields two possible names, of which both refer to the element of Fire. The traditional name is Kenaz, whereas the alternative is Kaunaz. The symbol's meaning is divided into internal and external fire, reflected in the double naming of the Rune. Symbolically, the element stands for knowledge, creativity and skill, and it is linked with the transformational powers of the dwarves.

Traditionally, the k-Rune is called Kenaz, after the Old English Rune name Cen. The Younger Futhark, however, has Kaun, rendering Kaunaz as a possible name for this Rune. Although Kenaz has become the accepted name for this Rune in recent times, it is fair to say that Kaunaz comes nearer to the truth. The Younger Rune names are more reliable because they were not contaminated by the Christian influence as were the Old English. Additionally, the Gothic alphabet has *kusma* for K, sharing its meaning with Old Norse *kaun*. This alternative name means sore, boil. The traditional Kenaz means torch.

There is no image more suited than a torch to represent the element of Fire. However, sores and boils refer to fire also. A related word like inflammation is founded on the image of kindling a fire. The k-Rune for example denotes burnt fingers and blisters. Therefore, Kenaz stands for fire on the outside, whereas Kaunaz denotes fire on the inside.

The Old Icelandic Rune Poem has the lemma *flagella* as a Latin translation of *kaun*. The Old Norse word means a tender spot or a sore spot, but the Latin *flagella* means whip. For this reason I suspect the Rune refers to sword wounds. A received sword blow feels like the stroke of a lash. On top, torch was a kenning for sword (*brandr*). Etymologically, the alternative Kenaz is related to English 'keen' meaning sharp. On top of that, such wounds gave rise to ulcers and swellings. As a matter of fact, these wounds would have been tended to with hot steel.

According to Polomé, Kaunaz symbolizes a plague that strikes man. Fire would have been used to exterminate the plague. The Rune name suggests

those waves of epidemics flaring up at the worst of times, riding man and beast. *Havamal* 137 states that fire expels disease.

On a smaller scale, boils may simply be a sign of a boy coming to puberty. The Old Icelandic Rune Poem specifically states that *kaun* affects children. Interpreting children as youngsters, this may refer to acne. The inner heat of Kaunaz is readily explained as a boost of pubertal hormones. This inner fire does then not only stimulate growth on all levels, it also kindles the emotion of passion.

External fire is represented by Kenaz, which is confirmed by the Rune's triangular shape. The element has been mastered by mankind since Paleolithic times. Torches were made of fir. Incidentally, this makes amber the associated gemstone. Amber is essentially the fossilized resin of an ancient pine tree. Because of that, amber has the property of sustaining a flame when lighted, much like a torch. The myth of Freyja and the dwarves supports this relationship. The torch symbolizes man's control over the elements. The associated Celtic Goddess is Brighid.

Although Kenaz is the archetypal Fire Rune, different aspects of the element are expressed by different Runes. These aspects are more esoteric in nature, whereas Kenaz represents the physical flame. According to Alice Bailey's teaching, fire has three aspects, electric, solar and frictional. Electric fire corresponds to Thurisaz, symbolizing lightning. Solar fire is represented by Sowulo. Fire by friction is Nauthiz. It is said that solar fire is produced when Thurisaz and Nauthiz are brought into contact, because fire by friction represents matter and electric fire spirit. The resultant fire is that of the soul.

The torch is a small Sun. In Greek myth, amber (*electron*) was associated with the Sun deity. The torch represents light and enlightenment. In a spiritual sense, the Sun symbolizes wisdom as a continuous string of integrated insights. On the other hand, Kenaz symbolizes the single spark of a sudden realization. It guides you along for a time, but special effort is needed to keep the fire going. Once the isolated sparks of enlightenment overlap and complement each other in a self-sustaining continuum will the fire blaze like that of the Sun. For this reason, countless ancient mystery cultures kept eternal fires burning. They symbolized the Sun on Earth. On a psychological level, too, the torch's light drives away the dark. It repels shadow and ignorance alike. To wield the torch means to consciously throw light on otherwise unclear or invisible matters.

Whether in a sacred space, gathering or household environment, fire is always a focus. In the old days, the community gathered around the fire and recounted all kinds of stories; information was exchanged. In general, Kenaz stands for a focal point or centre, Latin *focus* simply meaning hearth. Nonetheless, this Rune is endowed with a stirring or exciting influence, because of the flickering quality of fire. The enthusiastic energy of Kenaz is almost tangibly contagious and encourages or motivates a group. Kenaz is the centre of a group. It focuses the group mind.

In ancient times, torches were used to mark ritual space. Its fire banishes the darkness and keeps animals at bay. During ritual processions farmers' fields were circumscribed with torches to ensure fertility. In modern ritual, candles are lit to make contact with the spirit world.

The *Zhuangzi*, a Chinese book on Daoism, says "the torch's resin burns away but the fire will always be passed on" meaning that words may die out but wisdom will not. *Havamal* has *brandr af brandi brenn*. The passing on of torches symbolizes the transmission of knowledge, although fire also signifies the imparting of cosmic knowledge by means of mediumship.

Information as a form of knowledge is ultimately futile because it has meaning only to one individual at the time. This aspect distinguishes wisdom from knowledge, because wisdom refers to a general understanding and is applicable in every situation. However, insights come through detail and through detail the greater whole is appreciated. Therefore, information is a necessary step towards wisdom, although it will always retain an aspect of isolation. This is why it can be profitable to specialize, whereas it is not necessary to know all trades.

Kenaz denotes a revival or an urge. Often it points to an urge to pass on knowledge. The energy of Kenaz is what forces the inspired poet to write. The k-Rune may also indicate opportunism. This Rune's energy represents a strong desire or real yearning. Someone having a strong Kenaz personality will tend to be hair-splitting.

In mythology, Kenaz is recognized as the blacksmith's fire, operated by dwarves. In Norse mythology, these are also known as Black Elves or Dark Elves, owing their nickname to their blackish appearance due to the soot. The process of forging refers to transformation and creativity. The patron deity of smiths is the elf Völund/Wayland. He is the Germanic Hephaistos/Vulcanus.

Dwarves transform mineral ore into all kinds of treasure. Their mythic function reads as a metaphor. In the subconscious, a particular principle processes bits and bytes of information. They result in treasured insights, surfacing sooner or later – and apparently belonging to the world of the Gods. But it is in the world of the Gods, that these treasures become meaningful. In the world of the dwarves, we only find the metabolic processes of transforming raw material. Svartalfheim is where the subconscious creative processes take place – beneath the earth; beneath the threshold of our consciousness. A lot of this raw material, be it information, self-generated thoughts or unrealized impressions, only gets processed in the dream sleep. Therefore, the energy of Kenaz is the motor behind your dream content.

Kenaz stands for insights, skills and art. As a torch, it reveals what before was hidden. As a sword, Kenaz helps to make clear cut decisions. Kaunaz indicates disease, hypocrisy and the superior power of Nature. Yet fire sterilizes wounds, so it has a healing quality. Fire possesses a cleansing aspect. Disease and fire are two sides of the same coin. You could posit that Kenaz is the positive side of this Rune and Kaunaz the more negative.

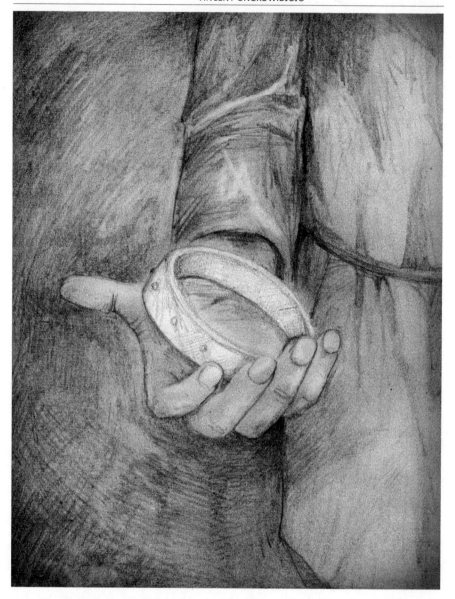

GEBO   X

Gebo means giving, while the Rune shape expresses the principle of equilibrium that compensates this concept. From Viking times, we know that the concept referred to gift, as well as marriage and luck. By a gift we also understand a talent. In ritual, Gebo is an offering. In myth, it is associated with the Valkyries who grant a share of the mead, symbolic of wisdom, to their heroes.

A gift ever demands a gift in return. This is one of the central ideas of Ancient Germanic civilization. Their whole diplomatic system was based on this principle. A gift ties one party to another, because a return gift is expected. A debt was redeemed as service and favours, the form being dependent on the relationship of the participants. In a way, the concept of giving pertains to karma and the law of cause and effect.

Mutual agreement and the principle of debt form the basis of any contract. In Viking times, transactions of all kinds were sealed with the presenting of a ring. Today, this symbol of commitment is still found as an attribute of marriage. The word *gebo* in reality refers to marriage. Also, when a king recruited a young warrior, he presented his sword to him girded with a ring. Rulers were named ring-breakers because they paid their crew with broken-off pieces of silver rings. In pathworkings, this gesture can be incorporated whenever a gift of some kind is apt.

Gebo means luck as well as gift. This luck was 'given' to someone and was bestowed by supernatural beings. There is a whole class of spirits of luck in Northern belief known as Hamingjur. At birth, however, one's fortune was fated by the Norns. In war, the Valkyries conferred luck upon the warriors. These creatures had the power to grant victory. They are associated with ravens, wolves and swans. All of these blessed beings are women.

Last but not least, Gebo also indicates atonement. We 'for-give' someone. In the olden days a truce was exacted by exchanging hostages. This is mentioned in the myth on the war between the Aesir, Gods of air, and the Vanir, Gods of earth. Thus, Gebo is regarded as a Rune of mercy.

To forgive someone can only be done when you have first atoned yourself; and in this lies the great power of this Rune. Debts demand to be settled, not only in matter, but on an emotional level especially. Gebo is generosity, to be capable of giving. And this means giving without making others dependent of you.

The Rune shape represents a kiss. In the olden days, a kiss sealed a contract, but is also a token of absolution. In Northern mythology, this truth is embodied by Kvasir. He sprouted from the spittle of Aesir and Vanir as a result of the truce agreed between both camps. Kvasir is the God of the Sacred Mead and personifies wisdom. After the killing of Kvasir, his blood was collected in three vessels, Odrerir, Son and Bodn. Odrerir is the generic name of this substance. Bodn refers to the bottom; it is the very last drop of the mead. Nothing may be spilled. The middle one, Son, refers both to the kiss and to absolution. The Old Norse word *són* is cognate with *zoen*, a Dutch word for kiss. The same word is found in Dutch *verzoening* which is synonymous with reconciliation, atonement, absolution.

Relating the myth of the Holy Mead to the act of bestowing wisdom, the Valkyries become strongly connected with the Gebo Rune. They dispense the mead. In the mysteries, they offer their horn of wisdom and magic to heroes and initiates. The motive appears in *Sigrdrifumal*. Names of Valkyries match those of the Germano-Celtic Matronae, many of which refer to Gebo, as there are Gabiae, Alagabiae, Garmangabis, Friagabis. From Viking times, Goddess names such as Gefn and Gefjon have survived. They all refer to the act of giving, the main Valkyrie motif.

From an esoteric point of view, the energy of Gebo strives towards balance, which is in itself an ideal. The Rune corresponds to Libra. In physics, the same corresponds to the law of the conservation of energy, the first thermodynamic law. Not just financial debts have to be compensated for, but those made of subtle energy as well. Wherever and whenever a vacuum occurs, energy must be supplied from elsewhere; and vice-versa. In history books, this phenomenon is known as transfers of power.

The financial aspect of Gebo is readily observed. In modern-day society, the balancing energy of Gebo is seen working in economy – or so it should be. Gebo is the system through which Fehu circulates. Through the medium of Gebo, the money finds its way, much like blood, to the necessary organs. Money is there to be spent. As Gebo represents the laws of finance, the seemingly subjective qualities of trust and goodwill can actually be measured by the fluctuations of stock markets.

The energies of Gebo stay balanced because they move all the time. Tiny adjustments are made all the time in order to keep the balance. It is the intelligence of Nature. Through this Daoist principle of equilibrium through movement Gebo remains stable. By its shape, it will drain excess energies or draw in needed extras. It is a *mobile perpetuum*.

The energy of Gebo is very gentle and favourable for hard sleepers or when to catch up on sleep. Its influence rounds off sharp ends and polishes rough faces. Gebo makes things uniform, although its energy is dynamic, in contrast with Berkana's. Gebo has an absolving and even appeasing effect; Berkana is static but pulsating.

Gebo indicates weddings, or any kind of relationship between two or more parties. Gebo is used to enter into engagements, to direct relationships and to induce luck. Atonement will be possible or maybe a more indifferent attitude will be assumed. Gebo denotes purification on an abstract level. It connects and ties loose ends. On a social level, the energy of Gebo can be used to bring people together, to get them connected. It also helps to have the energy in a group of people circulate more evenly. Often the Rune is associated with love. Gebo indicates a joyful event.

Ring Gods are Odin and Balder, and also Thor and Ull. Dwarves forge Odin's ring Draupnir. This ring generates eight new rings of equal value every ninth night. This way, Odin can financially maintain his troops. At Balder's cremation, Odin offers his son this magic ring.

The rings of Ull and Thor were used in oath taking. Thor's oath ring was attached to his weapon. The ring originally held the rope or chain with which the storm God swung his Bronze Age battle axe. The Old Norse word for the oath ring is *baugr*, which also means money, because pieces of the *baugr* were cut off and weighed as a means of payment. It is also the name of a giant, Baugi. In this instance, it refers to the oath ring attached to the temple's altar. The giant Baugi plays a role in Odin's quest for the Holy Mead. Odin is asked by Suttung to take an oath of honesty at the *symbel* he attends at the frost giants' hall. Once Odin sees an opportunity he breaks the oath and takes off with the mead that Suttung concealed there.

Thor is the God of marriage. With his hammer a wedding is blessed. This deity symbolizes faithfulness.

WUNJO   ᛈ

Wunjo has two meanings. Its prime meaning is joy, but it is sometimes translated as pasture. On the one hand, the Rune symbolizes friendship and on the other hand freedom. The concept of Wunjo refers to springtime celebrations, which is why this Rune is intimately linked with the Goddess Freyja.

The word for joy is etymologically related to verbs like 'to win, to wish, to ween, to wont and to want'. Additionally, it is cognate with sacred words like Vanir and Venus. Old Norse *vinr* means friend. This shows a series of connotations, all of which refer to a condition of fulfilment and success.

The Latin word *Venus* means passion, beauty and love. It has always puzzled me why the Goddess name Venus has a male ending in Latin. A similar puzzle is found in Northern myth. Tacitus mentions a Vanic earth Goddess Nerthus. This *Terra Mater* evolved into a male God over time, known as Njord. An analogous evolution is found in Mesopotamia, where the Goddess Ishtar is originally believed to have been a male war God. In Assyrian, the word *ishtaru* means God, whereas *ishtartu* means Goddess. Ishtar is also linked with the planet Venus and thus with Frigg and Freyja. This digression ties in with the motif of incest among the Vanir. Apparently, gender is interchangeable among the fertility deities.

Wunjo is a Rune of hope. As a Rune of joy Wunjo symbolizes friendship, togetherness and family. The shape of the Rune resembles a flag or banner, a symbol that typically unites people. Nowadays, this symbol equates with a company logo.

As a Rune of joy, Wunjo stands for the art of seducing, the so-called charming. The use of this Rune points to charms and enchantments. Wunjo denotes everything you are fond of and includes connotations of love.

Joy is a blissful feeling. In fact, joy is ultimately what people look for in life. Wunjo is a Rune of happiness and fulfillment. Its closing position in the first *aett* is therefore very fitting.

One expression of joy is laughter. Smiling relaxes the muscles and induces an inner sensation of liberty. Even a timid smile loosens the body as well as the mind and presents us with an opportunity to expand our inner world of awareness. In this sense, Wunjo refers to the exalted mind. Wunjo expresses a sense of purpose in daily life. If you want to connect to your soul, Wunjo is the Rune to work with. When a person meditates, a natural chemical substance called serotonin stimulates the production of DMT (dimethyltryptamine). This substance is also produced under extremely stressful circumstances, such as life threatening situations, near-death experience and ultimately death itself. The increase of DMT is then stimulated by higher levels of adrenalin, among other hormones, whereas in meditation, the levels of these hormones remain stable or even decrease. DMT is a substance associated with deep awareness. Plants that contain DMT have been used throughout history by South American shamans. In the human body, the substance is released from the pineal gland.

As a Rune of pasture, Wunjo symbolizes freedom. In actuality, the Rune name refers to the spring month when cattle were again allowed on the pasture, this point in time heralding summer. This moment was very important to shepherds and coincided with traditional celebrations venerating the Goddess Freyja, such as Walpurgis Night, Whitsuntide and the erecting of the Maypole. This was a time of enjoyment and festivities. Frey and Freyja are deities of joyfulness. Their names provided for the word 'frolic'. The Roman Goddess Laetitia may be associated with this Rune, too. She is the patron of any celebration. Her attributes of apples and wheat remind us of the Germano-Celtic Matrones.

As a Rune of pasture, Wunjo indicates a ritual space in the landscape. In ancient times, stones were piled up as an altar to indicate a holy site. These are called *hörg* in Old Norse and **harugaz* in Ancient Germanic. Another name is *vé*, or **wihaz*. They are often situated on elevations in the landscape. A *vé* is a consecrated area marked by wooden poles, torches or stones. Large ships made of standing stones still mark these sites. In heathen times, altar stones were blessed with sacrificial blood and sometimes blazed with a sacred fire. Cleasby and Vigfusson suggest that primarily the Disir were venerated at such sanctuaries. They are Goddesses akin to the Elves. The term *harugaz* may etymologically be linked with the Greek God name Hermes, who is an aspect of Odin. Additionally, Vé is a hypostasis of Odin.

Wunjo has an uplifting effect. Whenever friends meet, the energy of Wunjo is present. Its energy attracts the like-minded or calls new people into your life. The playful, temperate energy of Wunjo is capable of making you forget your cares. Its influence is including and enclosing. This Rune's power links, sometimes on a mental level, sometimes on the level of the heart. In group workings it symbolizes a spiritual leader or inner plane guidance. It may denote the egregore.

It is easily recognized that the Runes Kenaz, Gebo and Wunjo belong together. The hearth of Kenaz brings people together. It represents their joint focus. Gebo connects and harmonizes their energies – it represents their individual effort – so that the joy and fulfilment of Wunjo will be their part.

Wunjo stands for finishing a project, a positive outcome or a welcome visit, sometimes unexpected. In certain situations, Wunjo indicates increasing solitude. At other times, it stands for humour and free time. Often the Rune refers to family.

Odin, the God of wishing, who still acquits himself of this task as Saint Nicholas, is curiously associated with Wunjo. The Rune is linked in with the mystery of the Germanic triad of Odin, Vili and Vé. The Odinic triad is based on a w-alliteration. In Ancient Germanic, Odin's name used to be Wodanaz. This fact alone makes one realize that the Odinic Triad must have ancient roots. The sound shift that caused the initial W of Wodanaz to drop only occurred at about 500 CE. Therefore, the triad, Wodanaz-Wiljon-Wihaz, must have been very real in ancient Germanic times.

Of the triad, the Odin aspect symbolizes action. It represents the inspiration needed to start a working. The Vili aspect symbolizes intention, representing the magical will. The Vé aspect symbolizes the sphere of influence. It represents a sacred enclosure or magic circle. It is power in a spacious sense. All three are coordinates in the spiritual realm. Yet, Vé is the most physical of the three, Odin the most volatile and Vili the highest. They are matter, soul and spirit respectively. So, Odin and his brothers symbolize a triad of magical ingredients. Vili is the will to achieve something. Vé is the plane of action and possibly the target. Odin is the energy and power needed for expressing the will. The symbol of Vé is a V or triangle, reminiscent of Wunjo itself! The same V-shape was used to delineate sacred space. At the same time, Wunjo is the expression of all three combined.

HAGALAZ   N

Hagalaz literally means hailstorm. To Viking Age poets the term referred to war. Because of its association with death, the Underworld Goddess Hella rules this Rune. The symbol's energy is used to tune into the darker aspects of one's personality.

Usually, a hail storm only lasts for a handful of minutes and is always fathered by a thunderstorm (Thurisaz). But for the short time it lasts, it causes serious damage. In the old days, people mostly feared for their livestock and crops. Even then, no-one nowadays likes to get caught in a hail storm. In a metaphorical way, hail expresses the proverbial cold shower, or either an unexpected, painful experience. This often involves a public humiliation, for the reason that one is forced to show face. For this reason, the Rune is considered to be an ill-omened one. When you meet Hagalaz on your way, you can expect opposition. This layer of meaning is nonetheless only a generalization.

Hagalaz represents battle. To the Ancient Germanic people, hail was a kenning for war and battle, like a 'hail of bullets'. In German, they still speak about *Pfeilhagel* 'a hail of arrows'. The hailstorm therefore symbolizes the destructive result of an inimical volley of arrows. In the days of the Ancient Germanic people, it probably involved a hail of spears.

Snorri's *Skaldskaparmal* corroborates that missiles are often termed hail, snow or storm. Arrows are called the 'hail of the hand bow', and 'storm of spears' is a frequent kenning for fighting. Hence Hagalaz denoting a fight, threat or attack. On the other hand, Hagalaz stands for acquiescence and submission.

Jan Fries observes that in Neolithic Europe "while farming produced more wealth than before, the ever increasing communities led to an increase of diseases and warfare". Then, he goes on to say that larger communities imply more laws and regulations. His observation links the Runes Fehu, Hagalaz and Teiwaz as one complex of historical momentum. The more you

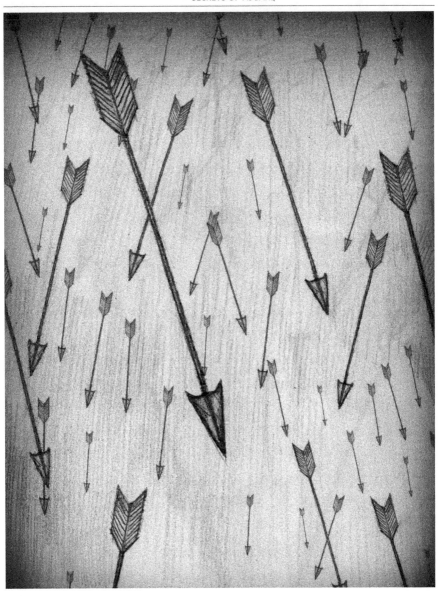

have (Fehu), the more you want to protect (Hagalaz) and the more social regulations are needed (Teiwaz).

Psychologically, war symbolizes inner conflict. Daily, people make choices as a *persona* that do not correspond to the nature of their real self. As a result, greater and lesser psychological issues are created that become suppressed or disregarded by the waking consciousness. Together they build up the Jungian shadow, corresponding to the Hagalaz symbolism. A small exercise can be done to face this much dreaded subconscious garbage. Visualize the Rune. This may be either Hagalaz or Nauthiz (fear). Hold it firm in order to consciously accept its existence. That is a first big step. Then slowly have the Rune disintegrate before your mind's eye until absolutely nothing is left. However, if you feel the need, you can afterwards fill up the Rune with a flow of brilliant gold light. If Nauthiz was used, it can afterwards be bent into a golden Algiz Rune.

The Celtic alphabet contains two alien letters. One is the letter H and must have had a Germanic origin. Incidentally, the Celtic letter Huath means both horror and fear, which matches Hagalaz's symbolic meaning. The other alien letter is the Celtic Z. The meaning of this letter is uncertain, but its kennings are known. Straif or Zraif is known as 'the strongest reddening, the increase of secrets, and the seeking of clouds'. The word for secrets is *rún*, cognate with Old Norse *rúna*. Possibly, the kenning translates as Great Secret (Algiz).

Psychological patterns are formed by conditioning ourselves in response to recurring circumstances. People usually remain unaware of these although these patterns exert on the individual's behaviour an influence that is not to be underestimated. Hagalaz represents these hidden routes of our consciousness. Therefore, this Rune offers an insight into our own patterns of behaviour and into those aspects that overshadow the self. Once these elements in the self have been unveiled, they lose (some of their) power. The individual will subsequently be more capable of being in harmony with himself.

In case one does not come to terms with one's own shadow, the role of the victim is played. Psychologically, Hagalaz denotes those people who profile themselves as victims. This passive and dependent attitude contrasts well with the first Rune of the third *aett*, Teiwaz being a Rune of activity. Yet Teiwaz can also be ascribed to the anti-hero.

To a large extent, the Goddess Hella, daughter of Loki, is associated with Hagalaz. She is the Underworld Goddess who represents a person's shadow. The realm of the dead symbolizes the subconscious, because that is where 'dead' thoughts and ideas go to. Some other ideas are deliberately suppressed by our consciousness, the realm of the Aesir, because they appear as hostile. Consider the myth of Gullveig in this light. The myth is also an example of how the power of Hagalaz destroys the happiness of Wunjo. Hagalaz and Wunjo symbolize the ever alternating poles of war and peace.

Hurling a spear is associated with Odin. His weapon is named Gungnir and has the ability to start a war. Esoterically, this ability possesses an initiating quality. Odin is also a death God.

The Goddess of snow is Skadi, who can also be associated with this Rune. She is a skilled archer. On top of that she symbolizes the contradistinction between giants and Gods in Norse mythology.

Hagalaz has a disrupting effect. It has the same effect as when someone stirs a puddle. Mud clouds the water. This mud symbolizes the settled past. Essentially, this Rune is used to stir up past and delicate issues from the depths of our unconscious. Yet Hagalaz is also experienced as a warding power. The Rune exposes and confronts the individual with difficult issues.

Hagalaz symbolizes inner conflict, but also indicates a personality clash. This Rune frequently stands for an unexpected event or turn of events that is sensed as being negative. Afterwards, it usually appears that these situations could have been avoided. Generally, Hagalaz signifies damage.

NAUTHIZ

This Rune means need. It implies everything ranging from instinct and desire over pressure and stress to resistance and fear. Nauthiz is associated with wyrd and is ruled over by the Northern Ladies of Karma, the Norns. In Ancient Germanic times, the word referred to a ritual known as the Need-Fire.

In daily life, the need of Nauthiz refers to all kind of needs, such as sleeping, eating and drinking. These needs are primarily a pressure created by our biological nature to take certain life sustaining actions. A large part of our life is spent fulfilling these requirements. Hence, this Rune symbolizes our basic instinct and strategy to survive. It depicts the side of life in which we are asked to perform our duties or to conform to society, including our social and work-related obligations next to our basic biological needs.

Metaphorically, Nauthiz indicates a precarious situation or crisis. Whenever need arises, it builds pressure on our emotional body; often it results in a mental collapse. It feels as if you are standing with your back against the wall having no room to manoeuvre. The pressure is too high to yield so that resistance and paralysis occur (Isa). In relation to Hagalaz, Nauthiz represents our response to disrupting, upsetting events. In the face of fear, people respond either by fighting or by running or by growing totally rigid. The complex of Hagalaz, Nauthiz and Isa relates to the fight-or-flight response.

From a historical point of view, Nauthiz symbolizes the Need-Fire. This is a Germanic ritual that involves the kindling of a fire by means of friction. The function of this ritual was to remedy disaster. These fires were made in times of dire need, as when an epidemic or famine occurred. In his work *The Golden Bough*, Frazer gives a full account of how the ritual was done. To start with, every fire in the surrounding area of the Need was put out. Then people gathered at the appointed place. Two selected individuals (Algiz) rubbed wood together, usually oak, until it caught flame and used it to kindle the bonfire. When the fire had somewhat died down, cattle and horses were driven through it and people ran through it. When everyone returned home,

they took bonfire torches with them to rekindle their own hearths. These torches are associated with the fire giant Surt. His name means black and refers to the charred wood.

The ritual explains the magical and purifying quality of fire. The poem *Havamal* confirms the fact that fire dispels disease. Moreover, it links Nauthiz with the ability to find a way out of trouble. Nauthiz is not only a Rune of trouble and affliction but also of alleviation and liberation. In this we recognize the Christian motive of suffering.

In Scandinavia, the midsummer fires, which are a formalized Need-Fire ritual, are dedicated to the Sun God Balder. Frazer mentions that annual fires, like those of midsummer and midwinter, go back to an original Need-Fire ceremony. These bonfires have been lighted in Europe until well into our own times. As in the Need-Fire, the Yule log was usually of oak.

The Need-Fire ritual seems to have served as a model for constructing healing charms. Many Viking Age charms include nine n-Runes (sometimes nine kinds of wood were used to kindle the fire). Some of them mention a stone called Surt, whereas associated healing rhymes instruct heating the stone. These three ingredients, the n-Rune, Surt and heat, refer to the Need-Fire ritual. At least one such charm indicates that the stone is situated at a holy place. For modern use, we can imagine a black stone on an altar encircled by nine n-Runes. A sick person holds the stone until it becomes warm. This way, the disease is transferred from the body into the stone. Complementing this, a German custom is recorded in which the community would walk up to a sacred White Stone on Whitsuntide. There, they would break off branches of a nearby yew tree and take them home to ward their houses and stables with.

The kindling of these ceremonial fires well expresses the energy of Nauthiz. Much like rubbing wood, rubbing your hands creates warmth. This heat is the result of friction. Fire by friction is based on the principle of resistance. Physically, resistance between objects results in energy accumulation. Metaphorically, the same is true for resistance between what two individuals or two parties might emotionally experience, or within the mind of one person between what the individual feels and thinks. They result in conflict, internally felt and/or externally expressed. Resistance creates pressure and therefore the need to respond. The ceremonial kindling is also a metaphor of the kindled heat of passion between lovers. Hence, the Rune stands for sexual contact.

According to Greek mythology, Hermes first invented fire by rubbing two sticks together. Hermes also governs boundaries, both marking and transgressing them. Nauthiz certainly stands for psychological boundaries. The energy of Nauthiz is mainly restrictive. Nauthiz denies passage, a responsibility accorded to Syn in the myths.

The Norns are associated with Nauthiz, because they preside over fate. Their names are Urd, Verdandi and Skuld, but every person has a personal Norn too. They create the life path of man. Some are akin to the Aesir, others to the Elves and still others to the dwarves. These three races represent the three levels of life; the mental types, the spiritual types and the emotional types.

Fate is often associated with karma. In the Northern tradition we have the concept *wyrd*. Karma is often interpreted in a negative way, and the same applies to 'fate', but that should not always be the case. The nature of events is merely the result of deeper causes. In the present you create your own circumstances. This is where the power of Nauthiz lies.

The power of Nauthiz compels. It makes you do something. It is the adrenalin that rushes through your veins when you want something done right away. This Rune is capable of delivering an ultimatum. Excitement, too, can be a result of this Rune's energy. The energy of need is the driving force behind all creativity. The energy of this Rune is easily visualized, but it must not be mistaken for the object of desire. Nauthiz is only a subjective feeling. It is the ego's power to strongly hold on – out of fear of losing it. In contrast, Isa holds things on a neutral basis.

On the other hand, this Rune often leads to putting things off, resulting in a lack of change. In this way, its power symbolizes futile attempts. After all, it is a Rune of frustration. Nauthiz is when you are not able to get the most out of a situation. The related feeling of regret belongs to Eihwaz.

Nauthiz also has a binding effect, since its power restricts your freedom of movement. It has much in common with Thurisaz and the planet Saturn. The Old Icelandic Rune Poem explains the Nauthiz Rune as thralldom: *nauð er þýjar þrá*. You are bound by whatever drives you against your better judgement. It may even drive you towards insanity. The thralldom of Nauthiz is the oft feared fetter of addiction. However, this emotional condition is a great opportunity to break through illusion in order to gain a greater sense of independence.

Nauthiz indicates pressure of time. Its energy is that small amount of pressure needed to keep on performing. If this pressure is handled in the wrong way, an unhealthy kind of stress arises. Psychologically, the Rune indicates fears and inhibitions. Esoterically, Nauthiz holds the power to release the soul.

In divination, the Rune advocates immediate action. Yet the presence of this Rune sometimes tells you that any action at all will be in vain. These actions will be carried out anyway, although they will lead to nothing or even to negative results. The Rune denotes a denial of something you think you have a right to. Sometimes it simply means denial. Nauthiz stands for indecisiveness, but also for serious efforts and hard work. The Old Norse Rune Poem glosses this Rune *opera*, which is Latin for 'work'. Nauthiz symbolizes difficulties.

ISA

The Rune Poems describe Isa as cold, slippery, glistening, clear and treacherous. These icy qualities offer a wide range of symbolism. On the one hand, Isa stands for chill, rigidity, invariability, and obstinacy. On the other hand, Isa stands for clarity, splendour, the deep, and the even. Isa represents the absolute zero of physics, a temperature at which both time and space cease to exist.

Isa reminds us of a cool or icy personality, a sudden silence in a discussion or an uncomfortable situation. Once 'the ice is broken' distance dissolves. It indicates situations in which two individuals are emotionally well tuned but psychologically unable to express it. Distance is guarded in spite of mutual understanding. In comics, icy speech bubbles are used to denote a cool and distant answer.

The ice to which the Futhark alludes is a surface. When winters are relatively severe the upper layer of water freezes over on ponds, lakes and rivers. This phenomenon holds the vice and virtue of Isa, since it is not always perceptible whether the ice will bear the weight of a man or not; hence the saying not to walk across one night's ice. This proverb is already included in *Havamal*, where this piece of advice is to be taken literally. Frozen rivers offered an excellent opportunity to walk across the water instead of crossing a real bridge. That is why the ice is called the 'broad bridge' in kennings. Germanic tribes crossed the frozen Rhine to invade Roman territory in December 406 CE.

In Isa we find the capacity to build a temporary bridge. From a deeper understanding this is achieved through concentration, one of key words of Isa. The clear, glassy constitution of ice looks much like crystal and symbolizes focus, clarity of mind and flow. The aspect of flowing through ice is physically demonstrated by inventions such as superconductors that conduct energy at a greater speed when they are kept at the lowest temperatures possible. Isa technically represents the absolute zero. Practically, absolute zero cannot exist, because it would mean the end of our universe. However, this

observation links Isa to Thurisaz, because of its relation to entropy. At the same time, Isa represents meditation and contemplation. The slippery-as-glass surface is treacherous on the one hand, but on the other hand offers the possibility to introspection and 'reflection'.

Before you want to venture on the ice, you must be well prepared. If this is not the case, chances are you lose control and have a bad tumble. The coldness of the ice does not only stand for paralysis, but also for death itself. In a figurative sense, this denotes postponement or abandoning a plan. Isa stands for an unwilled end result. Its power of paralysis makes this Rune a valuable aid in achieving and maintaining the cataleptic state necessary to astrally project. Then invoke the Eagle. Or the Helicoptre.

Isa has a freezing power. Its energy is cold and pure at the same time. It draws heat from the body and life force from the environment, but it sharpens the mind as well, deepens awareness and allows a thorough grounding. Isa has the power to call things to a stop.

The magic of Isa is meant to congeal an energy complex. Isa makes manifest. Its power cools down an abstract realization into something real, because Isa does not just freeze things as they are at a certain time but also makes the inherent crystalline formation of the thought form apprehended come into view. This is the real power of Isa. It makes things crystal clear. The work of Masaru Emoto has shown the reality of this. Additionally, in combination with Sowulo, this insight reveals the true meaning of the old formula *solve et coagula*. The magic of Isa also simply holds things.

In divination, Isa points to possible danger, maybe treason or an insufficient preparation. When Isa appears, prudence is called for. Sometimes it denotes someone who secludes himself from his surroundings; someone lonely. In general, Isa indicates a standstill, silence or break. Depending on the context, this break is welcome or not. Isa also denotes an absence of energy, pointing to a degree of incapacity to carry out a certain act of one's will. On the other hand, Isa represents pure will power.

In mythology, this Rune is linked with the frost giants. These rime thurses live high in the barren mountain ranges. One of those frost giantesses is reckoned as one of the Gods. Her name is Skadi and she is married to Njord. She is called 'shining', possibly alluding to ice. She is a winter Goddess. Her male equivalent is Ull. Perhaps we might reckon the mythical giant Ymir as belonging to Isa too, since this primal being is created from ice and in fact embodies the crystallization of fire and water; spirit and matter. Cosmic Fire is related to Fehu, whereas cosmic water is an aspect of Laguz, this Rune being the medium for ice anyway. The alignment of these three Runes in the Futhark diagram well expresses their relation. From Ymir the Earth is created, represented by Jera.

Since Thorsson's work on the Runes, Isa has traditionally been held to be Fehu's counterpart. However, more in tune with the actual lore, Isa is complemented by Sowulo, and Fehu by Uruz. In spite of that, it makes sense to set Isa against Fehu. It is the discipline with which the diverging power of Fehu can be harnessed. Fehu is full movement, whereas Isa is total stillness, which cannot be said of Uruz.

JERA

Jera is a Rune of time, life and death, evolution and all kinds of cycles in general. The symbol represents the investment on the one hand and reward on the other. The deity associated is Frey, the God of plenty.

The name of this Rune refers to harvest time. Only later on, the word became to mean year. Therefore, Jera refers to the harvest seasons of summer and fall in the first place. When explaining 'harvest' as a metaphor Jera signifies the result of hard work done.

To the Ancient Germanic person, Jera referred to the agricultural year. To farmers, tilling the earth usually means a lot of hard work. There is a long period of toil that precedes the actual harvest and even then, bringing in the harvest means effort too. On the one hand, Jera symbolizes the fruit of your efforts and on the other hand working towards a goal. A certain extent of investing is always necessary in achieving anything, although this can be done on many levels. Most often, Jera stands for work, but it can also denote a financial or social investment. Jera then indicates those advantages you can count on in the future, like help from your friends or your retirement pay. The Rune Poems emphasize the positive result oriented aspects of the Rune.

In a figurative sense, the harvest symbolizes reaping the results of your past actions and accepting responsibility for what you have caused to happen. As you sow, so you shall reap. Therefore, Jera corresponds to the inevitable Law of Karma. At a certain level, Jera symbolizes death. It is the Grim Reaper in full action. Saturn is known as a Lord of Karma.

As a Rune of time, Jera represents cycles. On an individual level, this Rune expresses the four seasons of man. More esoterically, Jera refers to the soul cycling in and out of incarnation. It implies the cycle of involution and evolution. On a grander scale it represents the cosmic age. In physics and astronomy, it refers to precession. The Rune's shape resembles a galaxy's.

As the embodiment of a time cycle, Jera represents steady progression and natural evolution. Jera symbolizes growth and development. The power of time can be wielded in creating favourable circumstances. Jera indicates those circumstances when the right person is in the right place at the right time. With this Rune time is manipulated. Magically, the energy of Jera sends your intention into the field of time. As a result, it is then everywhere, but of course you give it direction. When you put a magic in the energy of Jera, you release it into the medium of time. Of itself, the magic will operate. And it will only be able to work at the right time.

As a harvest Rune, Jera offers wheat, of which both bread and beer are made. Consequently, this Rune is involved in acquiring food. A connection with Fehu cannot be avoided. Money is what is earned by hard work. In addition, the sequence of Jera, Eihwaz, and Pertho refers to acquiring food, albeit in different ways. Jera refers to farming, Eihwaz to hunting and Pertho to gathering. Grains have been the first plants to be domesticated. Rye and wheat were first cultivated from around 11,000-9000 BCE. In Northern and Western Europe, this only happened from 7000 BCE onwards. Even later this led to a sedentary type of life.

In his book, Olsen explains well the relation between Fehu, Jera and Gebo as the process of an investment towards an envisioned goal. It struck me as relevant that these three Runes form a triangle in the Futhark diagram. Once visualized, the triangle can be expanded on, adding Teiwaz and Othila. Material gain is then visualized by the descending Runes Fehu, Jera and Othila, as Fehu represents money and Othila ownership. Spiritual gain would be visualized along the rising line of Teiwaz, Jera and Gebo.

Frey and Njord preside over Jera. These Gods are responsible for a good yield. Frey and Njord are also considered to be Gods of peace. This is exactly because they provide food for the community. Another fertility God associated with Jera is Thor. With his fiery lightning bolts it is Thor who fecundates the land. The Ancient Germanic people and the Vikings dedicated ploughed land to the God of Thunder.

In divination, Jera shows a gain. It also indicates fecundity, growth, maturity, and an appreciation of life. Its gentle energy allows one to go with the flow of life.

EIHWAZ

Eihwaz represents the yew tree (*taxus baccata*). This evergreen unites the concepts of life and death. Typically, bows were made of its wood, which is why Eihwaz symbolizes hunting. Ull is associated with this Rune.

The foremost feature of yew is that it is evergreen. The fact that this conifer remains fresh in winter makes it a symbol of life and immortality. It symbolizes the continuity of life during the stages of death. Druid lore associates the tree with immortality and resurrection.

Conversely, the yew tree is known as a Tree of Death. About every part of the tree is poisonous. Arrows and spears were dipped in yew sap changing them into lethal weapons. In a wider sense, poison signifies corruption, disease and paralysis. Someone with a poisonous tongue will sow discord and disunity. Often a deliberate and sneaky action is suspected in these cases. The positive side of poison is that the substance can be used medicinally.

Traditionally, yew trees are found at burial places. According to folklore, the spirits of the dead reside in the trees or among the tree's roots. Through these associations, Eihwaz is a symbol of the Underworld. It gives access to this world.

On the other hand, the magic of yew wood was said to keep witches and wizards away. The wood protects against sorcery, and yew talismans were commonplace in the old days. In German folklore, a piece of yew wood was worn on the body to keep safe from sorcery. In Sweden, the living room was decorated with green yew twigs in order to keep out evil. Spiteful dwarves, known to cause disease in Germanic belief, were driven out with twigs of yew. Maybe jinxed computers can be remedied with the energy of Eihwaz, too.

The practical worth of yew, however, lies in its elastic quality. Bows were made from this wood, the Greek tree name *taxus* meaning bow. According to Jan Fries, bows became popular from Neolithic times onwards because forests quickly started to grow thick after the last Ice Age. The bow and arrows outrivaled all other weapons to hunt game. Therefore, Eihwaz stands for

hunting. The act of hunting is associated with focused attention. It is known of cats that their minds go into alpha state when they are about to attack. The energy of Eihwaz is certainly able to bring you into a deeper state of consciousness. The chemical substance associated with hunting is dopamine.

In prehistoric times, bows were made of elm. Unfortunately, this kind of tree practically disappeared at around 4000 BCE, so that another species of tree took its role. In fact, this incidentally explains the myth of Ask and Embla. They are bow and arrow, Embla being the female bow and Ask representing the darting male arrow. Moreover, the Dutch word for elm, *iep*, is cognate with 'yew'. Bow and arrow also seem to be linked to Loki's parents Laufey and Farbauti. In the Yr stanza of The Old Icelandic Rune Poem Farbauti is connected to the arrow. The name Laufey occurs in the Bjarkan stanza and refers to the suppleness of birch wood, alluding to the bow's strength. Laufey's alternative name is Nal 'needle' explaining her name to refer to a conifer. Loki's own association with the arrow is found in the myth of Balder's death. In addition, Loki is associated with poison (*laevatein*).

Eihwaz expresses the action to step up to a certain goal. Aim your arrows towards your target and fire. Accordingly, this Rune denotes purposefulness and pursuing ideals. To the spiritual person, hunting symbolizes the quest for Truth.

Eihwaz can be used to succeed in achieving a clear-cut objective, like finding a job, a house or a partner. Keep in mind though that this Rune requires sacrifices. To achieve what you want you will have to give up something else. Thus Odin took his own life to acquire the wisdom of the Runes.

The Rune is a symbol of discipline. Often Eihwaz indicates tough luck or a trying situation. Its energy challenges you and puts you to the test. Its power teaches you to hang on and not to let complications or hindrances of any kind throw you off balance. It wields the energy of competition. In divination, Eihwaz may indicate a person harassing you.

The God of the hunt is Ull. He excels in archery and lives in Ydalir, the Valley of the Yew. He is venerated at midwinter. About the same time of the year the Christmas tree is decorated, which is a Germanic yew cult vestige.

The Goddess of the hunt is Skadi. She too is a winter Goddess. On top of that, she is associated with venom. When Loki was bound, she hung a snake above his head so that Loki would be tortured by the poison dripping onto him. Poison associates the serpent with Eihwaz. Snakes as well as the yew tree are attributes of the mystery God Odin. Snakes dwell amid the roots of the World Tree.

The shape of the Eihwaz Rune recalls a staff and I like to recognize Odin's spear in the glyph. The Rune shape also resembles the *was*-sceptre of Ancient Egyptian iconography. These staffs were held only by supernatural beings and were usually the length of the body. The top was bent and the bottom had a hook. The sceptre symbolizes the alignment of the chakras in the human body. Similarly, Yggdrasil unifies the Nine Worlds. Because of this, Eihwaz has a great bearing on consciousness.

Eihwaz's shape is evocative of the spinal column. But because Eihwaz is essentially a mind Rune, its energy directly relates to the nervous system and its subtler counterpart, the etheric body, and consequently to the chakras. These subtle energy centers are usually represented as wheels, which links Raido to Eihwaz. Completing the triad, Laguz symbolizes the energy flow whirling the chakras and vitalizing the etheric body. We find thus three kinds of movement in this triad: free energy (Laguz), structural energy (Eihwaz) and connective energy (Raido).

Along esoteric lines, Jera and Eihwaz form an interesting pair. In our world, energy exists in two forms, life and consciousness. These two concepts resound in Jera and Eihwaz. Jera represents the ever pulsating energy of life. It moves and whirls and ever continues. Eihwaz is connected with the deep mind. It links the physical brain with the etheric and astral body through the energy centres and through an ever present awareness. As an esoteric version of the Isa Rune, Eihwaz represents supreme self-consciousness and the ability to deepen the mind. The movement of the mind along the axis of different mental states can be compared to travelling up and down the Yggdrasil tree. In meditation the mind is guided by a conscious effort along the vertical axis of the spiritual dimension.

PERTHO   ᚹ

Pertho is an interesting Rune because the word as it has come down to us has not been explained adequately. Traditionally, it has been translated as 'dice cup'. In my opinion, it has a Celtic root and refers to the apple tree. As such, Pertho is associated with the Goddess of youth, Idun. In later medieval Rune lore, the Rune sign explicitly refers to Ginnungagap. Therefore, Pertho symbolizes the subtle reality behind all manifestation. Psychologically, it refers to the collective consciousness.

The meaning of the Pertho Rune is somewhat obscure. The word is found in none of the modern Germanic languages. The translation of the Old English variant *peorð* as 'dice cup' is likewise uncertain. In any way, the shape resembles some sort of receptacle. Perhaps the Pertho Rune refers to a cauldron. Perhaps it metaphorically refers to receiving and gathering subtle energy and information.

Possibly, the name of the Rune is derived from the Celtic word for 'apple tree', *quert*. Indo-European languages divide into families retaining an original qu- or changing to a p-; compare Latin *equus* to Greek *hippos*. This shift happened in the first millennium BC. Central European languages changed an original sounding *quert* into **pert*. This word strongly resembles the Old English *peorð* and the corresponding Gothic *pairþra* and *qairþra*. The Gothic letter shapes for P and Q both resemble the Pertho Rune, albeit in a different position. It therefore seems sound to posit that Pertho means apple. The word might be linked to Latin *quercus*.

The apple is a symbol of love. It symbolizes fertility, love, fidelity and affection. It is used in love magic and marital rituals all over Europe. Among many customs, De Cleene records the practice of offering an apple as a token of proposal. Apples were given to express your love to someone. In Germany, symbols were carved on the apple or a small paper was inserted in the apple. On the paper was written your name in blood. This was given to the person. The apple was also used to facilitate childbirth. There is an Old Norse tale in

which a king and queen are granted a child by eating a divine apple. Ultimately, this species of tree is related to the rose family.

In Northern mythology, the apple belongs to Idun. She is the Goddess of youthfulness and keeps the apples of youth in a maple basket. It is quite likely that the shape of the p-Rune represents this basket. I had a dream once that explained that the Old English Rune Calc was derived from Pertho. This makes sense, since the shape of the Calc Rune resembles Pertho very much. In addition, the Hickes' edition of the Old English Rune Poem shows a different shape for the original Perthro Rune suggesting that another Rune had taken over part of its function. This must be Calc. The very word means chalice, which links it with the concept of a container, such as a cup, basket or cauldron. The meaning is backed up by an alternative etymological explanation. It is possible that the Rune name does not derive from the Celtic word for apple but rather from the Celtic word for cauldron. The Welsh word *pair* means cauldron.

In my opinion, Idun's apples are the fruit of the World Tree Yggdrasil. So, a link is made to the previous Rune, Eihwaz representing the *axis mundi*. In Greek mythology, the golden apples of immortality were guarded by the Hesperides. These nymphlike Goddesses are associated with the western quarter representing nightfall. In the west lies the isle of immortality, known in the Celtic tradition as Avalon, the Isle of Apples. Here, the apple trees symbolize eternal youth. According to Ellis-Davidson, Valhalla, too, is situated in the west. These Hesperides are the Greek counterpart of the nine Invidjur who live in the tree, mentioned in the *Voluspa*. Moreover, the Greek tree of life is guarded by a dragon. In Northern myth, this creature is known as Nidhogg. A further association can be made with Mesopotamian mythology. The Sumerian Hulub tree housed a snake among the roots and an eagle in the top, reminiscent of the Germanic story. The snake, sometimes a lion, represents the Earth realm, whereas the eagle stands for Heaven. The Hulub tree housed a third creature, namely Lilith. In the Northern tradition, she is Freyja, but can be compared with the Hesperides and the Invidjur, since she represents the soul of the tree. In a temple in ancient Germania Freyja was depicted holding three apples in her hand. Incidentally, Saint Nicholas, a hypostasis of Odin, is attributed three golden apples resting on a book. These represent the three wishes of the average fairy tale. According to De Cleene, the apple was sacred to Balder.

The Gods have to eat Idun's apples to remain young. That is why Pertho is associated with eternal youth, recovery and rejuvenation. The Rune symbolizes the essence of life; the invisible side of reality. In Celtic mythology, the apple is emblematic of Avalon. Throughout many a tradition, the apple refers to paradise. On the one hand, the apple bestows knowledge, on the other hand longevity. Both may be related. The Chinese occult system was inherently construed to prolong life through various exercises. The apple is a symbol of immortality.

The Northern equivalent of paradise is Idavoll, the Garden of Idun. The mystical apple stands for poetic inspiration, because cider was made of this fruit. Furthermore, the apple is the key to the Otherworld. It is the instrument leading you from the physical realm to the mythical world; from the rational to the poetical. That is why it is associated with prophecy in the Celtic tradition and *spá* in the Northern.

Idun and her basket of apples remind us of the Matres/Matrones cult. This was a fertility cult popular among continental Celts and Germanics alike with sacred centres along the Rhine. These Mothers were shown seated in parties of three, often with a basket of fruit beside them. As a trinity, they may either correspond to the Norns or to the triple Goddess. Their late Celtic match would be Ériu, Banba and Fódla. The Mothers' season must have been autumn at which time offerings of fruit were probably given to them. The Celtic apple month, Quert, roughly corresponds to September. However, the Northern tradition celebrates the archetypal mother, Frigg, at Yule eve, which is called Mother Night. This celebration is related to the Disablot or Disting, at which the Disir were honoured. The Disir may have been maternal ancestors.

Because of its uncertain meaning, this Rune has been associated with the mystical altogether. Pertho stands for secrets and events that have not yet taken place.

In the late Middle Ages, the Pertho Rune represented Ginnungagap. The Icelandic Gapaldurstafur is basically a Pertho Rune turned so as to represent the vault of the sky. *Gapaldur* means 'the age of Ginnungagap'. In the same historical period, *ginnungagap* was synonymous with the vastness of the sea or the sky, the heavens. Snorri notes in his *Skaldskaparmal* that *ginnungagap* is a kenning for sky. In both is found the quality of the infinite. In mythology, Earth is also surrounded by *ginnungagap*. In the middle of this space Midgard was created. Consequently, we can imagine Ginnungagap to be deep space.

Pertho is associated with the night sky. This is an image not only of Ginnungagap, but of Mimir as well. Staring into the night sky will awaken spiritual ambition in oneself.

The morpheme *ginn* refers to the age before creation. It denotes the potential that is present in the chaotic and embryonic cosmos. *Ginn* is the quality generated when fire and water are activated, when positive and negative poles are juxtaposed. It represents the range of possibilities as suggested by quantum probability. Moreover, the Pertho Rune symbolizes the so-called Zero Point Field underlying all manifestation. Laszlo terms this field Akasha. The morpheme *ginn* is found in the English verb 'to begin', which gives a hint as to the meaning of Ginnungagap. *Ginn* is also found in the Dutch word *ontginnen* 'to extract'. As it is, the word is etymologically related to Greek *khaos*. According to Ovid, chaos precedes the ordered universe, cosmos.

As a pre-creative stage in history, Pertho psychologically refers to an individual's early childhood. From this point of view, the *ginn*-quality of Pertho corresponds to the innocent growing up of a child. Psychologists often claim that events at this stage of life determine future personality. In other words, it represents someone's established *örlög*. Our childhood corresponds to the early stages of becoming the person that we are meant to be and so to fulfill our destiny.

Magically, Pertho is used to obtain information from the collective unconscious. Ginnungagap is reflected in Mimir's Well. Moreover, Pertho can be used as a vacuum in which you will be able to create your own fate. In this way, the Rune is linked with Frigg and the Norns. It is the pool that all occult students drink from. As a symbol of the collective subconscious, Pertho teaches that information is not owned by anyone in particular, rather is it available to every mind able enough to resonate with the information looked for. It often happens that two or more people pick up on specific information in a creative way at the same moment in time but living miles apart. They both have a claim to original insight. Since this happens quite regularly, the work of both scholars is usually acknowledged. It is one of Pertho's pulls to create synchronicity. However, you may then wonder to what extent it is important to be able to claim innovation, since on the mental and spiritual levels it is ready to be perceived by all individuals fine-tuned enough to pick it up. More importantly, the resultant thought-form will circulate. No one can claim knowledge, because it is in the ether. The thought-forms contacted were created by the merging of minds. It must come into existence first, and then it can be picked up on. It only needs those few able minds to manifest. On the genius of a few, progression depends. But a lot more work is done than appears in science papers.

The next Rune in the row, Algiz, may be seen as the radar with which to attune oneself to the knowledge of Pertho. A person only responds to energies that he himself is working with. He has trained his mind to consciously receive certain impulses only. A person trained in mathematics will rarely have innovating ideas on psychology. The same is true within the limits of a school of mystery. Those working with the Runes and the Northern tradition will automatically drink from the same pool and mentally connect through their study. However, it will be less likely that they will be making headway in yogic philosophy or Jewish mysticism. Of course, one can always train oneself in different traditions at the same time, though you must be aware of the cost.

Pertho offers insight into the different layers of existence and into the possibility to creating your own reality. Cause and effect are one in Pertho. This Rune symbolizes the input and addition of data. Pertho is the book of the cosmos. Pertho is a storehouse of memories. Secrets of the past become the potential for growth in the future. Any recollection of past experience, whether in the body, the mind or on the astral level, is a grand opportunity to heal.

In divination, Pertho indicates an unexpected event. It may denote karma or it may denote exploiting a one time opportunity. Someone guided by the energy of Pertho will unexpectedly but intentionally change the course of his or her life. Such a person will take another direction. The future is open to all ends.

ALGIZ Ψ

Algiz means both elk (*Alces Alces*) and protection. In addition, it was the name of a twin deity. The Rune's alternative name, Alhaz, is based on the Gothic letter name and refers to a sacred place. The Rune's meaning seems to draw heavily on shamanic practice. On a deep level, Algiz symbolizes the subtle reality of man.

Algiz refers to a twin God that the Roman historiographer Tacitus calls Alcis. This twin God has been compared to the Greek Dioskouroi. They are a pair of brothers idolized as young men and associated with the oak tree. Tacitus mentions that the Alcis were venerated in a certain wood in Germania and reports that the high priest approaches them dressed up like a woman. Not much more is known about the Alcis, except for the fact that the name translates as both 'protection' and 'elk'. Evidently, there must be a connection between Alcis, protection and elk. The concept that underlies this connection is either hunting or shamanism.

On the one hand, Algiz literally means protection and among the Gothic people refers to a sacred site of some kind. This foremost meaning is found in Greek words like *alke* and *alexein*. On the other hand, elk is an epithet of Odin (Old Norse *elgr*). From , it is known that Odin dresses up as a woman to practice *seiðr*, which is a version of shamanism possibly having its roots in Finnish shamanism. The elk's antlers are emblematic of early shamanism. The Hallristningar show both horses and people covered with them. In his *Helrunar*, Jan Fries mentions that sets of deer antlers were found that were made to fit human heads. The symbolism of the elk's antlers compares to the horned crowns in Sumerian iconography. Supernatural beings in Ancient Sumer are always depicted wearing them as a sign of divinity. It is very likely that all these connotations are somehow interwoven, so that Algiz denotes the site, the person, the deity and the animal that form part of a certain shamanic ritual.

Ellis-Davidson mentions that shamanic rituals were performed in connection with the elk hunt. These ceremonies were held on secluded

locations and were specifically designed to show respect to the animal world; a sort of thanksgiving for being allowed to hunt game. At these sites the shaman carved symbols on the rocks. The ceremony formed the spiritual side of the once necessary practice of hunting deer. The elk was hunted by specially trained dogs. Prey was raised into a lake. There a party of hunters lay waiting firing arrows and spears to kill the helpless animals. This kind of hunt is referred to in both *Havamal* 90 and the Ur stanza of the Old Norse Rune Poem. One kenning for ice is 'gallows of the elk'. Among the Inuit, raven talismans were worn to hunt elk, since these sacred birds were able to stealthily approach the animals.

All in all, Algiz symbolizes divine protection. The Rune shape corresponds to a posture of worship that is adopted almost automatically when a person calls on the Gods. The Algiz energy is very warding and offers a sense of security. To call upon the Rune's capacity of protection, place yourself in the middle of its energy.

Algiz has a consecrating energy. Items and rooms can be hallowed with its power. The Rune emanates a sort of holy quality. Algiz enables you to make contact with the higher realms, with the divine or celestial energies. You could use the Algiz Rune to replace the pentagram of other traditions.

This Rune stimulates the flow of energy from the subtle dimensions towards our realm of physical reality. To man, this Rune expresses the pull of the spiritual dimension. When the hands are lifted towards the heavens they express a person's desire to walk among the Gods.

The Algiz energy indicates ambition, because this Rune refers to the desire to take things to a next level. This can be expressed socially, professionally or spiritually. Frequently, the Rune indicates divine protection. Your deeds are supervised from above. Psychologically, this compares with the intuition. In esoteric circles we speak of guides. This Rune makes you feel as if you have been chosen.

Algiz indicates a good mental receptivity. This means that you pick up a lot of useful information – stored in Pertho. Algiz is a Rune of awareness, which is a quality readily associated with Heimdal. Consequently, the Rune reflects heightened states of awareness.

The God Heimdal is frequently associated with Algiz. He stands guard over Asgard and administers access to the realm of the soul. He rules Bifrost Bridge, which is the pathway that leads to celestial promise. The bridge is visualized as a rainbow and described as having three colours. The number corresponds to the Rune's fork. Being the seventh Rune in the second *aett* the Rune's number also reminds us of the seven colours of the rainbow. According to *Gylfaginning*, the Bridge's main ingredient is fire.

The shape of the Algiz Rune is a glyph with deep symbolism. It represents the Antahkarana as it is understood by Alice Bailey and others of the same tradition. Antahkarana means Rainbow Bridge, immediately linking it with Bifrost and explaining the Northern concept's esoteric meaning. In the Younger Futhark, the same glyph symbolizes a person (Madr). Its shape recalls a person's physical body, but it also reflects the individual's inner framework. Inner man is an amalgam of etheric, astral and mental bodies, connected to the spiritual through the soul and the monad. The three lower bodies comprise the so-called personality. Thus three inner levels arise. They are represented by the top, centre and bottom area of the Algiz Rune. In a more detailed way, the symbol's shape outlines the individual's inner framework. The heart of the Rune symbolizes an individual's personality. From this point, the personality is branched into the different bodies. The physical body is represented by the nethermost point of the glyph; the vital, emotional and mental bodies are represented by the symbol's fork. Algiz as a whole then stands for a person's inner alignment. Once the different bodies are integrated, the individual contacts his or her soul. In occultism, this is known as 'bridging the soul'. As a personality, the individual will attempt to incorporate the quality of soul into his life, whereas the soul will attempt to contact the lower levels of man via the mental body. In the Northern tradition, Bifrost bridges the heavens from the Earth upwards while the Gods descend from Asgard downwards.

SOWULO   ⟩

Sowulo is a very potent Rune. The word means Sun and refers to the Northern Sun Goddess. Sometimes she is called Sól, sometimes Sunna. She drives across the skies in either a ship or a cart. She is also pictured as a whirling wheel, and 'Elf-Wheel' is one of her names. The Rune is associated with the swastika. As a symbol of light and life, Sowulo stands for the light of the soul and for success in life.

The number 16 is strongly connected to solar symbolism in esoteric numerology. 8 is the number of the Sun and Sowulo is the eighth Rune of the second *aett*, while 16 itself refers to the swastika. The number 16 also adds up to 7, which is the number of cosmic Rays in the tradition of the Ageless Wisdom, the number of colours in a rainbow, and the number of planets in classical astrology.

The symbolism of the swastika is intimately connected to the Sowulo Rune. The so-called *fylfot* is made up of two entwined s-Runes. Nonetheless, the swastika can also be seen as a bind Rune of Jera and Eihwaz; the point of stillness and the moving All.

Sowulo represents the solar Goddess Sól. A whole complex of myth surrounds her. Her brother, Máni, is a lunar God. They are fathered by Mundilfœri, who named his children Sun and Moon because of their beauty. The solar Rune is a symbol of all that is beautiful. Every day, Sól drives the solar chariot through the skies. This cart carries a spark of the Fire World Muspelheim. It is out of this spark that the Aesir created the Sun. In this way, cosmic Fire is added to the world of Midgard. The spark's blaze is so hot that it has to be cooled down by iron (Isa), if not it would burn the mountains and boil the seas. The Sun Chariot is drawn by a team of horses, called Arvak and Alsvin (Ehwaz). In Greek mythology, the Sun Chariot is driven by Helios and pulled by four horses.

The Sun Goddess is also named Sunna. Her name means 'in the south'. From the Old Norse Rune Poem it appears that every morning she was greeted with a solemn bow. Grimm mentions a similar custom.

Beauty is one of the main aspects of this Rune. Sowulo is therefore associated with the Light Elves. Snorri Sturluson says that the Elves are more beautiful than the Sun to look at. Maiden giants, too, are reckoned to be the most beautiful creatures. In *Skirnismal* they are an expression of the Sun's beauty. According to Northern myth, their white skin shines like the Sun. The colour white is associated with the Sun and the Sun Goddess. Figuratively, the giant maidens express the power of attraction and desire. Esoterically, they represent the power of subtle energy radiation.

As a source of light and heat, the Sun determines all life on Earth by means of the seasons, the tides and the rhythm of day and night. Sunlight is essential to good health, and a sunny day will render anybody more happy. When the Sun comes out, people do too. Metaphorically, this feeling relates to expressions such as 'bringing in sunshine' and 'brightening up the house'. A person like this is always cheerful, his mood often being infectious. This connotation of joy is also found in the Dutch saying 'after the rain comes the Sun again' which means as much as 'after a storm comes calm'. All in all, Sowulo stands for good times, happiness and general prosperity, much like Wunjo. The storm mentioned refers to Hagalaz, emphasizing the duality of H and S. These three Runes thus create a dynamic triangle of force.

Therapeutically, the heat aspect of the Rune's energy is able to dissolve any frozen area in body or mind. Some parts of you may take more time and energy than others to melt. Still, all Isa problems can be solved by means of Sowulo. Frigidity, lethargy and stagnation will disappear as snow to the Sun. But whatever was captured in the past by the holding power of Isa will then be released. Often, with this kind of work the energy of Hagalaz surfaces. But if healing is done in a gentle way, then Hagalaz's dark power is easily handled.

In the Futhark, Sowulo is the antithesis of Isa. Sowulo is the natural enemy of ice, because her warmth will thaw the frost. The Old Icelandic Rune Poem says *sól er ísa aldrtregi*. This physical relation works well in a metaphysical way too. From a depth psychological point of view, Isa stands for the ego or lower self and Sowulo stands for the soul or Higher Self. Once the power of the Sun increases, the ice must give way. A parallel is found in the first *aett*, as shown by Freya Aswynn, where Thurisaz stands for the lower will and Wunjo represents the true, higher Will.

Essentially, Sowulo is a Light Rune. In fact, the Rune's shape recalls the wavelike property of light. More to the point, light is an electromagnetic wave, which means that light is in fact a double wave, as the electric and magnetic component travel perpendicular to each other. Light waves also spiral. I imagine a cross section would look like a swastika. The Rune's shape has also been interpreted as a lightning flash or snake.

In the Younger Futhark, the Sol Rune could represent both light and dark. By changing the direction of the symbol, the different parts of day were portrayed. It could therefore be used for night magic. For example, the so-called sleep thorn was drawn by inverting Sol (Los). More elaborate forms were made of a combination of Thurs and Sol, the initials of the charm's name.

The Sun was venerated in every ancient society, and Midwinter celebrations are still very alive in Europe today. In ancient times, the winter and summer solstice were always celebrated with a fire festival, Fire representing the Star's power. More emphasis was laid on the winter solstice, because more depended on the Sun's ability to increase in strength than its decrease at Midsummer.

Frazer notes that at European Midsummer festivals burning wheels on oaken poles were carried along. These represented the Sun. Rock engravings all over Scandinavia show elements of this ceremony. Processions of heathens with a spoked wheel on a pole are recognized in the Bronze Age carvings. This wheel symbolized the Sun and was sometimes attached to a ship. In Viking lore, the Sun is also known as the Wheel of the Elves (Alfrodul), pointing to the Sun as an archetypal image of the chakra. In the Hindu system, the chakra is Vishnu's weapon. Again, this whirling missile is a solar image.

In many cultures over the world the Sun wheel is depicted as a disc or swastika.

According to Scandinavian Bronze Age iconography, the Sun's four steads were linked to certain power animals. At night, the Sun disc is associated with a fish symbol. In the morning, the Sun is drawn up by an eagle. By midday, the Sun is pulled by a horse. In the evening, a snake takes charge of the disc.

Midwinter or Yule symbolizes the return of the Sun's power. Christmas is founded on this tradition. The days lengthen and Sól gains in strength. In Christianity this represents the birth of Light, personified by the Christ. In the Northern tradition this corresponds to the birth of Heimdal or the rebirth of Balder. In Scandinavia, the death of Balder is linked with Midsummer (Baldr's Balar). Heimdal is named 'the White Ass' and 'the Brilliant God', the colour white symbolizing the Sun's brilliance. It alludes to beauty. Sometimes Frey is regarded as a Sun God. He rules over sunshine and rainfall. He rules over Alfheim, the World of the Elves, and possesses a shining sword. He is above all a summer God.

Two Runes herald the Sun Rune. These are Wunjo and Algiz. As a morning and evening star the planet Venus guides the Sun. Sometimes Mercury acts as the Sun's guiding star, but both planets correspond to Wunjo. The relation is supported by Sumerian mythology, where Venus is regarded as the Sun's sister. Inana is a sister of Utu. In Sumerian mythology, the father of Utu and Inana is the Moon God, Nannar, who, at the same time, is a brother of Earth. Wunjo heralds Sowulo's reign. Wunjo hides the promise of the Sun. The temporary joy of Wunjo has grown into a steady attitude of happiness.

As a morning and evening star, the planet Venus symbolizes the duality of life and death. This is the cycle the Sun goes through every day (Dagaz). In a symbolic way, Wunjo and Sowulo may represent the lower and higher self respectively. They might also refer to the alignment of personality and soul, in which case Dagaz may denote the monad.

Algiz also heralds the Sun. This Rune of protection symbolizes the gate to the Otherworld. Through this door the Sun passes daily. An upside Algiz refers to the eastern quarter and the rising Sun, and symbolizes life. An inverted Algiz refers to the west and the setting Sun, and symbolizes death (Zigla). Algiz guards these portals. In Sumerian mythology, this gate is guarded by twin Scorpions.

As a symbol, the Sun represents inner guidance. The Sun symbolizes the so-called higher self. In other traditions, the same idea is known as the Holy Guardian Angel. I believe, in the Northern tradition, we could speak of a Holy Guardian Alf. The Sun also symbolizes unconditional love. Her fiery energy reflects the monad. Every Star is a Sun.

Magically, the Sowulo Rune can be used to aid in astral travel. Its power, more than that of Algiz, irresistibly pulls you upward. The falcon, which is traditionally a solar bird, can be of help here. Frigg and Freyja both possess a falcon dress with which they travel the worlds. As a metaphor, it plainly refers to astral projection and the art of shapeshifting. Both Goddesses are associated with Venus and therefore Wunjo.

Sowulo stands for life force and the richness of life. The Rune denotes merriment, leadership, happiness and the power to act. Sometimes it denotes vision. Sowulo is a person who has found his life's purpose. It may also indicate a journey or holiday. Sowulo stands for a break in which, nonetheless, activity is present. Sowulo symbolizes a promise. It typically indicates success.

The Sun's virtue is found in her fair judgement. She shines as often and as bright for any of us always. Nonetheless, her power must be channeled; otherwise she would scorch all life. Sowulo is power.

In a negative way, Sowulo is a person who ignores others. This person imposes his will, or is always in the spotlights. The Sun attracts other people, but is essentially supposed to serve herself. Although a Sowulo personality may seem impressive to others, it is this person's job to be unconditionally ready for others and not to have others carry his or her load. Such persons will always be the centre of attention and will draw attention toward themselves.

The energy of the Sun is used to emphasize the positive. Sowulo embodies positive thinking and optimism. Since the Sun symbolizes universal life force, her power can be harnessed for healing purposes (*qi*). The Rune helps you to gain a clearer picture of your current situation; and it brings joyfulness. The power of this Rune is capable of destruction, but will as easily support constructive projects.

On a final note, the second *aett*, concluded by Sowulo, is mainly a story of overcoming internal trouble. At the start of the row, there is Hagalaz representing the Dark. At the end, there is Sowulo, representing Light. The dualism of this pair is so striking that I would readily associate Hagalaz with the Moon, as Sowulo already symbolizes the Sun. They are night and day. War and peace.

TEIWAZ

Teiwaz is the elder name of the Norse God Tyr. He is a sky deity who has authority over war and justice. Etymologically, his name refers to light. In a person, T stands for valour and wisdom. In a situation, it stands for triumph. As an abstract concept, Teiwaz stands for truth. It is the Rune of the initiate.

No myth except for one has survived about Tyr. All the same, he must have been one of the chief Gods in earlier times. When the Futhark was first designed, Tyr headed the Germanic pantheon. His hierarchical position is reflected in the Rune row: he appears as the first Rune of the third *aett*. Moreover, in coded runic texts, the third *aett* is taken as the first one. As a result, Tyr heads in front. Teiwaz is a Rune of leadership.

Originally, the term *teiwaz* indicated a priest. The Old Icelandic Rune Poem remembers *tyr* as the 'warder of the temple' (*hofa hilmir*) and the older Negau helmet inscription has *teiwa* as a reference to a cultic functionary. Teiwaz connects with the divine. The root of this God name is shared with all Indo-European cultures. Teiwaz is cognate with *deva*, *deus* and *theos* and found to be the root of other supreme deities, such as Jupiter and Zeus. The proto-Indo-European root **dei* means Bright One or Divine One, referring to the heavens. In Northern mythology, a whole class of beings is named after this word. Maybe these Northern *tívar* could be regarded as the Devas or Angels of other traditions. However, the Northern Tivar are always concerned with battle.

Teiwaz is the archetypal Sky Father. And as such, an Earth Mother is expected. This the Futhark immediately provides for. Teiwaz's female counterpart is found in the next Rune. In relation to the t-Rune, Berkana is the archetypal Earth Mother. Teiwaz represents the male principle; Berkana represents the female principle.

The same polarity is portrayed differently in another runic pair. The s- and t-Rune match in meaning when it comes to qualities of leadership and triumph, but they also represent the polarity of male and female energies. They are the War God and the Sun Goddess. And their symbolism

complements each other well. The attribute of the War God is a spear or a sword, symbolic of action and initiative. The attribute of the Sun Goddess is the orb, symbolic of receptivity. On an abstract level, they bring together the two fundamental qualities of any symbol, the line and the circle. Every symbol is a combination of both. Every shape is a combination of both. The line is found in the arrow, spear or sword of the War God and the circle is the archetypal image of the Sun. On a very basic level, they correspond to the seed and the egg cell.

In medieval times, Tyr was associated with Mars, the God of war, and was invoked in battle. Many sources confirm that Tyr was called upon for victory. In *Gylfaginning*, Tyr is described as both valiant and wise. He does not hesitate in taking action. His character exemplifies that of the initiate. The sword as his attribute is the weapon the magician takes his oaths on. It is the power of Teiwaz that the magician pledges to wield. The sword symbolizes the power to make decisions. In the right hands, it becomes an instrument of Truth.

One specific Scottish inscription is of interest here. At Housesteads a votive altar is found on which Tyr is mentioned as *Mars Thingsus*. The deity's name is accompanied by the names of Valkyries. That is why Tyr is seen as both a God of war and jurisdiction. He not only rules warfare but also presides over the Germanic folk assembly. This fact illustrates his role as a former chieftain among the Gods. On a symbolic level, this means that Teiwaz is a Rune of truth and truthfulness. In other sources, Tyr is called Teutan, making him a God of the people. In this respect, Tyr embodies the folk soul.

Only one myth of Tyr has survived into our times. That is his confrontation with his mythical adversary the wolf Fenrir. In the Futhark, the story is summed up in the triad Fehu-Hagalaz-Teiwaz. Fehu represents Fenrir, Hagalaz symbolizes the binding and Teiwaz refers to Tyr.

One more relevant characteristic of Tyr has to be discussed. Typical of Tyr is his hairstyle. It has the same shape as the top of the Irminsul, the World Tree. This cultic object is shown on the German Extern Stone, while

Tyr's hairdo can be distinguished from the Trollhättan Bracteate. Consequently, the Teiwaz Rune symbolizes Yggdrasil. Nearby this mythical tree the Aesic court assembled. In smaller settings, the World Tree was represented by a pole with a nail hammered into it and dedicated to the Regin Gods.

The Teiwaz Rune is used to ensure victory. The Ancient Germanic people and the Vikings carved this symbol in their war gear. In our modern times we are less confronted by actual combat, but battle and victory have become symbols of problems and their solutions, challenges and successes. Therefore, the Rune's symbolism is still applicable today. The energy of this Rune wholeheartedly encourages you to do something, but at the same time makes you address your common sense. The energy of this Rune changes the consciousness so that intent and awareness will keep their purest quality. Of all the Runes, Teiwaz expresses your intention the clearest. You are very clear about *why* you are doing something.

Sometimes Teiwaz means that a certain battle will have to be fought on your own. Possibly, this Rune denotes your mission in life or finding your path in life. The Rune will bring purpose to your life. It stands for straightforwardness, truth and efficiency. As a Rune of divinity and discipline, it represents the energy of a cosmic Plan. A negative Teiwaz stands for defeat, lack of power, or plain laziness.

BERKANA ᛒ

Berkana is the Goddess of the birch tree. She is celebrated at May Day, when the maypole is erected. A connection with Freyja is inevitable. It is a Rune of love and caring. Besides, its energy is strongly associated with motherly affection.

Berkana is a typical Ancient Germanic tree Goddess. Unfortunately, she was only barely remembered in Viking times. Still, the b-Rune Bjarkan is still named after her in Old Norse. Although the Anglo-Saxon Futhark did not retain this, it is supported by the Gothic b-name Bairkan.

The Ancient Germanic word for birch is *berko. The suffix -an found in the Rune name alludes to a numinous entity. That is why Berkana refers to the spirit of the birch tree, and not necessarily to the tree itself. The same suffix is also found in the name Wodanaz, for example. The suffix is etymologically related to ansuz and Latin anima meaning 'spirit, breath of life, inspiration'. The proto-Indo-European root *ane means 'breath, wind', and is cognate with Old Norse önd. The name of this tree means brilliant white and refers to the silvery bark of the tree.

Birch (Betula) is a typically Northern European sacred tree. It does not grow in the area of the Mediterranean. The suppleness of this species made the tree first to reappear after the Ice Age (8000 BCE). The tree grows fast and has a protecting mission in nature. Birch is considered to be a pioneer among trees.

As a tree of motherly protection, Berkana symbolizes concealment. In the Örvar-Odds Saga, the hero Odd dresses himself in birch bark. When he comes to a king's court, no-one recognizes him. Birch may hide your true identity. Psychologically speaking, this conforms to Jung's idea of the persona. 'Birch bark man' is a kenning for outlaw. The wood was also used for making shields. And in Britain, birch twigs were hung about the house as a protective charm, against lightning especially.

Birch bark was also used for roofing. Being waterproof and long-lasting, it made the perfect material to cover roofs with. Turf was laid on top of it.

The bark contains a substance called betulin, which makes it very durable. In medicine, the substance is used to fight cancer. Birch bark was also used as parchment since the early Iron Age (600-500 BCE).

Berkana symbolizes the feminine principle. As such, it is the counterpart of Teiwaz. Berkana, too, is associated with the tree of life. Birch was regarded as a World Tree in Siberia. It channeled celestial energy into the world of men and made it possible for human queries to be heard by the Gods at the same time. Siberian shamans carved either seven, nine or twelve notches in the wood to represent their number of worlds. Perhaps the Ancient Germanic people had a similar custom to depict the Nine Worlds of Yggdrasil. Among the Saami, a nail was hammered into the birch post to represent the Pole Star, associated with Teiwaz. This custom was taken over from Germanic traditions, where these nails are known as *reginnaglar*. The motive is found in folklore and fairy tales where the hero swings his sword in a tree. The condition of the sword indicates the hero's condition.

The ritual related to Berkana is the erecting of the maypole. This involved a springtime celebration associated with the Goddess Freyja. The annually performed ritual, which still survives to this day, was usually held on the first of May, although the exact date differed from place to place. Villagers go into the woods and fetch themselves a birch tree to take home. It is then erected in the middle of the town, danced around and decorated. These birch poles symbolize the world axis. Ribbons were woven around the birch to accentuate the quality of centrality and interconnectedness. They represented the rainbow via which the shaman travelled to the upper worlds to walk among the Gods.

Because the maypole was erected in springtime, Berkana is linked to this blossoming season of promise and energy. The Rune's energy rouses the sap in trees. Berkana stands for renewal of life and rebirth, and a fresh start in general. At springtime, youngsters and cattle were struck with a Rod of Life made of birch twigs to promote fertility and health. Spring is also the season in which Freyja is honoured. She is said to dwell in the birch tree.

According to De Cleene, birch was sacred to Thor. Moreover, the tree protects against lightning. The tree is sacred to witches. And then there is Frigg, who does everything in her power to keep Balder from harm. It demonstrates her motherly love and concern. Frigg is associated with the birch tree because the tree represents the weeping Goddess, much like Freyja. The act of weeping refers to Uruz. Both Uruz and Berkana come second in their respective *aett*. In Germanic, Siberian, Baltic and Slavonic traditions, birch was a symbol of purity.

Berkana is a Rune of love – in a playful, tender, joyous, innocent way. In Germany, birch twigs were used to predict whom a girl would marry. Pliny mentions that birch is the most favoured kind of wood to make wedding torches from, a reference to Kenaz. The k-Rune's flaring energy is found in the spring aspect of Berkana. Birch bark is easily inflammable, too, so that it was used to kindle fire. Torches of birch bark were still ritually used in the Low Lands and Russia until the 17th century. In Germany and the Low Lands, cups of birch wood were used in *symbel* rites until the 16th century.

The energy of Berkana is sweet and nurturing. The energy of this Rune strengthens the body when it is weak. It prevents the aura from dissipating when you are tired. A negative Berkana sometimes acts as a smothering influence or denotes allergic reactions. The power of this Rune is able to anaesthetize, but its power is also warding. There is a very soothing and lulling energy flowing from the birch Rune's power centre. Birch was known as a Tree of Healing and rituals are known of transferring one's disease to birch. Eihwaz on the other hand is about hunting. Its male energy much contrasts the caring nature of Berkana. As a team of archetypal trees, they make a dynamic pair of opposites.

Berkana stands for new beginnings and pioneering. Her protecting and endearing nature translates itself into motherhood. This energy may, however, lead to attachment or even dependency. The Rune hints at pregnancy, or the desire to have children. Hence Berkana referring to maternal instincts and issues. The shape of the Rune is easily compared to a pair of breasts but it also resembles a woman with child in profile. The Rune may denote nurseries or those who take care of others. Its astrological equivalent is Virgo. Berkana's meaning really matches the sign's esoteric symbolism of nurturing the Christ principle. A Berkana personality is a guarder of peace.

EHWAZ   M

Ehwaz means horse and refers particularly to sacred horses. The horse plays a prominent role in Northern mythology, the best known one being Sleipnir. Different aspects of the horse symbolism are reflected in the myths, where they are celebrated for their strength, speed, awareness and health. They were beasts of burden and transport, and they were a symbol of status. The symbolism of the horse is connected with the shamanic Underworld. Ehwaz stands for the dream body.

Wild horses represent freedom. Although this animal has been domesticated by man (3800 BCE), horses still retain a will of their own. They have a strong sense of individuality. Domesticated horses were introduced in Europe by the Celts, just as the wheel was, together with the ritual use of beer and mead. The animals were held as status symbols and steeds of war. In addition, horses were exploited as beasts of burden too. The horse is associated with hard labour, but its most excelling characteristic is its speed, and that is what the human rider has turned to his own advantage.

The best horse of all is Sleipnir. This magical mount has a range of distinctive attributes. The horse has eight legs, is dappled, and has Runes marked on his teeth. Having double the amount of legs as that of a normal steed makes Sleipnir a faster horse than any other. Its number of legs stresses the animal's swiftness. On the other hand, the Runes on Sleipnir's teeth cause him to be the very picture of health. A horse's health is gauged by its teeth.

Being a grey horse, Sleipnir is a horse of death. He has the ability to guide his rider to the Underworld. Shamans use the image of the horse all the time to travel to the Underworld. In the myths, Sleipnir carries some of the Gods to Hella's Underworld.

In relation to a horse's association with the Underworld, it must be remembered that in Germanic society, 'horses of the sea' carried the departed to the realm of the dead. 'Horse' is a kenning for ship. That makes this Rune a symbol of all kinds of free-moving vehicles and transport in general. In Greece, horses were sacred to Poseidon.

In ancient times, the horse was a status symbol reserved for chieftains and priests, who are associated with this Rune. These animals were regarded as incarnations of the Gods. White horses in particular were sacred to the Ancient Germanic people. Priests prophesied the outcome of battle by means of their neighing.

There is an obvious connection between Raido and Ehwaz, so much so that in the Younger Futhark, *reiðr* takes over all the meanings of Ehwaz and covers all of its connotations too.

The Celtic horse Goddess was called Epona, cognate with the Rune name. The Germanic equivalent would be Ehwana. She is said to have been a triple Goddess. Incidentally, Ehwaz is the third Rune of the third *aett*.

Psychologically, the horse represents instinct, emotion, passion and the astral body (*hamr*). In earlier days, people dreamed of horses, nowadays they dream about cars. But the symbolism remains the same. The horse stands for the *persona* of Jungian psychology and symbolizes someone's libido. On the other hand, it might also denote a person's *anima* or *animus*. In Ancient Scandinavia, horses were associated with the *fylgja* concept: *marr er manns fylgja*. This relates Ehwaz to the soul concept, since the Old Norse word for Guardian Angel is at least once glossed as *fylgju-engill*. The word means follower and refers to a person's double.

In divination, Ehwaz stands for efficiency, a journey, and moving towards a goal. Often the Rune is associated with marriage and relationships, because of the intimate bond between rider and animal. That is why Ehwaz stands for complementarities and cooperation. Ehwaz stands for team work. An inverted Ehwaz stands for competition.

Ehwaz is the link that exists between two beings. Celtic tales often feature pairs of birds that are linked with silver cords. In the story of *the sickbed of Cuchulainn*, a pair of birds is linked together by a golden chain. The story of *the Dream of Angus* features paired swans linked by silver chains. Accordingly, Ehwaz connects two persons, or a person and his power animal, or a person and a business. Persons married to their jobs experience this power. The Rune's energy glues together and transmutes dualities into unities. Occultly speaking, this power is central in handling magical tools. Ehwaz is also a Rune of trust, since a rider must trust his mount.

Ehwaz stands for a long term project. Sometimes it denotes flight, sometimes a quest. Always it symbolizes loyalty. Sometimes it indicates a game or competition, a bet or competitor. An Ehwaz personality is full of energy and is able to act quickly, but may at the same time remain very tranquil. Ehwaz stands for physical labour and efforts. It also refers to sports. The Rune's energy helps in recovering from physical strain. Ehwaz brings the mind down to the body.

Frey and Odin are both traditional horse Gods. In this respect, they operate as priestly figures, but have been regarded as leaders as well. In a mythological context, horses are connected to the realm of giants. When they go to Thing, all the Aesir ride horses. The names of their horses are Sleipnir, Gladi, Gyllir, Glaer, Skeidbrimir, Silfrintopp, Sinir, Gisl, Falhofnir, Gulltopp and Lettfeti.

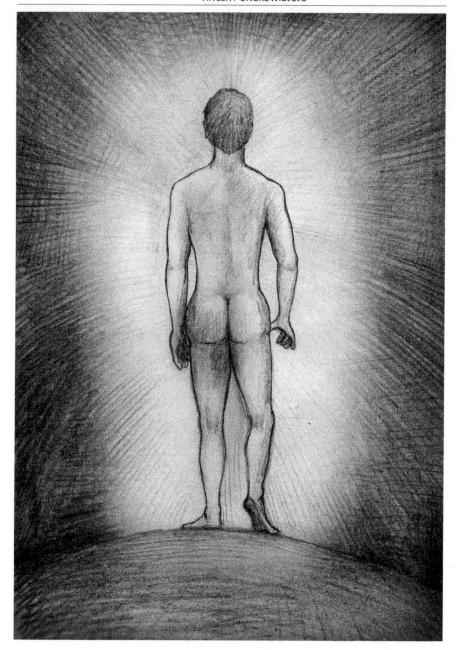

MANNAZ ᛗ

Mannaz is YOU. The secret of this Rune should be sufficiently known to each and every one of us, because it symbolizes a human being. What makes this Rune so powerful is its ability to connect all humanity. Mannaz does not only stand for an individual, but for the whole of mankind too. The mutual connectedness between every human life is deeply present in this Rune.

Humanity distinguishes itself from the animal kingdom, represented by Ehwaz, for the reason that we are able to use the rational mind. Self-consciousness and mental abilities are the key elements of this Rune. Mannaz represents the intellect, the capacity of introspection and meditation, but also contemplation, telepathy, and communication in the broadest sense. The latter aspect forms the key to our sense of being connected. Ultimately, the root of this word is related to 'mind' and Latin *mens*.

As a Rune of mankind, Mannaz embodies the collective soul. On an archetypical level, this image is presented as the concept of the perfect man. In the Kabbalah, he is known as Adam Qadmon. Thus, Mannaz symbolizes everything that Man ambitions for. On an individual level, this is expressed as self-realization. On a collective level, this is expressed as social activity.

According to Tacitus, a deity existed by the name of Mannaz. He was the son of Tuisco, who corresponds to Teiwaz. The God Mannaz had three sons, of which Inguz was one. As a progenitor of humanity, Mannaz embodies the Adam Qadmon of the Northern tradition. He is the over-soul of which all folk souls are only aspects.

Humans look out for each other, and individuals try to find their soul kin. The spark behind this desire is directed from the pool of Mannaz energy. Like-minded people will find each other and people come together to support each other. Mannaz is the Rune of soul mates and mutual understanding. Its energy synchronizes minds. According to the Old Icelandic Rune Poem 'man is the delight of man'. Two things can be said of this expression. Firstly, human beings have the need to be with others and to be recognized as an individual. Secondly, the power of Mannaz attracts joy.

Freya Aswynn is right when she suspects Mannaz to be a double Wunjo Rune. In the transition period from the Ancient Germanic alphabet to the Viking Futhark, the m-Rune transformed. The original younger shape of this Rune was formed like a common variation on the elder Inguz Rune. Indeed it looked like two elder Wunjo Runes joined together back to back. Moreover, the Rune Poems confirm this interpretation. The stanza on Madr is a clear reference to Wunjo and simultaneously expresses the meaning of the m-Rune.

Mannaz indicates mass gatherings, such as at a gig or market day. Its energy is easily experienced at peak hours at the underground station. The Rune indicates your social attitude and your self-esteem. A Mannaz personality is mild and easy-going.

Magically, Mannaz expands the mind. This Rune is especially beneficent in developing telepathic abilities or to induce lucid dreaming. The energy of Mannaz will bring the individual in touch with his or her soul. As a Mind Rune, it closes a row of three. Berkana symbolizes the body, Ehwaz our feelings or astral vehicle and Mannaz our thinking. A person's soul might be associated with Laguz.

The Mannaz Rune refers to the creation of mankind. According to the myths, the Gods travel about at some point in prehistory and find two logs of wood. From these they shape the first pair of human beings. The three Aesir who worked on this are Odin, Vili and Vé. Sometimes they are Odin, Hœnir and Lodur. They created two individuals from tree trunks. The logs symbolize the still unconscious, physical body, while the Gods offer them consciousness, the breath of life, insight, understanding and similar faculties.

A series of Runes is found in this myth. The Aesir create man and woman from breathing life into logs of ash and elm. This connects Mannaz to Berkana and Ansuz. Linking up these three Runes, a square is formed in the Futhark diagram. The office of the Aesir is matched with Ansuz. They step down the energy of consciousness into a physical form, Mannaz. The medium to hold this energy is wood, referring to Berkana. Completing the square is Uruz.

The energy of this Rune is on the same level as Ansuz, but its function is that of Berkana. Uruz symbolizes the blueprint or shaping energy, reflected in Berkana on a lower level in the same way as Mannaz is a reflection of Ansuz. In the square, the upper Runes represent energy and force on the Inner Planes; the lower Runes express their qualities on a concrete level. The left Runes represent the form aspect, the right Runes the mind. The end result is a creative process initiated by the Aesir through the medium of two wooden logs. Laguz represents the location of the myth.

Another story tells us of Heimdal, disguised as Rig, initiating the triple hierarchy of mankind: slaves, freemen and rulers. The class of slaves is regarded to comprise everyone who serves. The class of freemen contains farmers and warriors alike, and the ruling class consists of kings, judges and priests. It is self-evident that a spiritually developed individual will strive towards a balance of all three aspects.

LAGUZ   ⎰

Water is the element that Laguz refers to. Traditionally, water stands for the emotional world, the astral realm, illusions and dreaming. At the same time, the Rune's power has a healing and cleansing quality. As a concept, Laguz refers to the wishing well tradition.

Laguz is a Rune of water. The symbolism of this element is very elaborate. The flowing nature of water symbolizes life and energy, and flowing life force. Water is always moving and shows in many different forms, like rain, rivers, wells, clouds, mist, and the sea. All these phenomena add their own real associations to the symbolism of this Rune.

First and foremost, Laguz is a Rune of purification. Taking a shower or drinking water cleanses the body on many levels. Drinking lots of water detoxifies the body. It reminds me of the myth of Herakles. The first task he is given is clearing out the stables of king Augias. In order to cleanse the sty, Herakles redirects the course of a nearby river to flush the sty. The river's name, Alpheus, is related to our word 'elf' and means white or shining.

This Rune is very powerful in healings. Laguz helps washing away all your emotional and psychological unhygienic garbage. The power of flowing moves around everything that starts to become silted up. On top of that, the energy of Laguz strengthens the blood, nourishing the etheric and astral body.

Rivers and springs are widely known as sacred sites of healing. In relation to this, the Ancient Germanic ritual is mentioned of bidding the Gods for victory before going to combat. When the Gods did grant them their victory, the warriors solemnly offered them the enemy's weapons. Swords and shields were broken and cast into the water. Similar practices go back a long way. To illustrate this, stone axe heads have been found as votive offerings in Scandinavian lakes dating to at least 3700 BCE. Nowadays, we toss pennies in wishing wells to invoke good fortune.

The Gods and the spirits are addressed at a body of water because these places function as gateways to the Otherworld. An example of this is the

story of Mother Hulda or Frau Holle. In addition, ancestral sibyls were consulted at these sites. In the myths, the archetypal prophetess appears as Saga, who dwells in a bog. Frigg, too, lives in the marshlands.

The whole mythological complex of the three cosmic wells Urd, Mimir and Hvergelmir is associated with this Rune. They represent creation, divination and energy flow. Laguz is the water of life on which every soul feeds. It is the wide kettle in which the drops of our every thought and deed are gathered and shared. Through the cosmic wells all life/consciousness is connected.

As a Rune of Water, Laguz can be considered as a symbol of illusion. The reflection on its surface deforms real images. Nonetheless, the surface has also got a hypnotizing effect promoting clairvoyance or inducing a trance.

In a literal sense, Laguz refers to the sea. In Northern cosmology, this location represents the unconscious, being the realm of the giants. In this place Loki of Utgard dwells. As an alchemical element, Water has been associated with the emotions. Correspondingly, skalds use the image of a ship to represent control over one's emotions. A troubled sea stands for an unhealthy dominance of the world of emotions.

In the skaldic poems, sea is a kenning for blood. Mythologically, this is explained by the fact that the primal giant Ymir is slain by Odin and his brothers. His blood filled the void Ginnungagap and created the primordial ocean. From these primal waters Earth was created.

One of Odin's names is Thund, referring to an overflowing river. This image symbolizes uncontrolled emotion, like anger or sorrow. Thor has a connection with Thund as well. Of all the Aesir, he is the only one able to cross the rivers to the Gods' Thing without a horse. Another myth relates how Thor crosses a river in Jotunheim. A giant maiden weaves a spell and waters start to rise. Thor saves himself from drowning by clinging to a rowan tree. This flooding symbolizes the overpowering impact of the giants. They represent our desire nature and our emotional body in general.

Overcoming the urge of desire is a real challenge in our civilized society in which desire and the vice of possession are meticulously cultivated. The media today are responsible for a great deal of misleading upbringing on all levels. Through the astral world they manipulate the masses by creating illusions or empowering illusions that already exist in people today.

The hazards of the astral world are well attested in folklore. Many traditions confirm that spirits cannot cross a running stream. It would shatter their ethereal body. Likewise, the Gods take Bifrost bridge to ride to Urd's Well and the dead cross the bridge Gjallarbru leading into Helheim. A great river separates the world of the Gods from that of the giants. This river is Yfing and it is said that it never freezes over, preventing giants from crossing it. Even the binding of the Fenriswolf takes place on an island. No escape is possible. Then again, this makes isles natural sacred places.

In divination, Laguz represents those things you distinctly prefer; certain occupations, friends, TV-shows. This Rune indicates deception, depression, or exactly the opposite like frivolous pleasures and wants. Sometimes Laguz indicates a choice you make against your better judgement. A positive Laguz denotes healing and improvement. You are sorting yourself out or coming to terms with a situation.

Magically, the energy of Laguz is perfect to help you let go of things. Imagine how the flow of a river washes away your issues. They are never really gone, but you will no longer hold on. The thoughts you offer will be taken there where they are meant to be. When you hold on you have only one thing. When you let go, you have all.

INGUZ   ◇

Inguz is the name of a God who was known in Viking times as Frey. The Rune's energy is like the God's, gentle, patient, sunny, heroic, and full of life. The Rune symbolizes a seed. It is the archetypal child. From an occult point of view, Inguz represents the Law of Attraction.

Allegedly, *inguz* means young man, but as a suffix it denotes 'son of'. The English noun suffix –ing denotes one of a kind. As a result, this Rune symbolizes progeny, the promise of a future generation and the power of youthfulness. Inguz epitomizes the archetypal child. The Ancient Egyptian mythographer would associate him with Horus.

The Rune name also refers to a deity known in antiquity as Yngvi and known nowadays as Frey. Etymologically, Frey means lord. Most likely it was originally Yngvi's main epithet. Later, Frey became the name of this deity and the original God's name was only found in personal names like Ingrid, Ingeborg, Ingimund, etcetera.

I believe the Rune shape developed from what is known as a cup mark. These are cup shaped hollows made in the surface of megalithic monuments. They consistently occur on monuments throughout Europe, among which the Bronze Age Hallristningar of Scandinavia. They are frequently found on British megaliths, and even as far as India. They were installed to create sacred spaces altering the energy field of Mother Earth. In my opinion, they are symbolic of the female principle. In Scandinavian folklore, these marks are known as elf-mills.

In inscriptions, the Inguz Rune is frequently presented as a bind Rune of Isa and Inguz. I take this sigil to be the integration of feminine and masculine energies. As Inguz stands for the female genitalia, so does Isa represent the male. They are the *yoni* and *lingam* of the North, governed by the twin deity Freyja and Frey. As noted by others, the Old English Rune looks like a DNA double helix. The image corresponds to the Vanic pair of Freyja and Frey.

According to the Old English Rune Poem, Ing or Yngvi arrived from over the sea as a baby. Later he returned homewards in a chariot. Furthermore, they call him 'hero' in the poem. These three ideas offer some insight into the nature of the God Yngvi and the symbolic meanings of the Inguz Rune. The stanza may refer to a ritual procession. The chariot links Frey to Raido. He is a celebrated leader bestowing peace and prosperity.

In the myths Frey appears as a fertility and vegetation God. He is invoked for growing crops. He offers the necessary rains and sunshine. Nonetheless, the story that characterizes Frey the most is told in *Skirnismal*. In this poem he woos Gerd, a daughter of giants. She embodies the fertile earth, but only gives in to Frey when he threatens her. Frey's desire is typical and Inguz may hence be regarded as a Rune of falling in love and attraction. From a religious perspective, the sacred marriage of Frey and Gerd was celebrated in high summer. Furthermore, Inga-Gerd is a name for Freyja.

From the sagas, Frey appears as a very warm person. This can be taken literally. It is said in *Gislasaga* how the burial mound of his devotee stayed clear of snow in winter. In the *Ynglingasaga*, Frey appears as a priest responsible for conducting ceremonies (*blót*). His power animal is the boar, which animal is still associated with luck and festivities in Continental thinking. Of this the German word *Glückschwein* attests. In the Celtic world, the boar stands for priesthood.

Magically, Inguz has an including power. Its force is warding, in particular regarding families and children. As a result of the enclosing energy of Inguz, this Rune takes hold of something. In Inguz energy is stored. This quality is observed when we fall in love and internally long for the other. In late medieval times, this Rune became associated with the Moon. In pathworkings, the Rune can be used to teleport yourself.

In divination, Inguz indicates a period of promising waiting and looking forward. At the same time, Inguz refers to children or pregnancy. The Runes Teiwaz, Berkana and Inguz stand for the energy triangle of father, mother and child. Inguz advises to be patient. Inguz is the Rune of planting a seed and having the patience for it to grow and mature. A seed refers to real seed; it also refers to seed thoughts. This Rune power symbolizes our confidence in life.

The working of Inguz is similar to the Athanor of ancient alchemy, which symbolizes transformation. Inguz denotes those businesses that are kept hidden until the right time comes. Its energy stands for organic growth or natural recovery. An Inguz personality is rather introverted, but still waters run deep.

OTHILA ⊗

Originally, Othila referred to the complex of a person's character. Later on, it referred to the concept of inheritance. Nowadays, the word is usually translated as 'piece of land'. On a grander scale, Othila is interpreted as the planet Earth. As a symbol, the Rune refers to ethics, traditions and everything that holds together civilization.

The concept of Othila refers to inherited goods. Originally, this included all kinds of objects handed over in the family. In this manner, swords were marked with this Rune. Later, the concept specifically referred to lands and properties. This is why the Rune now denotes a piece of land. Othila implies the law by which a piece of land is rightfully claimed by a family, and by which the family can keep the land even after the passing away of the *pater familias*.

Out of this construction, the landed nobility arose in the North of Europe and from this word is derived the Dutch and German word *adel* 'noble' as well as the Old English word *atheling* 'prince'. As a result, Othila refers to the upper social class. Today, we may regard celebrities as a modern equivalent of that old caste.

Connotations of words like noble and nobility apply to the symbolism of Othila. This Rune stands for the aristocracy, and at the same time for noble principles, noble-mindedness and a certain connotation of excellence. In an extreme way, this becomes exclusiveness.

The Othila Rune symbolizes hearth and home and the feeling of being at home. It signifies the family as a unit and the individuality of that family. As a consequence, Othila stands for the particularity of every individual. Originally, the word literally referred to a person's character. Othila symbolizes someone's personality and comprises the entirety of someone's values and ideals. The power of this Rune is present in those who stand up for their rights, those people who fight for their ideals and for their home country, in every way.

On the whole, Othila consists of an estate, a house or farm and the family with its servants. This complex has ritual significance. And it can be expanded on. The triad Gebo-Algiz-Othila symbolizes a working in a magical area. It refers to priesthood and dedication. Gebo symbolizes the Gods. Algiz is a priest. Othila represents the temple. The combined Rune energy translates as 'a sacred space of sharing'.

The shape of the Rune represents a house. The two upper strokes refer to Teiwaz and symbolize heaven. The cross beneath is a reference to Gebo and stands for the four quarters. In this way, Othila combines the principles of Heaven and Earth in the human body. On a different scale, the estate of Othila is our solar system, or even the expanse of a universe.

Given that Othila has the connotation of 'home' it symbolizes the place where things come from. From a spiritual point of view, this is the soul, the world of the soul. From a material point of view, it refers to the genetic information that is passed on from generation to generation, associating the Rune with ancestor veneration.

This Rune has a close tie with the Goddess Jord, Mother Earth, and therefore creates a close bond between man and planet. Othila helps you to ground yourself when you are up in the clouds too much or when you have lost the connection with your body. Herein lies a great healing potential. Othila takes you back into your body. This Rune's power teaches you to bring down your ideas into the material world.

Othila has a conserving or lasting influence. At the same time, the energy of this Rune attempts to slowly lift existing circumstances to higher levels, hence the eagle being the Rune's sacred bird (Dutch *adel-aar*). Othila, therefore, symbolizes ambition and measured growth. You may compare this growth to the endless expansion of a city.

Othila marks possession. In this respect, Othila has a certain warding function, because its energies immediately react when something that you regard as holy is stirred in a negative way. In a figurative sense, it symbolizes steadfastness, although it also means all kinds of opinions.

In divination, Othila may point to old-fashioned behaviour. Or else, that one adheres too much to what has been achieved in the past. Usually, the Rune stands for security, both in home and profession. The Rune stands for firmness, fundamentals, long term projects and finding your way in life. In more subtle cases, Othila may indicate a certain attitude of arrogance. This Rune stands for traditions, legacies, and heredity.

Odin is closely related to this Rune because he is the aristocracy's God. As king of Asgard, he heads all the Aesir. The Othila Rune was used to decorate bread offerings to Odin as also Yule cakes. Heimdal, too, is a king; and he watches over Asgard. This protecting aspect is found in Thor as well. He is well known as a warder of Midgard, synonymous with Mother Earth. The warding aspect of this Rune reveals that Othila symbolizes the border between the familiar and the unfamiliar, between the desired and the anomalous.

DAGAZ   ᛞ

Dagaz means day. The number 24 refers to the number of hours in a day; twelve in the day and twelve in the night. The meaning of the Rune name is associated with both daybreak and nightfall. As such, Dagaz is a Rune of both awakening and concluding. On a mental level, it symbolizes the cycle of different states that the mind goes through in the space of twenty-four hours. Dagaz is a symbol of light, visualized as the blue vault of heaven. It stands for lucidity.

The Rune itself is made up of two Thurisaz Runes, one complementing the other. Both Dagaz and Thurisaz are Fire Runes. Correspondingly, Dagaz represents the sublimation of the raw power of the Thurses. It may be likened to the sublimation of libido. This energy is made 'noble' after the initiation of Othila.

The clear blue sky of day and the light thereof symbolize lucid consciousness. The Rune symbolizes presence of mind and a clear vision. For that reason, Dagaz is a good Rune for dreaming since the blue heaven symbolizes lucid dreaming. Staring at the day sky is good practice to develop this ability.

The light of day is ideal to discuss weighty matters. The setting induces an atmosphere of openness and truth. It is therefore no wonder that the Germanic custom of the governing Thing assembly is related to this Rune. Icelandic sources recount that a Thing could only be held in the full light of day. It was held in the open. Dutch words such as *dagen* 'to summon' and en *verdedigen* 'to defend' are related to *dagaz* and recall this tradition. English has the expression 'to let daylight into an issue'. Other old words that relate the Thing assembly to Dagaz are Old Saxon *dagething*, Old High German *tagading* and Old Frisian *deithing*.

The Thing was usually held under an oak or lime tree, while either four or twelve wooden poles marked the *vé* of the Thing. These were either made of oak or hazel. The number four nicely links in with the shape of the Dagaz Rune.

The original meaning of Dagaz seems to have been 'heat' or 'fire'. It represents the inner warmth of life itself. It also points to the consuming fires of Ragnarok.

Again from the linguistic point of view, Dagaz refers to the moment of 'dawn'. Metaphorically speaking, this breaking power of Dagaz symbolizes the dawning of insights. These sudden understandings are like an opening door. It may be compared to the power surge of an initiation which is like a fresh wind rushing through you when all the doors and windows of your being are open wide. Dagaz has the power to ignite a spring-cleaning in the soul.

Dagaz has a reviving power. The Rune awakens life within and galvanizes the mind. The early morning power of this Rune is so strong that sleep will irrevocably be driven away. Because sleep symbolizes unconscious actions, Dagaz must mean awareness. It also stands for discoveries and revelations. Its power revitalizes.

The animal associated with awakening is the rooster. Every morning the cock's cries wake up the world. In mythology, the cock has exactly the same function. On Ragnarok's morning three roosters cry out and summon different supernatural beings to the final battle. Gullinkambi stirs the Gods and the Einherjar, Fjalar stirs the giants, and last but not least, there is a cock crowing in the Underworld, stirring the dead.

In the Germanic belief system, the cock is a symbol of resurrection. In Scandinavian folk tales a killed cock comes back to life when he is flung over the gates of the Underworld. The animal also appears in the story of Mother Hulda. Generally, the cock symbolizes transformation. Dagaz stands for the twilight zone between life and death.

Although the day breaks with the magical morning glory, in ancient times day used to commence at nightfall. Both moments of time lie in between light and darkness, and are neither of both at the same time. Both moments in time reflect a phase of fragile equilibrium. The word 'evening' literally refers to this. That is why Gebo is found in Dagaz.

As an evening Rune, Dagaz has an inwardly directed power. This power wraps things up. Dagaz rounds off, although at the same time a new day begins. Thus, Dagaz represents an ending as well as a new beginning. This Rune denotes that moment in time between two activities in which there is complete emptiness – when you fall into a sort of limbo. Dagaz may stand for a transitory period. Its energy naturally makes you doze off when the body or the mind needs rest.

Cosmically, Dagaz represents the fulfillment of all creation. Everything that has been set up by the first breath of the Lords of Muspelheim will be consummated at Dagaz. At the same time, Dagaz holds the seeds of a new era. On an energy level, Dagaz may be akin to the quality of *ginn* found in the Ginnungagap.

During the twilight hours the power of Dagaz is experienced in its fullest essence. After the Sun has set, colours fade, so that even white is no longer distinguishable from black. For that reason, Dagaz is used in spells for invisibility and blending in.

Spiritually, Dagaz symbolizes cosmic consciousness. This Rune aligns an individual's personality with his soul. As a Rune of light, Dagaz symbolizes a positive attitude in life. Its awakening energies express themselves in an open mind and in being open towards others. Through its disclosing energy, Dagaz will always out the truth.

In the Prose Edda, Dag appears as a deity. This fact is confirmed in the poem *Sigrdrifumal*. The deity of the blue skies is Heimdal. His name refers to bright light. Dawn is associated with Ostara. She rules over the eastern quarter.

The energy of Dagaz is dawning, awakening, expanding, enlightening and clarifying. Because of that, this Rune relates to the mind. Its energy is used to place something between or above the worlds. This Rune represents the transcendent. The Rune can be drawn in the four quarters of a magical circle.

Dagaz cautions not to draw conclusions hastily or to shout victory too early. *Havamal* 81 tells us to praise the day at nightfall, and this proverb is still known today. The wind changes often in a day. That is why Dagaz may indicate sudden and unexpected turns.

Usually, Dagaz denotes optimism or an elucidation, sometimes an unexpected positive event. Sometimes it alludes to secrets and denotes the impotency to reveal the truth. This Rune symbolizes a closing phase or a new start. Certain issues may come to light.

ᚠ ᚠᛖᚻᚢ	cattle, wealth; gold
ᚢ ᚢᚱᚢᛦ	aurochs; water, drizzle
ᚦ ᚦᚢᚱᛁᛋᚨᛦ	thurs, giant, troll, the Strong one; thorn; Saturn
ᚨ ᚨᛋᚢᛦ	God, forefather, Áss, Odin; mouth; Jupiter
ᚱ ᚱᚨᛁᛞᛟ	to ride, horse riding; road
ᚲ ᚲᛖᚾᚨᛦ ᚲᛖᚾᚨᛦ	torch, sword / ulcer, boil; lash
ᚷ ᚷᛖᛒᛟ	to give, gift, talent, marriage, luck
ᚹ ᚹᚢᚾᛟ	joy, pasture
ᚺ ᚺᚨᚷᚨᛚᚨᛦ	hail storm, war; grain
ᚾ ᚾᚨᚢᚦᛁᛦ	need, Need-Fire; toil
ᛁ ᛁᛋᚨ	ice
ᛃ ᛃᛖᚱᚨ	harvest, year, summer
ᛇ ᛃᚢᚹᚨᛦ	yew, bow and arrow
ᛈ ᛈᛖᚱᚦᛟ	apple; dice cup
ᛉ ᚨᛚᚷᛁᛦ ᚨᛚᚺᚨᛦ	elk, protection, Alcis / sacred site, temple
ᛊ ᛊᛟᚢᚾᛟ	Sun, Sól; wheel
ᛏ ᛏᛃᚢᚱᚨᛦ	Tyr, the Brilliant One, divinity; Mars

ᛒ ᛒᛅᚱᚲᛅᚾ	Bjarkan, the Birch Goddess, silver birch
ᛘ ᛘᚢᚱᚱᛦ	horse, sacred horse
ᛉ ᛉᛅᚾᛦ	man, human being, humanity
ᛚ ᛚᛅᚷᚢ ᛚᛅᚢᚲᛦ	sea, lake, water, blood / leek, garlic
◇ ᛁᚢᚱᛦ	Yngvi, Ingi-Frey, youngster, son; hero
ᛟ ᛟᚦᛁᛚ	estate, inherited property, nobility
ᛗᛗᛅᚷᛦ	day, dawn

Germanic Metaphors

What makes the Runes symbols of magic is their combination of meaningful shape, name, arcane history, mythological background, some historical facts and their modern use. At the height of the Elder Futhark, the Rune row was intentionally altered to suit certain needs. The Rune row was reduced from 24 to 16 Runes which did not involve linguistic needs. Rather, its inherent magicality catered for this reorganization. For about two centuries the Elder and Younger systems coexisted, sometimes appearing in one and the same inscription. At the same time, Rune poems were being composed, like the *Abecedarium Nordmannicum* dating from the 7th or 8th century CE. Later the Icelandic and Norwegian Rune poems developed. They all have a rather cultic content and refer to mythological themes. Likewise, many of the Rune names refer to Northern mythology. We may conclude that the Runes were deeply linked with the religious life of the Germanic people.

Magic and religion are philosophy in practice. To give body to religion it was expressed through a corpus of myths. These stories are in turn a reflection of the layered human mind. Consequently, the Runes link in with human psychology and the mental world. It also grants the Runes a divine origin. In a way, the Runes become the interface between humans and Gods, symbols being their mutual language. Magic complements religion in that it represents the Will with which the Runes are wielded. Magic defines as a person's attitude towards life.

On the Symbolism of Runes

It is unavoidable that some of my discussions resemble those of others. Nonetheless the exposition is firmly founded on my own understanding. It is backed up with traditional lore and own experience.

This is exactly why it is important that any Rune student explores the meanings of the Runes for himself. Read and write about them. Look around and recognize the Runes in nature; or, in your daily decisions look for those elements relevant to one Rune or another. Look for images. Any visual or textual material relating to the runic concepts will do. Slowly you build a storehouse of associations. Read more on Runes and consult the insights of others. Discuss the topic. Make mind maps. Enter into a dialogue with the Runes, and so forth. The runic symbols represent archetypal structures to which every individual will give his own personal interpretation.

```
                    ┌──────────────┐
                    │  Rune Sign   │
                    │   (shape)    │
                    └──────────────┘

                         Rune

┌──────────────┐                    ┌──────────────┐
│  Rune Name   │                    │ Rune meaning │
│   (sound)    │                    │    (idea)    │
└──────────────┘                    └──────────────┘
```

As it is, the symbolism of the Runes is mainly expressed in three ways: shape, name and concept. On the one hand, they are represented by the sign's shape, on the other hand by the sign's name. The underlying concept of the Rune name or the Rune shape determines the symbolic content and explains the esoteric meaning of the Rune characters.

As an example Jera and Eihwaz are given. Their respective shapes are j and y. The shape of Jera represents a cycling movement. The Rune name refers to both 'year' and 'harvest'. Therefore, the secret of this Rune is the concept of time, which has been observed by other Runesters. The shape of the Eihwaz Rune represents a pole or staff connecting the upper worlds with the netherworlds. Its name means yew referring to the tree as a representation of the cosmic axis. Therefore, the secret of this Rune expresses inner alignment.

The ideas of power, sound and concept make up the triad of practical aspects of the Rune symbols. The power of the Rune is its cosmic essence (life), which is experienced when its energy is invoked. The sound is connected to the Rune name and allows us to resonate with the Rune energy (quality). The concept translates in ritual and folk custom (appearance).

Returning to our two exemplar Runes, it is noted that Time is the power behind Jera and Alignment behind that of Eihwaz. The ritual custom hidden in Jera is that of the calendar. The seasons dictate the rhythm of sowing and reaping, and the yearly evolution of farming helps to keep track of time. Festivals mark the different stages in the mystery of crop growing. The ritual custom hidden in Eihwaz may relate to hunting. In the very early stages of shamanic times hunting was a sacred art. It also involved aiming well to achieve your goal. Focus is needed to hit your target. Mind, instrument and target align.

3
THE
AETTIR

The Futhark is divided into three equal parts. Germanic gold bracteates from the 6th century already show this division. Among the best known examples of this are the Swedish bracteates from Vadstena and Mariedam and the Grumpan amulet. In all probability, the threefold division was a natural aspect of the runic alphabet from the very start, determined by the number of Runes. The division is based on the sacred numbers three and eight, combining the qualities of fire and earth.

The threefold division recalls earlier alphabets such as the Greek and Hebrew ones. The Ogham too is divided into three groups of letters, altogether termed *trilithon* referring to standing stones. In the Northern tradition, these groups would not be associated with megaliths but with the giant roots of the World Tree Yggdrasil.

In the Northern tradition, these groups of eight are called *aett* 'family'. Cognate with the Old Norse word is the Scottish *airt* indicating the cardinal points of the compass. Ogham terminology has the Celtic word *aicme* for 'family, clan' which is used in the same sense as *aett*. The understanding of this term implies the intricate relation among the Runes of one group.

In the Celtic tradition, every group of letters was represented by a standing stone and every letter by a tree. In the Northern tradition, however, every group is a family and every letter a secret. The head of every family is traditionally a God, corresponding to the first Rune of the respective group. Similarly, each Celtic *aicme* is named after its first letter. We can therefore say that every Rune in a family shares a common principle, and in the Northern tradition this is expressed by the energy of the ruling deity.

The names of these *aettir* are known from Viking times. The first eight Runes are headed by Frey. The second *aett* is ruled by Hagal and the third by Tyr. Since these Gods refer to the initial Runes of every group, the original *aett* names might have been simply Fehu, Hagalaz and Teiwaz. We can only be certain of the Viking names, however, and these are implicit in the Viking Alphabet. That is why the Old Norse names are used.

Despite the reduced number of Runes in the Younger Futhark, the *aettir* division was still respected. These were no longer rows of eight, but they still started with the same three Runes. This means that the three heading Runes, Fehu, Hagalaz and Teiwaz, constitute a basic pattern in *aettir* symbology.

FREY

ᚠ	ᚢ	ᚦ	ᚨ	ᚱ	ᚲ	ᚷ	ᚹ
Fehu	Uruz	Thurisaz	Ansuz	Raido	Kenaz	Gebo	Wunjo

HAGAL

ᚺ	ᚾ	ᛁ	ᛃ	ᛇ	ᛈ	ᛉ	ᛋ
Hagalaz	Nauthiz	Isa	Jera	Eihwaz	Pertho	Algiz	Sowulo

TYR

ᛏ	ᛒ	ᛖ	ᛗ	ᛚ	ᛜ	ᛟ	ᛞ
Teiwaz	Berkana	Ehwaz	Mannaz	Laguz	Inguz	Othila	Dagaz

The God names of every *aett* and the Runes of every *aett* provide a clue as to their fundamental meaning. Frey was a God of peace and prosperity. He is associated with farming and fertility. Therefore, the first *aett* is mainly occupied with principles of self-preservation and the preservation of the species. It is all about the basic needs in life and attaining a certain degree of physical comfort to live that life. It is sometimes called Freyja's Aett. Unmistakably, the Runes of this *aett* are under Vanir dominion.

The Second Aett is named after an unknown Goddess called Hagal. The name clearly refers to the initial Rune of this group. Therefore Hagalaz sets the tone. It immediately becomes apparent that this *aett* symbolizes the complete opposite of Frey and Freyja's docile family. Hagalaz is the emblem of war. On a psychological level, Hagal's Aett represents inner strife. We can therefore conclude that the warlike Aesir rule the Runes of this middle *aett*.

The Third *Aett* is ruled by Tyr. He is a God of justice and truth. He presides over the sanctuaries and keeps the balance of warring opposites. This *aett* represents the synthesis of the previous two. It is ruled by the Regin, a class of Gods formed by Aesir and Vanir alike. At this level, they come together to reach a compromise. Occasionally, the Gods are collectively known as the Tivar. They are called this when they fight side by side for a common cause, as with Ragnarok. It is the *aett* of reconciliation and cooperation.

From a symbolic point of view, every *aett* reveals an aspect of creation. Gods, giants, elves, dwarves and other beings are created in the first *aett*. Together they shape the world as we know it. But this world is also ruled by cosmic laws that seem to be inanimate, like time and space, cause and effect. These aspects belong to Hagal's Aett. The third *aett* harbours the forces of evolution and growth. For this very reason, the Gods made the Nine Worlds. There are trees and plants, human beings and spirits, animals, land and sea and daylight. Consequently, the three *aettir* together tell one story of creation. The myth starts with Fehu, Hagalaz and Teiwaz. The next step in evolution, on all planes, is embodied in the Runes Uruz, Nauthiz and Berkana. Ultimately, creation will conclude itself in Wunjo, Sowulo and Dagaz. In this respect, it becomes self-evident that Runes can be read in vertical triads, some of which have been discussed earlier.

Eight Triads

The triads themselves may refer to a multitude of things. The number 8 refers to the cardinal points, the Wheel of the Year celebrations, the octave of Western harmonics, the I Jing trigrams of the East, as well as the information grouped in one byte. It is also a reference to the spider, the scorpion and the octopus.

When the runic triads are linked to the process of creation, then we might recognize in them the energies of the first eight esoteric numbers. Following this, FHT stands for the absolute, UNB stands for the manifest, ThIE stands for evolution, AJM stands for the form aspect, RYL stands for the life aspect, KPNg stands for the spatial aspect, and so on...

The Triangles of Force of FHT, RYL, GZO and WSD have already been touched upon. Nevertheless, an added note on the Raido-Eihwaz-Laguz triad may be of value. The triad symbolizes the expression of three layers of subtle force in the physical body. Raido: a person's energy on the mental level expressed through the glandular system. Eihwaz: a person's energy on the astral level expressed through the nervous system. Laguz: a person's energy on the physical/etheric level expressed through the blood system. Beside this, the triad also indicates shamanic work.

For the sake of completeness the four remaining triads are briefly presented. The complexes UNB and ThIE both deal with the subconscious. AJM refers to the anthropogenetic myth. The theme covered in the triad Kenaz-Pertho-Inguz is childhood.

A further word on the Uruz-Nauthiz-Berkana triad might be insightful. This triad deals with Devic activity. Here the Uruz energy stands for blueprints. It symbolizes the archetypal forms underlying all physical manifestation. Correspondingly, Nauthiz symbolizes creative force. Berkana refers to the spirits themselves.

Last but not least, the number eight is commonly associated with the compass points. It ties in with the phases of the Moon and the stations of the Sun. But in order to understand this better in an occult way we refer to Bertiaux's work. In his chapter on the Point-Chauds, he introduces us in the setting up of consciousness. He says that "the orientation of the temple ... is really the way in which the symbols ... work as magickal engines". He describes eight directions and assigns them to the points on the compass. In my opinion, these pathways correspond to the Nine Worlds, Midgard being the magician's base camp. Bertiaux further explains how these pathways can be used for time travel.

1	ᚠᚾᛏ	N	Midwinter/Yule	Midnight	New Moon	Past	Absolute
2	ᚺᛰᛒ	NE	Imbolc/Disting		Waxing Crescent	Distant past	Manifest
3	ᛁᛉ	E	Spring equinox/Ostara	Morning	First Quarter	Distant future	Evolution
4	ᛈᛋᛈ	SE	Beltain/Walpurgis Night		Waxing Gibbous	Future	Form
5	ᚱᛇᛏ	S	Midsummer/Balder's Balar	Noon	Full Moon	Near future	Life
6	ᚲᛟ	SW	Lughnasadh		Waning Gibbous	Present	Space
7	ᛉᛏᛉ	W	Autumn equinox	Evening	Last Quarter	Present	Matter
8	ᛈᛋᛞ	NW	Samhain/Alfablot		Waning Crescent	Near past	Christ consciousness

The eight runic triads may also correspond to the eight planes of existence: physical, etheric, lower astral, upper astral, concrete mental, abstract mental, lower spiritual and higher spiritual.

Heimdal teaches the Runes

The *aettir* system reflects the different stages of evolution, in particular the evolution of consciousness. The three successive *aettir* represent three stages going from the gross material to the subtle spiritual. The first stage embodies the world of sensory experience and contact with the physical world. This stage is ruled by the feminine principle. It is the womb from which creation is born, holding the foundation of experience. This stage corresponds to Frey's Aett. Hagal's Aett symbolizes the development of consciousness. It represents the experience of suffering and the world of feeling and thought. Through these, contact can be made with the soul and beyond. Lastly, the third stage transcends the duality of masculine and feminine powers. They blend. It therefore represents the assimilation of polarities in an individual's personality. Then the perfected Man will arise, expressed in the m-Rune. Whenever a person walks through these stages of initiation, for that is what they are, he trains himself in the art of life, starting off as an apprentice and graduating as a master. The arrangement of the *aettir* moreover corresponds to the formula of thesis, antithesis and synthesis.

All of these spiritual truths are reflected in human society. According to Dumézil, ancient Indo-European society is based on a three-leveled hierarchy. The lowest class consists of farmers and workers. They produce the food on which the whole society depends. The second class is represented by fighters. It is their task to defend the goods of the workers. The upper class consists of kings and priests. They rule the other classes and organize their life. You can see how the whole fundamentally depends on the first class.

Frey			
Vanir	Body	Farming	Creation
Hagal			
Aesir	Mind	Warfare	Destruction
Tyr			
Regin	Soul	Politics	Organization

These three classes more or less correspond to the different races of Gods inhabiting the Nine Worlds. The Vanir are connected to the land and represent fertility. Both physical matter and fertility are expressions of the creative force shared by all Vanir. This constructive energy is balanced by the warlike Aesir of Hagal's Aett. Warfare is easily associated with death and destruction. As metaphors, death and destruction suit well the sacrifices of the Second Aett. Nevertheless, fighting implies a marked aim and realized ideals that are worth the trouble. Tyr's Aett represents the world of rulers and politicians. They organize, define, lay laws and determine fate. That is exactly what the Regin do. Daily they come together at Urd's Well to discuss matters and determine the fate of the worlds. The mythological poem *Voluspa* relates how the Regin organize the world by defining the different aspects of creation.

In the Northern tradition, the symbolism of the threefold hierarchy is preserved in the *Rigsthula* poem. The text describes how the God Heimdal descends upon Earth and visits three couples successively. Every couple bears a son of his blood and represents one of the classes. Heimdal's first son is called Thrael. His name means thrall or slave. The boy marries a girl called Thir. From them the *þraela aettir* stem. They till the land and herd the cattle. Heimdal's second son is Karl. His wife is Snör and from them are descended the *karla aettir*. The Old Norse word *karl* designates a free man. Heimdal's third son is Jarl. His wife was Erna. From them are descended the *jarla aettir*. A *jarl* is someone of noble birth and the word is cognate with English 'earl'. Jarl and Erna have a son called Kon. Him Heimdal teaches the Runes. In this context, teaching the Runes means preparing for initiation. Apart from these three classes there is a fourth group that counters all the above. In the myths, this power is known as *jötna aettir*, the families of the giants.

The sequence in which the sons appear reflects the different stages of development in the human race and mind. As a slave, Thrael symbolizes a will-less person. He conforms to society but does not feel the inner need for self-development or revolution. He represents the masses. Karl represents quite the opposite. As a free man he represents free will and embodies the desire to express this. At a certain stage, Karl experiences that free will implies responsibility. This is its spiritual aspect and is expressed in the life of the jarl. Thus, the ignorant man becomes Karl when he realizes he has got a will of his own and *wants* to use it. He becomes an individual; as it is expressed in the *Voluspa* 'once three came from among the host'. The individual distinguishes himself from the masses. Later still, Karl transforms into Jarl, wielding free will from a spiritual point of view. Jarl's son Kon represents his inner child or higher self. Esoterically, the jarl's class refers to the initiates, individuals who have achieved a certain degree of spiritual development. The jarl does not look just after himself, no, he serves the community. In this way, the evolution from the masses to the individual and from individual struggle to group life is present in the successive *aettir*.

Mythology grants us a further insight into the different classes. *Harbardsljod* contains the following words: 'Odin owns the earls, who in battle fall; but Thor owns the kin of thralls'. Odin is the patron God of high society. The word 'earl' ultimately derives from *erilaz*. Thor has always been the most popular God, representing the common people. He is called 'karl of karls'. The myth, however, assigns the fate of slaves to his hands. This leaves the middle class open to speculation, although it would be natural to assign Thor to it as well. Yet I would suggest the Goddess Freyja as ruling Hagal's Aett. According to *Grimnismal*, Freyja claims the fallen before Odin does. More than Odin, Freyja embodies the spirit of free will.

Frey	Þræll	Slave	Mass	*ósnotr*	Thor
Hagal	Karl	Free man	Individual	*meðalsnotr*	Freyja
Tyr	Jarl	Prince	Initiate	*snotr*	Odin

These three classes and their symbolism reflect a quality present in every Rune of each *aett*. Note how the Runes of Tyr's Aett refer to jurisdiction, perfection and magic. Similarly, Fehu, the first Rune of Frey's Aett, refers to food. Frey himself is a God of vegetation and fertility. Hagal's Aett contains Runes that are easily read in a psychological way. Their symbolism reveals inner conflict and outer struggle.

Evidently, comparing the threefold division and archetypal social hierarchy we observe certain patterns of inner development. Frey's Aett symbolizes serving the community. It awakens the quality of unconditional love in a person. Maybe an ignorant person would consider this a form of submission. From a spiritual standpoint, it is all that matters. It teaches us to remain humble in the face of grandeur. Devotion and loyalty are aspects of Frey's Aett. The other two *aettir* are supported by the first one. They cannot blossom without its teachings.

Hagal's Aett symbolizes freedom – or at least striving towards the ideal of freedom. Through the process of binding, all the Runes of this *aett* eventually lead to liberation. Tyr's Aett symbolizes control over the former two. For this to happen one must be free and independent; I would almost say, without karma. Tyr's Aett stands for responsibility. Its qualities of leadership, organization and teaching will pull the masses up from the darkness.

In the Stars it is Writ

A meaningful link exists between the *aettir* and astrology. The three crosses of astrological lore neatly correspond to the symbolism of the three successive *aettir*. The mutable cross stands for principles of moving and orientation and corresponds to Frey's Aett. The fixed cross stands for principles of integration and discipline corresponding to Hagal's Aett. The cardinal cross stands for principles of transformation and initiation and corresponds to Tyr's Aett. Esoterically, these crosses express the ideal evolution of man.

The mutable cross expresses the life of change. It stands for the cycle of life and birth. It is also expressive of conditioning circumstances playing on the outer life of an individual. The energies of this cross, whether expressed as Runes or star signs, produce periods of change, swept by desires, ideals, disappointment, and long sought after satisfaction. Thus, the first *aett* represents the wide range of accumulated life experience. As a foundation, this external conditioning is needed to turn the mind inward. This first cross is associated with the masses and so the allied *aett* symbolizes herd instinct. Therefore, the keyword of this *aett* is instinct. Frey's Aett represents the Path of Evolution, treaded by average man going at the regular pace of evolution.

In the second *aett* of the Futhark, the keyword changes to intelligence. Man becomes conscious of his own power in life and redirects his actions. An individual arises from the crowd of mankind, referred to above by the quoted *Voluspa* line. The corresponding fixed cross expresses the influence of the soul conditioning a person's inner life. The energies of the fixed cross represent points of crises leading to inner changes, as Runes such as Hagalaz, Nauthiz and Eihwaz testify. It is therefore an *aett* that is primarily psychologically oriented. This cross is called fixed, because the individual earnestly adopts a vision that directs him onto the spiritual path. He fixes his gaze upon the inner life instead of upon material gain. Such a person is esoterically called a disciple. We would call them Einherjar. Or Valkyrjar. Thus, Hagal's Aett represents the Path of Discipleship.

The third path is called the Path of Initiation. Through the full range of inner and outer life experience the disciple becomes initiated in life. The cardinal cross stands for achieving exalted states of awareness and spiritual attainment. In this *aett* are integrated the inner and the outer, so transcending the duality of man's earthly world of experience. The energies of this cross represent points of synthesis, culminating in Inguz, Othila and Dagaz. The shapes of these Runes say all. The cardinal *aett's* keyword is intuition, which is a concept symbolic of the spiritual world and the inpouring cosmic energy. The individual's focus will change again from himself towards others desiring to serve humanity as a whole.

ᚠ	**Mutable Cross**	Mass	Personality	Path of Probation	*instinct*
ᚾ	**Fixed Cross**	Individual	Soul	Path of Discipleship	*intelligence*
↑	**Cardinal Cross**	Group	Monad	Path of Initiation	*intuition*

As the three *aettir* outline a story of evolution, so do the crosses describe the way leading a person from blind ignorance through the realization of individuality to eventual spiritual attainment. One deed leads to another. The mutable cross, and therefore Frey's Aett, concerns the form nature, the body and the physical world. Its energies train the lower aspects of man, such as the physical, emotional and mental body. In this *aett* an individual's personality is shaped. This can be called the *stage of theory*. Then follows the fixed cross, symbolic of the *stage of practice* in which experiment and experience become of paramount importance. The process of necessary learning goes hand in hand with much suffering – or what may be called the working out of karma. The energies of the fixed *aett* make it possible to contact the soul. This *aett* is therefore concerned with the alignment of soul and personality, which is made possible through the experience of the pairs of opposites symbolized by Hagalaz. The alignment itself is embodied in the Rune shape of Eihwaz. And its consummation is represented by the Sun glyph. As the mutable cross corresponds to the personality, the fixed cross to the soul, so the cardinal cross corresponds to the influence of the monad, the spark of inner divinity. The cardinal *aett* can be termed the *stage of spiritual expression*, to use the terminology found in Alice Bailey's writings.

In Northern cosmology, the three realms of Utgard, Asgard and Midgard and their mutual relations express the energies of these three stages. These three worlds combine the horizontal plane of everyday awareness with the vertical axis of spiritual experience. Frey's Aett corresponds to the horizontal plane of outer life and is ruled by the Vanir. On this plane, Midgard, the world of man, is opposed to the forces of Utgard. Hagal's Aett corresponds to the vertical plane of inner life and is ruled by the Aesir. Here, earthly Midgard is set against the celestial world of Asgard. Tyr's Aett combines both axes in one great whole, itself representing the principle of synthesis. There is no longer a circle and a line, but a globe of radiating power. This last *aett* is ruled by the Light Elves, who also belong to the class of Regin Gods.

The crosses also correspond to aspects of the mind. The cardinal cross embodies the power of Will. Intention is in particular a power attributed to Tyr and the Teiwaz Rune. The fixed cross represents aspects of consciousness, through which wisdom is gained. This is more generally described as awareness. The mutable cross embodies the energies of inherent intelligence. This spontaneous aspect is typically attributed to the Vanir. The aspects are related to the Odinic triad.

FREY FEHU	HAGAL HAGALAZ	TYR TEIWAZ
Appearance	Quality	Life
Matter	Consciousness	Spirit
Material	Psychological	Social
Physical body	Nervous system	Energy system
Etheric	Astral	Mental
Water	Air	Fire
Substance	Force	Intention
Intelligence	Awareness	Intention
Active Intelligence	Love and Wisdom	Will and Power
Goodness	Beauty	Truth
Mutable Cross	Fixed Cross	Cardinal Cross
Mutable Planets	Fixed Stars	Galaxies
Planetary	Solar	Cosmic
Personality	Soul	Monad
Path of Probation	Path of Discipleship	Path of Initiation
Mass	Individual	Group
Comfort	Conflict	Balance
Thesis	Antithesis	Synthesis
WUNJO	SOWULO	DAGAZ

The Story of Frey

The Vanic deities Frey and Freyja rule this first *aett* of gentle conditions, fertility and basic requirements. The Vanic elements of Earth and Water point to the physical nature of this *aett*. As 'form' and 'formation' these elements are necessary principles in the manifestation of the universe macrocosmically and the personality microcosmically.

As expressions of basic principles, these eight Runes symbolize simple and material things such as money, health, conflict, intelligence, control, knowledge, temperance and pleasure. They convey simple truths and cater for the basic comfort in our lives. As an expression of this, none of the First Aett Runes is grafted on a double stem, whereas the Second Aett begins with one; Hagalaz represents the challenge of dualism. As an expression of basic needs and physical conditions, these Runes have much bearing on our bodily health.

Yet these principles can be explained on many levels. Generally, the Vanic powers of this family are associated with feeling, responsiveness, sensing, sympathy, and life energy. As Runes on the initiatory path of life, they represent energy, understanding, action, inspiration, ritual, discipline, generosity and friendship. As a pattern, the path of Frey's Aett evolves from the ignorant masses to a sense of brotherhood and community. The Fehu Rune represents the collective. Conversely, Uruz extracts the individual from that collective. In Runes such as Thurisaz and Ansuz, the individual attempts to express himself. Still further upon the path, the skill of sharing experience in Gebo will enable him to be an accepted part of the greater whole of humanity. Wunjo symbolizes kinship, brotherhood and group awareness.

As a family of creative powers, the Vanir as well as Frey's eight Runes set things in motion. They shape and they brainstorm under the auspices of inspiration. Vanaheim grants these runic powers the fertile fields in which the first cosmic principles can be sown, so that they will mature, work out and come to fruition in later times and *aettir*. This first *aett* symbolizes the foundation on which the other two are built. As such, these Runes reveal the patterns of creation and, in my opinion, correspond to the emergence of the Nine Worlds. After all, Frey's Aett is the first off in the Rune row story.

Because these eight Runes belong to one family, they share common characteristics. One of these is the associated meaning of leadership. Frey himself was a leader of sorts (Fehu). The myths relate how Frey leads the Aesic host. Ansuz symbolizes authority. Raido and Kenaz symbolize leadership as the ability of showing the way. Wunjo refers to a chieftain. Its shape is reminiscent of the battle standard carried high in combat. Uruz and Thurisaz represent a leader's qualities. These are courage, persistence and will power. Gebo too represents a much needed quality in management, which is the understanding and relation of a lord to his warriors; a superior to his employees.

From the foregoing, it is clear that many stories can be told using the eight Runes of Frey. The following paragraphs will sum up some of these in a methodical way. It mainly discusses how the First Aett underlies the progression of a project. The same pattern is then illustrated in different ways. It will be clear that Frey's Aett is the *aett* of development. Ideas become results.

As a finite pattern of eight, the Runes of Frey's Aett well express the different stages of a project. It guides you along a cycle of development, from nil to result. It all starts with an idea. It all starts with Fehu, the impulsive power of a desire or an urge to realize something, to achieve or possess something. It signifies the positive impulse with which a project is started.

FEHU

Fehu represents a sensed initiative; a creative spark from Muspelheim. There is an impulse, an urge to create, or the idea to start a project. Fehu also symbolizes the generic pool of human thought from which inspiration can be drawn.

URUZ

You follow up this desire to express the idea by elaborating on it. Uruz is the receiving womb of Mother Earth in which the seed of Fehu is planted. It cools the iron into shape. Then it must be hammered still. In other words, it blueprints your ideas, but these blueprints have to be developed. Uruz symbolizes the slow process of individuation from the collective mind of Fehu.

THURISAZ

Often one meets opposition in working out a plan. Difficulties arise in executing the plan. This is a natural and necessary stage that forces you to go deeper and to specify your goals. It makes you reorient.

ANSUZ

Ansuz symbolizes solutions. Any difficulty that may have startled you at Thurisaz will lead to a valuable insight. Meditating on the situation clarifies your position and helps finding answers to your problems. The Ansuz Rune always offers a solution. Ansuz clarifies while Thurisaz obscures. At Ansuz, you have a clear idea of where you are heading. This is carried out in Raido.

RAIDO

Then you get back on track again. Raido is the 99 percent transpiration, whereas Ansuz may have been the inspiration. This stage usually comprises the bulk of the project, the heavy lifting.

KENAZ

The k-Rune stands for perfection. Every detail of the plan is tuned. Furthermore, your skills now enable you to communicate your ideas to the outside world. Kenaz stimulates within you the desire to share your gained experience, skill or knowledge. It becomes public.

GEBO

Gebo signifies both the implementation of your project and its relation to others. It also stands for a windfall. Sometimes outsiders are needed to finish your project. Gebo amplifies the need of relations with others. Sometimes Gebo stands for profit. At Gebo is won what earlier had to be given up to achieve your goal.

WUNJO

Wunjo marks the finished project as your very own. It stands for completion, the finishing touch, claiming ownership, fame and so forth. It is the fulfillment of the first spark sensed at Fehu, maybe years ago.

The meanings of the last two Runes complement each other. Both stand for joy. Both stand for friendship. Both symbolize any kind of relationship. Their causal relation may be expressed as follows. Promises, contracts, and exchanges lead to friendships, delight and synthesis. Their meanings overlap and seem to be dependent on each other.

The pattern of development evidently links in with the story of creation, but from a different perspective, it also illustrates the growing up of a child. In the creational process, Fehu represents the creative fire. This Rune fuses the project or the life with the energy needed to complete it. But creation involves birth. Therefore, Fehu may be associated with birth. In that case, Uruz stands for feeding the child (Audumla). Thurisaz symbolizes the child's will to become independent. In Ansuz, self-awareness is attained and the growing child learns to express itself. Raido stands for the years of growth. Kenaz represents puberty. Gebo may signify marriage or first love. It may also refer to an individual's marriage to his or her soul. Wunjo may be the resulting family. From a more inclusive perspective, this family unit is nothing less than humanity.

In the body, the all pervading life energy of Fehu is seen as vitality or health (Uruz). A well maintained health results in a strong immune system (Thurisaz). A balanced body results in a free mind. Your attention can then be directed towards self-awareness, self-expression and grasping the meaning of life (Ansuz). This is a process of individuation that leads to treading a spiritual path symbolized by Raido. Along the way, insight in the self will enable you to grow (Kenaz). Once this is established, you turn your mind outward again (Gebo) and seek harmony with those around you (Wunjo).

FEHU   energy, life principle

URUZ   vitality, health, blood stream, etheric body

THURISAZ   immune system, aura

ANSUZ   breath, voice, desire to express oneself

RAIDO   a goal in life

KENAZ   know thyself

GEBO   giving in a balanced way, teaching, harmony

WUNJO   living true

Complementary to this table would be Gundarsson's interpretation of this *aett*. He relates the Runes of this *aett* to the necessary qualities of the magician. His insights on this are worth elaborating on. As we go along, I will use the car metaphor to clarify the concepts.

According to Gundarsson, Fehu represents magical force or energy. It is the power needed to fuel your operation. It can therefore be likened to fueling a car. Fehu is a vehicle's food. Uruz symbolizes the creative energy. It forms and shapes ('vital shaping power'). Similarly, the engine of a car transforms gas into movement. In order to move, one has to press down the accelerator. This 'dynamic, active force' is none other than Thurisaz. The Rune allows you to go full throttle if needed. The inspiration and *galdr*-technique of Ansuz comprise the Words of a ritual. The rhythm and timing of Raido comprise the Gestures. It is also symbolic of the ritual total. Expanding on our metaphor, Ansuz represents the destination you want to go to, it is your map – so carefully formulated in your *galdr*, and Raido represents the navigation. Kenaz is associated with controlling the summoned energies and using your skill to forge them into your set thought-forms or complexes. It corresponds to driving your car in sometimes stressing traffic. Gebo represents the exchange of energies. It encompasses giving and receiving power. I would suggest it corresponds to keeping to the rules of traffic; yielding being the archetypal example. Wunjo represents the magician's will. It is the magic straight staff of his intention. In our car story, Wunjo symbolizes arriving at the desired destination.

The Story of Hagal

As opposed to the physical and temporal world of Frey's Aett, we now enter the dimension of the immortal. The principle of the soul rules this world. Hagalaz symbolizes realizing the transitoriness of life.

Once the fleeting reality of the material world is realized those big questions in life as to the meaning of it all are triggered. The arising questions are found in Nauthiz and Isa. If the person is spiritually inclined he will look for answers. Thus starts the never-ending quest for absolute truth and grasping the immortal, the immaterial, through life experience and wisdom. The quest is characterized by Runes such as Jera, Eihwaz and Pertho. Algiz symbolizes aspiration. In Sowulo, the individual identifies himself with his living ideals. The immortal is then definitively sensed.

Deities governing this family vary from Hella to Heimdal to Odin. Hella as well as Odin seem apt to rule this Aett. They both demonstrate a twofold nature, an internal and an external. First there is Hella. She is pictured as half dead and half alive. She is a giantess yet a Goddess. She rules the dead yet harbours Balder. Then there is Odin. He binds and releases. As a war God he decides the outcome of battle. One will triumph. One must fall. From a metaphoric point of view, Odin represents the consciousness aspect of this *aett*. Hella emphasizes the psychological aspect. As an Underworld Goddess she rules the subconscious.

This second *aett* takes life from everyday awareness and comfort deeper into the less explored realms of the mind. Consequently, much mental and emotional turmoil and moral conflict arise from entering this path. Once Hella has granted you access to the deeper parts of the mind, you will have to face them. Hagal's Aett introduces powers outside human control, such as space and time, *wyrd* and *örlög*, or *karma* and *dharma*, the laws of nature and occasions of initiation and insight.

It is clear from the above, that the pathway of Hagal is a difficult and challenging one. It can be posited that this second *aett* ultimately represents a path of transformation. Whereas Frey's Aett kicks off with a constructive idea, Hagal's Aett begins with a destructive condition. Hagalaz indicates a difficulty or problem. But the rest of the *aett* presents us with the most likely way towards resolution. It guides us through the different stages of solving a problem, from inescapable fate towards final liberation. Just as with Frey's Aett all of these stages will be discussed in detail.

HAGALAZ

Hagalaz symbolizes the problem at hand or maybe a state of unhappiness. It denotes an event that disrupts or upsets you. Maybe a trauma. Maybe something that you carry with you from past lives.

NAUTHIZ

The Nauthiz Rune symbolizes the resulting need. Its power forces you to act. It denotes a crisis, such as a depression or panic. You realize that action must be taken to improve your state of being.

ISA

Isa represents the possible reactions to crisis. This is either to paralyze or to remain calm. Either you find yourself cornered and imprisoned by life itself. Or, you contemplate a possible positive outcome. Nonetheless, Isa can also be considered to be the aftermath of Hagalaz.

JERA

If the pressure of Nauthiz is strong enough, an answer will ensue. Time will give you the necessary opportunities. The old patterns are shattered and new ones will be built. Time heals. Improvement is in sight. Jera is able to slowly free you from the imprisoning fangs of ice. At that level, your old force becomes restored.

EIHWAZ

Eihwaz teaches you to endure in trying times. A second crisis may appear, maybe caused by disbelief or a victim attitude.

PERTHO

Pertho supports you in such a way that you will find new resources to speed up improvement and haul yourself from the doomed pit of despair. The Rune indicates help from people you did not expect it from; or you might be at a complete loss. This Rune also gives insight into the deeper meanings of your problems. You may look for answers in the occult.

ALGIZ

Algiz evokes from within you a sense of trust. It represents guidance from above and within. All will be well. Have faith!

SOWULO

Victory! The problem has been defeated, the darkness dispelled. At the level of Sowulo, the full process of learning has been integrated in your being. The crisis that started at Hagalaz has now been fully overcome.

This pattern reflects an important way of learning. The pathway of Hagal holds the quality of purifying the soul, because it transforms suffering into independence and freedom. In this *aett* karma is worked with and eventually cleared. Automatically, this process deepens your understanding of life and this understanding will enable you to find a higher standard of living.

One atypical example of recovering from a disrupting incident, however, is the integration of a near-death experience. Sutherland discerns four phases in processing such a powerful experience. They are denial, standstill, gradual improvement and increasing integration. These four neatly correspond to the Runes Nauthiz, Isa, Jera and Eihwaz. Of course, Hagalaz represents the actual experience. In his work on NDE, Van Lommel concludes that these patients show a long term reorientation towards the spiritual. This shows in Runes such as Pertho, Algiz and Sowulo. On the whole, the process of integration symbolized by the Second Aett reflects the observations of psychologists in working with traumatized patients.

In regard to dealing with an upsetting event, the first three Runes present us with three different ways of coping. Hagalaz stands for the fight response. Nauthiz stands for the flight response. And Isa stands for paralysis.

From a natural perspective, Hagal's Runes are all relevant to the season of winter. Maybe this should not be so surprising, since this row of eight comprises the *aett* of darkness and despair.

HAGALAZ	hail, snow
NAUTHIZ	the Yule fire
ISA	Ice, winter
JERA	Yule tide, return of the Sun
EIHWAZ	this is the Rune of Ull, a God of winter. Yew trees are a typical symbol of the winter season, because they are evergreen.
PERTHO	this Rune symbolizes the promise of life, waiting in the Earth. At the same time it symbolizes the reality of death.
ALGIZ	may refer to the contemplative mood typical of the winter season.
SOWULO	the winter solstice, the Sun

Feelings of loneliness, patience, darkness and silence complete these keywords. As a process, this row of eight symbolizes the turning of the year and the promise of a new season, expressed by the Sowulo Rune. These Runes have the power to turn your fate!

Mythologically, the two Runes at the extremes of this *aett* show that this *aett* recounts the myth of Balder's death. As a Sun God, Balder is identified with Sowulo, whereas his eventual destination of Helheim corresponds to Hagalaz. For that reason, we will now switch the normal reading direction and read the Second Aett from right to left. It symbolizes the young God's fey fate. Incidentally, this backward sequence symbolizes the path of destruction. The normal direction symbolizes a way of recovery.

Beginning with the last Rune of this *aett*, Sowulo represents the Sun God Balder. His death is remembered every year at Midsummer (Sowulo). Algiz refers to Frigg; once Balder's doom is known Frigg travels the Nine Worlds in order to ward off any possible evil. She protects her son (Algiz). However, there is one small item she deems harmless. Loki finds out. That is Pertho. Then Loki snatches the mistletoe weapon and guides Hoder's hand in aiming it at Balder's heart. The missile is Eihwaz. Jera refers to slaying the God. Isa symbolizes Balder's death. Nauthiz represents his funeral pyre. Hagalaz refers to Hella welcoming Balder in the Underworld. Afterwards, the Ragnarok war will break out and the Tivar will ride to Vigrid, which refers to the beginning of the Third Aett. On the other hand, Balder's youthful innocence reminds us of Wunjo. Consequently, the story makes a boustrophedon reading of the Futhark possible.

SOWULO	Balder, Sun God celebrated at Midsummer
ALGIZ	Balder protected by Frigg's magic
PERTHO	Loki discovers Balder's Achilles' heel
EIHWAZ	the mistletoe spear
JERA	Hoder slays his brother
ISA	Balder is dead
NAUTHIZ	Balder cremated at the Midsummer fire
HAGALAZ	Balder fares to Hella in his ship Hringhorni

The Runes of this *aett* not only refer to Balder but to the life of Odin as well. Some are very clear, such as Eihwaz and Pertho reminding us of his great sacrifices, but the other Runes too can be explained.

HAGALAZ

Because Hagalaz represents the Underworld, this Rune refers to Odin's travels to Hel where he consults the *völva* (*Baldrs Draumar*). In general, Hagalaz refers to any myth in which Odin consults a seeress, the poem of *Voluspa* included.

NAUTHIZ

Nauthiz refers to Balder's cremation. It therefore hints at Odin's mysterious decision to whisper a secret into his son's ear. He also gives him his ring Draupnir, which, transformed by the fire, drips gold ever after.

ISA

So far, the mythological references follow up the story of Balder's death. Subsequently, we can associate Isa with Rind. Her meetings with Odin are dealt with in Saxo's *Gesta Danorum*. Their child Vali will avenge Balder's death.

JERA

Jera refers to Odin and the Mead of Poetry. Before he comes to Suttung's halls to obtain the mead, Odin passes by the farm of Baugi, Suttung's brother. Disguised as Bölverk, Odin reaps the wheat of Baugi's fields. In return, he expects Baugi to help him obtain the mead from Suttung.

EIHWAZ

The Eihwaz Rune refers to Odin's initiation hanging at the gallows. Eihwaz represents both Yggdrasil, on which he hung, and Gungnir, with which he sacrificed himself. In the life of a human being, this myth represents the trials and hardships of the pledged disciple on the spiritual path. A conscious decision is made to grow spiritually often resulting in difficult ordeals initiating the individual in life's different qualities. It gives you a chance to work with your *wyrd*.

PERTHO

Pertho refers to the well of Mimir. At this well Odin sacrifices his eye for a drop of the waters of wisdom. *Sigrdrifumal* gives us the words presented by Mimir to Odin on that occasion. On top of that, *Voluspa* reminds us that Odin consults with Mimir at the onset of Ragnarok. This proves the order of the Runes to be in a chronological order. This is especially so because the myths also prove that the gaining of the Mead of Poetry happens after Balder's death, because Kvasir is only killed after Loki is bound at the end of *Lokasenna*. From this point of view, Nauthiz stands for binding Loki, Isa for Skadi's revenge and Jera for the slaying of Kvasir. In the life of the disciple, Pertho represents the cup or well of wisdom from which the individual is allowed to drink after the initiating hardships of Eihwaz.

ALGIZ

I would associate Algiz with Odin's royal might at Asgard. In our story, the Rune also refers to Heimdal blowing the horn to be ready for Ragnarok. On a spiritual level, Heimdal's rainbow bridge takes the human mind to the level of the soul. Communion is possible with the anima or Valkyrja; or with the animus or Einherjan. Algiz corresponds to Valhalla.

SOWULO

Sowulo can only refer to Ragnarok at which time Odin is killed by Fenrir – the wolf who tries to eat the Sun. After Odin succumbs, Vidar takes his place and slays Fenrir.

One more remark is in place under the heading of Hagal's Aett. The Old English Rune Poem promises that if need is heeded in time, deliverance will be near. And the words are true. Drawing a Nauthiz Rune, one first draws the vertical stroke representing the present moment (n). Then one begins to draw the stroke of destiny. In a sense this downward movement represents falling, but if heeded in time it can be restored and be drawn upward again. The exact timing to do that is none other than the present. If at that point fate is turned and the stroke extends upward you happen to create an Algiz

Rune (ᛉ). Algiz will always safeguard you from the dark shrouds of demon powers. Draw it often.

The Story of Tyr

Of the three the Third Aett is the most spiritually oriented. Not only does it synthesize the earlier two, but also does it symbolize synthesis in itself. Presided over by a God of heaven, the Runes of this family easily relate to cosmic principles. And Teiwaz being a Rune of discipline, vision and action, these Runes also embody a person's qualities when he treads the spiritual path. Teiwaz symbolizes the universal truth. This is the celestial *aett*.

Tyr stands for divinity, spiritual processes and communion with the higher realms. This God's radiation rings through in the Runes of this Aett. Justice and responsibility, self-sacrifice and self-awareness, devotion and faith all lead to the initiation that the first Rune promises. All these qualities are found in Tyr's Runes and in effect are the result of initiating processes. Creativity and art belong to this *aett* as well.

As a spiritual *aett*, Tyr's group of Runes provides the evolutionary plan of inner self-realization. As such, Tyr's Runes all relate to possible aspects of a person's spiritual path. Thus, Teiwaz symbolizes man taking on his first steps on the path of self-realization, while Dagaz symbolizes the initiation that can only be taken when all the preparatory steps have been walked. They therefore express aspects of inner guidance.

To begin with, Teiwaz sets the example. This first Rune reflects an ideal. Berkana nurtures a person's self-confidence. Its energy symbolizes the inner stirrings to express one's soul's workings. Ehwaz trains your intuition as Mannaz does with the mind. Mannaz also represents the perfected human being, which is an individual beyond the training of the earthly level. Laguz symbolizes purity and foresight. It also stands for mastering the astral realms. Inguz stands for mastering the physical plane. On the level of Othila, the individual lives in service of his fellows. Emphasis is laid upon service and group life. As a Rune of inner guidance, Othila inspires you to follow your ideals and principles. Listen to the whispers of your soul. Dagaz symbolizes clarity of mind. This Rune represents cosmic consciousness. The Runes of this *aett* reflect the spiritual development of man aligning his lower self with his higher self.

TEIWAZ

Teiwaz symbolizes a model or ideal. On the level of the personality, this ideal can only be expressed by setting a good example. On the soul level, it symbolizes an actual inner quality you consciously try to evoke. The Teiwaz Rune represents the Sky Father and hence spirit.

BERKANA

As an individual treads the path of self-development, a lot of time will be spent on the inner processes. The mind will be turned inwards. This mental reorientation is reflected in Berkana. In that space deep within you, you find trust and faith. Berkana helps you to gain self-confidence when and where needed.

EHWAZ

Ehwaz is generally understood to be the energy of intuition. Some connection is made between the individual's conscious mind (personality) and his soul. As a result, other thought patterns than only the logical are trusted. Ehwaz is linked with the associative part of the mind. The rational part is reflected in the next Rune.

MANNAZ

Mannaz symbolizes the deep mind. The root of the word *mannaz* is indeed cognate with the word 'mind'. On a psychological level, it symbolizes the integration of a person's inner polarity.

LAGUZ

Laguz holds the promise of developing paranormal abilities. They develop naturally according to a person's increasing spiritual awareness. The water element of this Rune initially leads you through the astral energies, but as you progress in developing your intuition, the astral experience will make downloading the higher energies easier. Laguz stands for foresight and premonition, and reading the signs. Laguz symbolizes the mysteries of life and death with which every human being is faced. The Rune's energy is expressive of life, love, light, meaning and purpose.

INGUZ

Frey is connected with the planetary body of our Earth. That is why the Inguz Rune is strongly associated with the body mind. From a practical perspective, Inguz reflects the art of meditation, because insight is gained through introspection. In the occult tradition, it is the soul that mediates the individual's earthly existence with its cosmic counterpart known as the monad. It is the divine seed in man. As a continuation of Laguz, second sight, second hearing and second touch come under the command of Inguz. Inguz also complements the mysteries found in Laguz. The individual gathers an understanding of the meaning of life through introspection and deep meditation. The opposite is true, too, however. By actively participating in the ritual of everyday life, all the necessary opportunities are met to learn the meaning and purpose of life. This is Othila.

OTHILA

Othila is the Rune of ethics, principles and conscience. A set of these is necessary in learning to deal with others as well as with yourself, with the planet and with your immediate surroundings, as well as learning discipline and the power of decision. Othila increases your awareness of the greater whole. The symbol represents the realization that the individual is only a particle in the greater body of humanity. The Rune's energy is connected with community and family. At the same time, it hints at ancestor worship. As opposed to Inguz, Othila teaches the value of experience. Insight is gained through daily life.

DAGAZ

The last of Runes represents cosmic consciousness. It leads a person from the earthly plane into the spiritual dimension. It is primarily a Rune of insight, as only insight enables one to advance in this world. Dagaz also stands for clarity of mind; and with this comes the power of Will. Now, no longer will anything stand in the way of the vision seen by the mage. Analogous to Othila, Dagaz increases our awareness of being a part of the cosmos. Humanity, and even the planet Earth, is only a particle in the cosmic body of the universe. In addition, the runic sequence ends with Dagaz expressing the rhythmic cycle of life and death, eventually transcending this. It is the door through which initiation is taken. Heimdal is its guardian.

In contrast with the earlier two *aettir*, there are two ways of going through this *aett*. There is a simple way and a complex one. Firstly, and much in line with the earlier two, Tyr's Aett is simply a metaphor for sending an intention. Secondly, the Third Aett stands for marrying two ideas. It is the Aett of synthesis.

In a most general way, Tyr's Aett outlines the path of any action. Teiwaz symbolizes an intention; the power of this Rune resembles launching a spear. Berkana gives birth to the intention in a more physical way. The relationship is much like that of Uruz to Fehu, Uruz being the vehicle to conceive the power of Fehu's impulsive thrust. Ehwaz represents the relationship between subject and object, which becomes established at Mannaz. Laguz is the flowing energy. Energy follows thought. It flows as it follows the focused mind of Mannaz. Inguz is the seed planted in the target. Othila is the target hit and Dagaz the intention having done its work.

Even this simple way of explaining the Third Aett reveals that the dynamics of opposites is involved. In the above, a relation is implied between a subject and an object. Teiwaz is the subject sending an intention, whereas Berkana symbolizes the object to be touched. Ehwaz symbolizes the connection that is made between the two, increasing in quality at Mannaz. The shapes of Ehwaz and Mannaz show how two opposites are first brought into contact and then merged. Laguz represents the natural response to the connection. Inguz symbolizes the unit of energy involved. Othila represents the full transference of force from subject to object. Dagaz earths the energies.

As a result, the dynamics of Tyr's Aett are entirely different from those of the previous two *aettir*. The third *aett* opens with two Runes and consequently demonstrates the interaction of any pair of opposites. Clearly, Teiwaz and Berkana comprise a duality on many levels. Ehwaz, Mannaz and Laguz all stand for union, the law of attraction and the binding power of Love. The last three Runes symbolize synthesis. Their shapes alone suggest this.

As a matter of fact, the shapes of Tyr's Runes visibly reflect their meaning as stages in a pattern of transcending polarities. Both Teiwaz ($\uparrow$) and Berkana (β) have only one stem. The next two Runes, as well as the final one, all have a double stem symbolizing the interaction and integration of two forces ($\bowtie$ $\bowtie$ $\bowtie$). Inguz and Othila, as well as Dagaz again, are based on a stemless design. They symbolize synthesis and totality ($\diamond$ $\times$ $\bowtie$). The shape of Laguz does not add to this symbolism, but the Rune's meaning is evidently related to the concept of mutual attraction. Moreover, its shape forms the basis of Runes such as Teiwaz, Ehwaz and Mannaz ($\uparrow$ $\uparrow$ $\bowtie$ $\bowtie$). And last but not least, the symmetry of Runes like Teiwaz, Ehwaz, Mannaz, Inguz, Othila and Dagaz reinforces the idea of unification ($\uparrow$ $\bowtie$ $\bowtie$ $\diamond$ $\times$ $\bowtie$).

Consequently, Tyr's Aett seems to be essentially a path of love. The story of Tyr's Aett adequately exhibits the union of positive and negative powers; of fire and water, proton and electron, father and mother, Teiwaz and Berkana. Its story echoes in love myths such as those of Frey and Gerd, Odin and Jord, and Arthur and Guinevere.

For example, the *Skirnismal* poem relates how Frey falls in love with Gerd. These two characters are symbolized by Teiwaz and Berkana respectively. Because Frey is unable to act, his servant Skirnir goes on the errand of wooing Gerd. His travels on horseback are a reference to the Ehwaz Rune. Gerd is rather unmoved by Skirnir's acting but is persuaded in the end

(Mannaz). She agrees to meet Frey in nine nights. Frey thinks this is a long time; and Laguz symbolizes his yearning.

The story of Odin and Jord is not so well documented, but clearly both deities are represented by Teiwaz and Berkana, since they embody Heaven and Earth. Their marriage is celebrated at Ehwaz. Mannaz symbolizes their son, which is Thor, the warder of Midgard. The other Runes of this *aett* may refer to Njord, Frey and Freyja, their coming to Asgard and the synthesis of Aesic and Vanic powers.

One of the key mysteries of the Northern tradition is the dispensing of the sacred mead to the initiate. The story has many variants in myth and legend, but always the hero comes before his Valkyrja and is allowed a drink from the mead. The best examples of this motif are found in the story of Odin and Gunnlod and of Sigurd and Sigrdrifa. This means that the mystery of the Grail is also to be found in this *aett*.

In summary, this *aett* symbolizes the Sacred Marriage of Heaven and Earth. As a pair, Teiwaz and Berkana symbolize the Sky Father and the Earth Mother. Their marriage (Ehwaz) results in the divine child Man (Mannaz). Ehwaz links spirit and matter. It brings about a union or marriage. This aligning harmonizes existing and formerly conflicting pairs of opposites. This Rune stands for the soul as a medium between spirit and matter. Mannaz symbolizes the consummation of the opposites. The energies blend. From that union is born the Divine Child who is a being of those two cosmic worlds. The central Rune, Laguz, expresses the Law of Attraction and Repulsion. Its energy feels like a continuous flow of Love, which binds two opposites and creates a third aspect. The resulting child completes the family (Inguz Othila). In Dagaz these children build their own families.

In a more general way, Ehwaz, Mannaz and Dagaz represent the union of Teiwaz and Berkana on different levels of consummation. Inguz and Othila stand for the third aspect produced by their union, like the neutron in the atom. Because pairs of opposites come in many forms, this *aett* can be explained as pertaining to everyday relationships between any two persons as well as to the life of the soul.

TEIWAZ BERKANA

The two first Runes of this *aett* represent any basic pair of opposites. Typically, they represent a man and a woman. In ritual, they may symbolize the high priest and high priestess, or the initiator and his *soror mystica*. In myth, they are the hero and his *anima*.

EHWAZ

Because opposite poles attract each other, the energies of Teiwaz and Berkana will seek out each other. At Ehwaz they are brought together for the first time. Their souls touch, so to speak. Or two individuals meet for the first time. On a physical level, the whole complex of interacting opposites manifests in electromagnetic phenomena.

MANNAZ

At Mannaz, the power of mutual attraction results in a more profound bond. A bridge is built. The two energies complement each other and are able not just to cooperate but also to think as one. They are fully aligned. Remember that the Rune Poems say that 'man is the joy of man'.

LAGUZ

Laguz actually represents the power that binds any two components. Of course, the power of Love has two sides. On the one hand it manifests as the Law of Attraction and on the other hand as the Law of Repulsion. How did the two poles interact at Mannaz? Did harmony prevail or did disagreement surface? In the end, everything depends on how the energy of Laguz is handled. This Rune makes or breaks a relationship. On the soul level, Laguz stands for the Valkyrja offering the hero his drink of wisdom.

INGUZ

Inguz stands for the third principle created by the original pair. It usually springs from marrying two principles, but it may also emerge from the opposite. If Laguz drives two people apart, then it may symbolize solitude. If not, it stands for fertility and even children. On the mental level, Inguz stands for psychological integration.

OTHILA

Othila stands for releasing all the foregoing energies into the world. It symbolizes the integration of a pair, or of the third principle, in society. Othila also stands for a child growing up to adulthood and a new generation in general. Othila also keeps the mysteries of ancestor worship, so that the link with the past is never severed.

DAGAZ

Dagaz may stand for fulfillment on every level. The Rune symbolizes the continuous energy flow between two people and between them and the rest of the world. Its power transcends any barrier.

TEIWAZ	south pole
BERKANA	north pole
EHWAZ	electricity
MANNAZ	magnetism
LAGUZ	electric current
INGUZ	electric charge
OTHILA	electromagnetic field
DAGAZ	photon

Because the sacred marriage of Sky and Earth is a universal myth, it is easily illustrated. This has been shown above in motifs from Northern mythology. In a more exotic example, Teiwaz and Berkana stand for the concepts of An and Ki of Sumerian mythology. They are Heaven and Earth. Interestingly enough, Sumerian mythology has a concept for what is between too. The term Lil is usually interpreted as 'atmosphere' and refers to the kingdom of Enlil. Then, Laguz denotes the Abzu, more or less analogous to the Celtic concepts of Avalon and Annwn. Inguz and Othila stand for the concepts of

Kur and Kalam. Kur, identified as the horizon, is a mythical region of fertile powers, whereas Kalam stands for the familiar world of man, civilization. These concepts compare to Northern tradition *utangards* and *innangards*.

TEIWAZ	An:	heaven
BERKANA	Ki:	earth
EHWAZ	Lil:	air
MANNAZ	Marduk:	man
LAGUZ	Abzu:	water
INGUZ	Kur:	third principle
OTHILA	Kalam:	society
DAGAZ	Me:	existence

In her book *Leaves of Yggdrasil*, Freya Aswynn points out that Berkana and Ehwaz represent the vegetable and animal kingdom respectively. She further explains Mannaz to mean civilized society, i.e. the world of men. Moreover, she associates the Teiwaz Rune with the Iron Age. I believe, the period she refers to may extend to the Bronze Age, since Teiwaz signifies the extraction of all metals. Her interpretation refers to the four physical kingdoms in nature. Consequently, Teiwaz, Berkana, Ehwaz and Mannaz represent the mineral kingdom, the vegetable kingdom, the animal kingdom and the human kingdom. Completing the sequence, Laguz would symbolize the kingdom of souls. And Inguz would refer to the devic kingdom. Othila and Dagaz are harder to explain in this way, although Othila may stand for that unknown but whispered about world on the inside of our planet. It might also refer to the planet Earth itself as a conscious being. In that case, Dagaz may refer to systemic or cosmic relations.

TEIWAZ	mineral kingdom
BERKANA	vegetable kingdom
EHWAZ	animal kingdom
MANNAZ	human kingdom

LAGUZ   kingdom of souls

INGUZ   deva kingdom

OTHILA   planetary relations

DAGAZ   cosmic relations

Finally, the three *aettir* as a whole read as one story. And as the first *aett* corresponds to creation, the last one refers to destruction. Indeed, Tyr's Runes can be linked with the story of Ragnarok. In the *Voluspa*, the Gods are repeatedly called Tivar when they engage in the last battle. This refers to Teiwaz. According to legend, the final battle was fought under a birch tree, representing the *axis mundi*. Berkana also refers to Balder waiting in Helheim. Ehwaz is symbolic of the charging Aesir on horseback. Mannaz symbolizes the human couple, Lif and Lifthrasir, hiding in Mimir's Wood. The Mannaz Rune also refers to the Einherjar. Laguz is the blood of the fight. The life containing corpse's sea will be the sacrifice that makes the rebirth of a new world possible. Inguz is Frey leading the Aesir into battle. Othila is the marked battlefield, known as Vigrid, which in the Hindu tradition is known as Kurukshetra. Maybe Othila also holds the promise of a new world. Dagaz is the last of days. The Sun is devoured and the Earth is ablaze by the fires of Surt.

There is one other myth that perfectly matches the Aett of Tyr, but it is not of Northern origin. The symbolism of all the different Runes of Tyr systematically relate to elements of the story of the Birth of Christ. To begin with, we have Joseph and Mary. They are Teiwaz and Berkana. The child Jesus is associated with Inguz. Together they look for shelter and, according to popular belief, find a stable (Othila). Usually, an ox and a donkey are portrayed. They are Ehwaz. Mannaz stands for the three wise men and their gifts. Laguz refers to the Herodes incident. The I-Rune stands for blood. Dagaz possibly corresponds to the angel Gabriel.

Patterns of Development

When the *aettir* are interpreted as patterns of development, then the Runes all stand for very distinct stages in these models. Because of this, any situation in life can be reduced to one Aett and one Rune, to one particular pattern and one particular stage therein. Therefore, when a personal situation is associated with a Rune, either intuitively or from a reading, a global scheme suddenly appears. The symbolism of the Futhark order then makes it easier to determine the root of your circumstances. Preceding Runes can be identified with past events while Runes that come after indicate a possible solution.

Given that the Rune row is divided into three *aettir*, each of these groups is regarded as relevant to one specific course of action. Depending on the situation at hand, you work with the first, second or third *aett*. The first two *aettir* cover most of the patterns. Frey's Aett commences with a constructive condition whereas Hagal's Aett starts with a destructive set of circumstances. The power of Tyr's Aett should be applicable to any event. Or it symbolizes stages in social relations.

Frey's Aett progresses as a pattern commencing with (1) an initiative (Fehu) and finishing with the completion thereof (Wunjo). Between those two Runes is depicted the pathway going from the initial intention towards the final result. Thus (2) Uruz symbolizes the will power to develop an idea. (3) Thurisaz symbolizes the obstacles met. (4) Ansuz renders welcome inspiration and outside help. (5) Raido indicates that all goes well and (6) Kenaz is the climax thereof. Kenaz symbolizes skill and perfection. (7) Gebo works two ways. You are communicating your project by informing the public, while at the same time the Rune foretells an unexpected gift that really finishes the project. (8) Wunjo symbolizes the end result.

Hagal's Aett begins with (1) a difficult or problematic situation (Hagalaz). This *aett* closes with Sowulo, assuring that a solution exists to any problem. After Hagalaz, (2) Nauthiz follows portraying the initial response to the crisis. A difficult situation increases the pressure to find a solution. (3) Isa represents the incapacity to come to a solution. (4) Jera on the other hand offers opportunities rising from among the clouds of inner conflict. A decision is made. This Rune foretells improvement. (5) Eihwaz symbolizes endurance. Eihwaz sometimes indicates that a hard choice is to be made as it signifies sacrifice. (6) Pertho symbolizes your faith and self-reliance. (7) Algiz is analogous to Gebo and stands for a sudden boost, which often comes from a third party. (8) Sowulo symbolizes triumphing over the problem.

Tyr's Aett can be explained in two ways. Either it signals the process any intention goes through, or it stands for two powers or persons making contact.

(1) The energy of Teiwaz represents an intention. (2) This wells up from inside a person and (3) manifests as a connection with the object that the person wishes to influence. (4) Mannaz symbolizes an established relation between subject and object, so that the one is influenced by the other. (5) The power of the intention works through the object and (6) the object is moved by the power. (7) Othila symbolizes the desired effect on the object. And (8) at Dagaz, the energies following the intention dissipate.

If Tyr's Aett refers to a social situation, the following sequence is obtained. (1) One person meets (2) another person. (3) At Ehwaz, their first contact is made. If the minds of these two individuals agree to develop their contact, (4) a stronger relationship ensues. (5) The quality of their understanding depends on the emotional responses towards each other. (6) Inguz symbolizes the natural product of their interaction, maybe a child, maybe a project, maybe just contentment. (7) Othila stands for how their relationship reflects on their immediate surroundings, the community, and society in general. (8) Dagaz stands for lasting relations.

A last remark is due, because it is obvious that the stages in these three patterns cross-refer. For example, the whole second *aett* fits in just one Rune of Frey, Thurisaz. Correspondingly, the whole first *aett* fits in Ehwaz of Tyr's Aett and the whole pattern of Tyr's Runes may fit in Hagal's Rune of contemplation: Isa. Consequently, the Thurisaz-Isa-Ehwaz triad symbolizes crisis. Likewise, the fifth triad too may signify a crisis.

Advancing through the *aettir*, it is observed that the different stages in each *aett* somehow resemble each other. The first triad sets off a chain of events. It stands for a beginning. Fehu, Hagalaz or Teiwaz symbolize the event that initiates the chain of responses. Then comes UNB, which energetically reflects the manifestation of the seed energy. UNB stands for the first and automatic response following the impulse of FHT. The third triad symbolizes a force that crosses the flow. It stands for a crisis response and conflict. It signifies the second response to the original impulse. The fourth triad, as the third, represents an energy that adds to the original impulse. However, AJM complements the energy. AJM symbolizes the planning aspect of a project. It signifies the third natural response to the original energy. RYL symbolizes the hard work part. As AJM symbolizes theory, so does RYL symbolize practice. This triad also stands for a second crisis. The complex of these three Runes represents decisionmaking. Raido considers right versus wrong. Eihwaz takes a risk or either makes sacrifices. Laguz doubts. KPNg symbolizes the seed energy coming to fruition. GZO symbolizes the integration of the energy into a greater whole, either the body, or the kith and kin, or society or the planet. The project is implemented. It stands for communicating the project to the outside world. The last triad symbolizes completion, satisfaction, feedback and grounding the different released energies.

ᚠᚺᛏ	Initiating event
ᚢᚾᛒ	Manifestation of energy
ᚦᛁᛖ	Conflict response to energy
ᚨᛃᛗ	Planning
ᚱᛇᛚ	Action
ᚲᛈᛜ	Result
ᚷᛉᛟ	Integration
ᚹᛊᛞ	Feedback

4

FROM URD'S WELL RISING

Runes you will find and meaningful Staves

Very strong Staves

Very stern Staves

Fimbulthul coloured them

And the Ginnregin created them

And Hropt of the Regin carved them

Odin with the Aesir and for the Elves Dáinn

Dvalinn for the dwarves

Asvid for the Jotun giants

I carved some myself

Reading the myths, it becomes clear that a group of Gods moots over the conception of runic powers. The above *Havamal* passage (142-143) reveals that the Runes come from the Regin. Different stages of creating the Runes are then described. After having fashioned them, the office of handling the Runes goes to the Norns. Consequently, the Runes are stored in the Well of Wyrd. Only afterwards did Odin hang himself at the very tree overshadowing the Well learning the Secrets of Asgard. Finally, at Ragnarok the entities that created the Runes will fall in battle and with them the Runes will disappear.

Who are these Regin? In the *Voluspa* they are called '*ginn*-holy' alluding to their primordial origin in the Ginnungagap realm. Their biggest exploit was the creation of Earth in the midst of this primordial space. Therefore, the Regin are first and foremost Gods of creation who lived in the time before time. Inventing the Runes was only one of their feats.

Several stanzas in *Havamal* and *Sigrdrifumal* mention that it was the Regin who made the Runes. What is more, this statement appears in different Ancient Germanic inscriptions in which the phrase **raginakudo** is used meaning 'coming from the Regin'. MacLeod and Mees read the phrase as 'made known by the Regin'.

Only then do the Norns appear. Once the physical world is created, their talents are needed. They handle the Runes and give substance to the different combinations of Rune energy – much as aspects in astrology work. The Regin invented these twenty four basic energies. But the Norns use them.

From a more historical viewpoint the word *regin* is related to Latin *rex*, perhaps originating from diplomatic contacts with the Roman Empire. Would it not be plausible that the Regin referred to as the inventors of the Futhark in fact refer to Roman chieftains who first inspired the Germanic people to use writing? It is beyond doubt that the Futhark as an alphabetic concept originates from the twilight zone of Roman, Celtic and Germanic civilization. It explains why Odin is regarded as the inventor of script. He was the *interpretatio Germana* of Mercurius/Hermes Trismegistos who invented the Latin/Greek alphabet.

Usually, the myths say that Odin and his brothers, Hoenir and Lodurr, or Vili and Vé, created the universe. The Regin however are an assembly of Gods, not a triumvirate. Their organization is similar to the Aesic court of later Scandinavian tradition. Again, in the *Voluspa* it is said that the divine Regin act whenever the need arises to come up with a creative solution to some cosmic problem. In this way, they created first space, then time, and then the dwarven race. Presumably, this holy assembly consisted of Aesir, Alfar and Vanir. *Regin* simply means advisor.

Because the Runes are designed by the creation Gods, they stem from a primordial era. They are therefore essentially *ginn*. They are created before time and space and thus form part of everything the universe is made of.

Shaping the Energy

The process of creating the Runes was completed in different stages. They are made, carved and coloured. According to *Havamal*, the making and carving was done by the Regin collectively, but the colouring was done by Odin. According to *Sigrdrifumal*, all is done by His Odinic Majesty. Stanza 15 of the poem explains that the Runes are devised, written and read. In the main, three stages are discerned.

Mind Runes you will know if you of all wish to have

The best of man's minds

Those he read – those he wrote

Those Hropt mentally conceived

From those waters leaking

From the skull of Heiddraupnir

And from the horn of Hoddrofnir

Combining both passages, the following sequence comes into view. The Runes are (1) mentally conceived and (2) physically given shape. Their mental conception involves a contraction of energy, whereas their shape implies a medium to harness the energy. (3) Each of these media is supplied with a visual symbol to represent the energy's quality. This is done by writing or carving the Runes. Finally, they are (4) coloured and (5) named. This last stage calls forth the energy of a Rune from the subtle realities into the planes of physical manifestation. A physical counterpart is added to make the link. Reading the Runes must be interpreted as an invocation.

Both passages agree that Odin plays a major role in the creation of the Runes. In this capacity, he is called Hropt, which is seemingly his Regin name.

According to *Sigrdrifumal* 15, Hropt is the one who invented the Runes. He literally thought them into existence.

In *Havamal*, Odin is called Fimbulthul when he stains the Runes. This is of interest as the name literally means Great *Thulr*. A *þulr* is a priest who recites cultic texts. The related verb *þylja* can be translated as chanting, mumbling, or reciting in a monotonous manner. A *þula* is an enumerating recital, like a list of names or Runes. It confirms that the Rune names were chanted while the staves were being coloured.

In *Havamal* 111, Fimbulthul's function is explained in more detail. Odin sits on the high seat of the *þulr* and gazes in front of him. More importantly, he is silent and pensive. On this throne Odin conceives the Runes. And this throne is situated at the Well of Urd, whose waters are associated with the drinking horn. The dripping mead to which Heiddraupnir and Hoddrofnir refer is the so-called dew on Yggdrasil's leaves, being collected in the Well of Urd. The names of these mythical creatures both mean 'bright dripping', alluding to the mystery of the Holy Mead. At the same time, Urd's Well is where the Regin gather.

From this it is understood that every drop of the well is a drop of wisdom. Every insight gained by man at any time adds a drop to this well. It then merges with the whole. Any drop drunk from the well contains all the information at once, much like a drop of blood that contains your DNA. Information added to any part of the body will settle in a person's DNA. This is the core meaning of the myth of Kvasir: synthesis. Each and every drop in the sacred well is an individual's spiritual contribution to the collective subconscious adding to the pool of universal wisdom.

Havamal 80 and 111 admonish to conceal the meaning of the Runes. The word for 'meaning' in this context is *ráð*, referring to reading and interpreting the signs. The interpretation of the Runes refers to actual divinatory practices. Furthermore, silence is elsewhere linked with foresight. Frigg knows the fate of every creature, yet she remains silent.

The action of being silent immediately follows staining the Rune staves. Esoterically, this indicates (6) a contemplative phase after chanting the Runes, they having induced a trance.

The fate of the Runes themselves is also described in the Edda poems. The Rune secrets possess their power as long as the Regin live. When they fall at Ragnarok, so will the Runes disappear. Yet the *Voluspa* reports that the Aesir in the New Age will still remember the ancient Rune staves of Fimbulthul. Since Odin has ingrained the Runes with his own life force, this much of his nature remains even after his death. Odin's power will always be essentially interwoven in the power of the Runes. He coloured them.

The Odinic Initiation

Odin's part in the creation of the Runes is unmistakable. Nonetheless, he learns the Runes' full potential only later in the history of the Gods. This is what the myth of his self-sacrifice is all about. *Havamal* 138-139:

> I know I hung on a windswept tree
>
> All nine nights
>
> By spear pierced and given to Odin
>
> The self to my Self
>
> On that tree of which no-one knows
>
> Where its roots are running
>
> Neither with bread nor with horn was I bestowed
>
> I looked down
>
> Up I took the Runes – screaming I took them
>
> Then I fell
>
> Thus Thund carved for the destiny of the folk
>
> There he rose where he had fallen

This oft-cited passage explains how Odin finds the Runes. At that time, the Rune signs are already in existence. He did not invent them at that time. He (re)discovered them. Considering the foregoing passages, it is only natural that Odin finds these secrets hidden in and amongst the roots of Yggdrasil.

The scene divides into different aspects. The setting consists of a tree, which must be Yggdrasil, and the Well of Urd, which is found at the World Tree. Then there is Odin, who does a number of things. He hangs and stabs himself. He goes into a near-death situation. He takes up the Runes. And he falls. His actions are generally considered to represent a shamanic ritual. The period of nine nights symbolizes a trance state. At the end of this period he falls down. This describes the event of reconnecting with the physical body. The sensation is common in dreaming. The different aspects will be discussed in more detail.

The myth of Odin's ordeal illustrates the willful act of how to surrender one's lower self to one's Higher Self. Odin's hanging therefore signifies initiation. He deals death to his ego while consciously giving himself freely into the hands of his eternal soul. This is the greatest possible offer: to destroy the ego in order to make way for the light of the soul.

The Odinic myth reflects one of the best hidden secrets of magic. As a magician you have to be prepared to make changes in your life and attitude, and in your personality, in order to let the magic flow. These changes require discipline, insight and daring. These are the sacrifices and Oaths so often mentioned in esoteric texts. Odin was prepared to let go of all the mud clouding his soul in gross materialistic or emotional gain. However, these changes do not occur overnight, nor in nine nights for that matter. The mythical number nine refers to a long and steady period of inner orientation.

The tree of which is spoken is in fact an erected pole symbolizing the world axis. It is man-made, which explains why no-one knows its roots. Furthermore, it may well refer to a gallows. One of Odin's names is Hanga-Tyr, as hangings were sacred to this God. However, context stresses the pole's function as a world tree used for shaman purposes. Remember the May Pole, too, has no roots. Vikings and Germanics would have had a good idea of what was meant in the Eddic verse. Never a real tree was intended.

When Odin looks down, what he sees is the Well of Urd. The Norns, who live there, use the Runes to carry out the decisions of the Gods. They are carven in the tree's roots and stained with mud from the well. These are the secrets Odin discovers.

In the *Voluspa* we read that the Norns come from out of this well and determine fate. This motif corresponds to the story of how the Runes originate from the well. According to *Sigrdrifumal*, the Regin shape the Runes out of a certain liquid (*af þeim legi*), which might be Urd's Well. However, the kennings used suggest that a drinking horn is meant. 'Skull of Heiddraupnir' and 'horn of Hoddrofnir' both refer to the golden colour of mead. The Old Norse word for liquid, *lögr*, is the same as Laguz. The sacred mead is unquestionably associated with wisdom, and a large part of the Northern mysteries is built on this idea. When Sigridrifa offers Sigurd the horn she says that the mead is mixed with Runes.

The Norns, surfacing from the well, symbolize insights in our past and future. These transpersonal beings are spirits of the water, warders of the tree. They embody intuitive counsels that gurgle up from the well of the subconscious into our waking surface minds. When Odin discovers the Runes it is this information that he gains.

Then, Odin takes up the Runes. He makes them his own. Therefore, 'taking up' the Runes is metaphorically translated as the integration of gathered information. In this way, the power of the Runes is able to settle in the mind. The Runes, as secrets, represent those bits of knowledge and wisdom you cannot yet put your finger on. They are your dawning insights – motivating to contemplation. But eventually... abstract ideas turn into solid concepts.

Then Mimir Spoke

The *Sigrdrifumal* poem continues to reveal Rune lore. In one famous passage Odin consults with wise Mimir. Stanzas 15-17 give the mysterious first words of Mimir's oracular head. They follow:

Runes have been wrought on the shield

that stands before the Shining God

On the ear of Arvak and on the hoof of Alsvid

On the wheel that whirls under Hrungnir's wain

On Sleipnir's teeth and on the sledge's irons

On the bear's paw and on Bragi's tongue

On the wolf's claw and on the eagle's nose

On bloody wings and on the bridge's end

On loosening hands and leeching tracks

On glass and on gold and on man's good luck

In wine and in wort and on the seat of the will

On Gungnir's tip and on Grani's breast

On the nail of the Norns and on the nose of the owl

Twenty four mythical items appear which have been inscribed with Runes. Context reveals that every one of these items is magical in nature. Moreover, the Rune inscriptions symbolize these magical qualities. In this way Mimir teaches Odin the necessary hints to use the Runes magically.

Á skildi þeim er stendr fyr skínandi goði. Runes are carven on the shield of the Sun Goddess Sunna. The name of this shield is mentioned in *Grimnismal* as Svalinn 'Cooler'. Its intention is to cool the Sun's energy so that it does not scorch the mountains nor boils the oceans. Isa is the appropriate Rune.

Á eyra Árvakrs ok á Alsvinns hófi. Arvak and Alsvid are a team of horses. They pull the Sun's wain across the skies. The Runes on their ears and hooves relate to the myth of the wolf who eternally pursues the Sun. The hooves make the horses run faster and their ears make them alert of their pursuer. The hooves' Runes are Raido and Ehwaz. The ears' Rune may be Algiz, because this Rune symbolizes awareness.

Á því hvéli er snýsk undir reið Hrungnis. The whirling wheel symbolizes chakras. In particular the solar plexus is meant because this is the gateway of the lower energies towards the higher centres. This work of transference is accomplished by the power of Thor who consciously faces the raw powers of Utgard in order to sublimate them. The whirling wheel is also a kenning for Thor's weapon, depicted as the swastika. His weapon has the power to annihilate any impediment to personal growth, such as fear, anger, hate and shame. Runes associated with Mjollnir are Thurisaz and Sowulo. Runes associated with the whirling wheel are Raido and Sowulo.

Alternatively, the paralleling text in the *Volsungasaga* reads 'on the wheel that stands under the wain of Rognir'. On the one hand, the verb 'to stand' indicates the nature of a shield more than a real wagon. The item is only called such because the giant stands on it. But on the other hand, Rognir is a *heiti* of Odin. However, it can also be interpreted as a kenning for 'chief' or 'warrior'. Traditionally, Hrungnir is named. In the myths, this giant is challenged by Thor. Before the fight Thor's squire Thjalfi tells Hrungnir that Thor will attack him from underneath. So, Hrungnir takes his shield and stands on it. Then Thor slings his hammer through the sky. Thunder resounds and the giant dies. Runes associated with shielding are Algiz and Thurisaz.

Á Sleipnis tönnum. Horses were examined by their teeth, because they give an idea about the animal's health and age; as the saying goes, 'never look a gift horse in the mouth'. The Runes on Sleipnir's teeth assure him of good health. Among these Runes may have been Uruz, Sowulo and Berkana.

Á sleða fjötrum. Clamp irons were used to fasten cargo to the sledge. Since the sledge is mentioned in a cultic context, I believe that it refers to the ceremony of fastening a ship on a sledge to carry it in procession. Many Bronze Age rock carvings show how ships are fastened on sledges. On these ships solar wheels are raised that resemble the Younger Futhark Sun Rune. The carvings probably depict a Midsummer ritual, akin to Balder's Balefires nowadays. Raido is the appropriate Rune.

Á bjarnar hrammi ok á ulfs klóum. I take the bear's paw and the wolf's claw to represent berserkers and *ulfhednar*. These warriors went into a rage when they were about to attack. In their frenzy, they got possessed by their totem animal; in this case either a bear or a wolf. The paw and the claw are expressive of attack. Possible Runes are Ansuz and Teiwaz. Nevertheless, both items may also refer to medicinal plants. There is a plant named Bear's Claw, better known as hogweed (*Heracleum sphondylium*). In Modern Icelandic it is called *bjarnarkló*. In Latin it is named after Hercules. This plant was a traditional healing herb. Wolf's Claw is better known as club moss (*Lycopodium annotinum*).

Á Braga tungu. In Northern myth, Bragi is the archetypal poet. The Runes on his tongue signify eloquence and wisdom. Mannaz and Ansuz are appropriate Runes.

Á arnar nefi. The eagle's beak might belong to the same category as the bear's paw and the wolf's claw, although a different interpretation is possible, because the eagle too attacks with its claws. Its beak it uses to fish. From Bronze Age Scandinavian iconography we know both the eagle and the fish to be associated with solar myth. Kenaz might be appropriate. On the other hand it may refer to the myth of the Mead of Poetry which Odin Bölverk snatches away from Suttung of the giants. In this myth, Odin steals the mead and then transforms into an eagle to get away, his beak loaded with magical mead. That is why he is called Farma-Tyr. Runes such as Uruz, Ansuz, Gebo and Laguz fit this fragment well.

Á blóðgum vængjum. The 'bloody wings' refers to a sacrificial ritual at which the ribcage of a condemned man was broken. His lungs were pulled out through the back, making them resemble wings. Runes were scored on the ribs dedicating the victim to Odin. The scene is described in the *Orkneyingasaga*. Ansuz or Othila is the corresponding Rune.

Á brúar sporði. The end of a bridge is a metaphor for reaching a goal after taking a risk. A bridge always implies crossing a border. Only when the end is reached, at either side, can we cry victory. Good Runes would be Dagaz and Wunjo. Thinking mythologically, Bifrost comes to mind. This bridge takes humans up into the celestial realms of Gods and Elves, but from the Gods' perspective, it takes them to the Well of Urd. Bifrost Bridge connects spirit and matter. It is a bridge that every man and woman has the right to walk. This is Algiz. It might at the same time refer to the symbolism of Isa.

Á lausnar lófa. From *Sigrdrifumal* is known a spell to ease the delivery of a child. Runes are written on the midwife's palms. Call upon the Disir. Nauthiz would have been among these Runes. The symbol refers to labour and deliverance.

Á líknar spori. According to sympathetic magic, Runes written in a person's footprints would affect that person. For example, certain Runes would increase a leech's healing powers, other Runes would protect the footprints' owner. Among these Runes may be Uruz, Wunjo and Jera. It also refers to a ritual of swearing blood brotherhood.

Á gleri. Runes in glass may refer to Runes carved in heathen altar stones. The fire's heat burning on the altar would glaze the top where the Runes would have been (*Hyndluljod* 10). We can imagine a dedication formula written in the rock. The magical formula *alu* as well as a whole Futhark row would have been part of it. Glass may also symbolize any kind of gem, for example amber.

Á gulli ok á gumna heillum. Gold refers to the golden amulets from Ancient

Germanic times known as bracteates. These were sometimes inscribed with Runes and runic formulae. Horses, birds and Gods were depicted. Gods included Tyr, Odin and possibly Balder. Frequently used formulae were *alu*, *laukaz* and *ehwaz*. Bracteates have been found carrying inscriptions to ask for good luck (*gibu auja*). As for *gumna heillum*, a person's luck and good fortune is known to have been conferred by spirits such as Hamingjur and Nornir. To sustain the link with the spirits people often kept, and still keep, lucky charms on their body, such as a rabbit's foot.

Here, the *Volsungasaga* version has 'on gold and on good silver', in which case, the reference is related to riches. Of all things, silver was used as a medium to pay. Runes may have indicated ownership. If so, then Othila would be among them. However, the *Volsungasaga* remembers the original line since *á gumna heillum* is slightly referred to later in the stanza. In an oblique position a twenty fifth item *í gumna holdi* is inserted, which means 'in people's skin' or 'in people's bodies'. The first may refer to tattooing. The second must refer to a person's character. The fragment is out of place but is clearly build on the *gumna heillum* entry.

Í víni. Runes in wine refer to the quickening quality of alcohol. There is an Icelandic saga in which a person is brought back to life by giving him wine to drink. According to *Grimnismal*, wine was all that Odin ever fed on. It is therefore an invigorating drink.

Í virtri. Wort is a liquid that is obtained in the process of making a strong drink such as ale or whiskey. Since it refers to the brewing process itself, it has a very alchemical tinge to it to add Runes at this stage. Runes of power and intention were carved on wood and then scraped off into the wort. The essence of the Runes was brewed in the ale. Uruz is an appropriate Rune.

Á vilisessi. In the alternative *Volsungasaga*, the Seat of the Will is explained as the seat of the *völva*. Such a prophetess usually sat on a platform to go into a trance to interact with the spirit world. Runes were carved in the wooden poles supporting the platform. A passage from one of the sagas mentions that Runes are carved in these poles to bring harm to the *völva*. Helpful Runes would have included Laguz, Inguz, Algiz, Ehwaz and Mannaz, as well as symbols to represent the Nine Worlds. These Runes not only helped the seeress guide her into the astral realm, they were also meant to protect her from harm. Well known seats include Hlidskjalf and the High Seat of the Thulr at Urd's Well.

Á Gungnis oddi. Odin's spear possesses the quality never to miss its mark. It therefore symbolizes achievement. Hurling a spear is a metaphor for sending an intention. Appropriate Runes are Eihwaz and Teiwaz. From a historical standpoint, spears were in fact decorated with runic signs. The lance head from Øvre Stabu shows Sun glyphs inscribed on it. The spear is also used to dedicate the enemy to Odin. We can interpret some of the archaeological spear inscriptions in this way.

Á Grana brjósti. After Sigurd slew the dragon, he meant to carry as much gold with him as he could. Unfortunately for Grani, the horse was destined to carry it all. Grani's withers symbolize physical strength. These Runes are the symbols of a beast of burden. Ehwaz would be among the right Runes, as also Berkana.

Again, the *Volsungasaga* offers an alternative. It has a Gygja's breast instead of Grani's. A *gýgr* is a kind of troll wife. It might in this context refer to mythical foster mothers. In the sagas it is told that heroes sometimes get lost in the woods and are looked after by a giantess who by the by teaches them all kinds of secrets. It is an initiation motif similar to that of the Holy Mead.

Á nornar nagli. The Norn's nail refers to a cultic object pinned into a temple's pillars or in a sacred tree. Similarly, in the *Eyrbyggjasaga*, the Regin's nails are hammered into the high seat pillars. This seat corresponds to the Seat of the Will mentioned earlier. The sacred nails guarantee blessing. Under Christian guise nails are still hammered in a ship's fore to procure blessing. In ancient Mesopotamia sacred nails were built in into the foundation of temples to keep the demons out. Nigel Pennick documents a similar custom in East Anglia, Great Britain. Exactly these nails sanctify a place, the reason being that it keeps out evil. Celtic folklore explains that fairies hate iron. Interpreting fairies as the evil eye, one would have good reason to hammer a few dedicated nails into a sacred pole. Algiz, Nauthiz and Eihwaz may serve the case.

Á nefi uglu. The owl has always been considered an omen of ill luck. Their cry portends death. Maybe this is the reason why it is mentioned last. The owl's beak in specific was used in the construction of curses. Appropriate Runes are Thurisaz and Nauthiz. However, according to Scandinavian folklore, the owl is also used to avert nightmares.

Introducing these mysterious stanzas, the poem almost biblically declares that Mimir's words are first, in one way or another. What is possibly meant is that these words are spoken in a time before time. They are uttered before creation, or at least form part of the process of creation. Afterwards, it is recounted how these Runes were gathered and mixed with the mead. Possibly, either Mimir's Well or Urd's Well is intended. The power of the Runes is then disseminated by the rivers that spring from the well.

> All were shaved off
>
> Those that were scored on
>
> And cast into the holy mead
>
> And sent on wide ways
>
> They are with the Aesir

They are with the Elves

Some are with the wise Vanir

Some has the human race

5
THE
ANGELS
OF
ASGARD

An essay on the magical system of the Northern tradition would not be complete without a small discourse on its Gods. A good selection of Aesir and Asynjur will walk along the catwalk showing off their main qualities and associated Runes. Of some of the Gods, their ceremonial postures will be discussed.

One of the key practices of ceremonial magic is the assumption of God-forms. The practice involves adopting the posture in which this or that deity is usually depicted. In his *Liber O*, Crowley particularly refers to the magical images of the Egyptian Gods. Naturally, the same can be done for the Northern tradition. However, only a handful of Scandinavian deities are known from the archaeological record. Figurines and statuettes of Odin, Thor, Frey and Tyr will be discussed.

ODIN

The chief of the Gods rules wisdom and war. These major themes are closely related, as any seeker readily acknowledges. War is a symbol of crisis. But when this is overcome, wisdom is usually reaped.

In battle, Odin claims the fallen heroes. They are known as Einherjar. Their physical death enacts a rite of initiation. They are consecrated to Odin. As Einherjar, these initiates-to-be are guided to Valhalla by the Valkyries.

These maidens represent the hero's anima – a theme well established in the Northern mysteries.

His wisdom Odin acquires through the act of sacrifice and through the act of love. He truly is a Lord of Love and Wisdom. Countless myths relate how Odin ventures into Jotunheim to pursue the daughters of giants, who represent his anima. Gunnlod is the classic representative. Jotunheim is regarded as a world of wisdom, since it is inhabited by very ancient beings; a fact confirmed by *Vafthrudnismal*. In addition, this is the place where Mimir's well is situated, where Odin offered his eye – gaining insight.

The Father of the Gods corresponds to Hermes/Mercurius/Thoth. His element is air. His presence is easily experienced in the wind and through the weather (Vidrir). In team with his brothers, Odin is a God of creation. His consort is Frigg.

Ansuz is Odin's main Rune, because he rules the Aesir and is called Áss. Archetypically, Odin stands for the complex of powers presented in the Ansuz Rune. Both Odin and Ansuz rule communication, good counsel and authority. Other Runes associated with Odin are Wunjo, Eihwaz and Othila. Wunjo is the initial Rune of his original name. In Wunjo, Odin's power to gather a host or to bring people together is found. Eihwaz stands for Odin's sacrificial act on the World Tree. The Rune is also a glyph of Gungnir. Othila refers to Odin as a king of Asgard and as a patron of the ruling class.

A small figurine of Odin is found in Lindby, Sweden, that pictures the God as standing upright with his hands on his sides. The figurine dates from the 7th century CE and is identifiable as Odin as he is shown with his right eye closed. His feet are set apart so that the whole reflects a recognizable Othila Rune. The posture may be compared to the bishop piece of the Lewis Chessmen.

In body language, this posture represents either an active listening attitude or a stance of teaching, even lecturing. Typically, this stance is assumed by parents lecturing their kids. Having the hands on their hips makes them look bigger. It is a stance of power and charisma.

Runes:	Ansuz, Wunjo, Eihwaz, Othila
Animal:	Raven, wolf, horse, eagle, snake
Plant:	Ash
Colour:	Blue
Element:	Air
Planet:	Mercury
Attributes:	Spear

FRIGG

As a Mother Goddess, Frigg presides over marriage and family peace. She corresponds to Hera/Juno. Frigg's power lies in foresight. Through her paranormal abilities she has access to information about the future. She knows every being's destiny. But in order to avoid preconception, she keeps all this knowledge to herself. She is the Goddess of silence, and consequently of secrecy. Her bond with fate is very strong, since she personally provides the Norns with yarn. She gets this magic wool from the dwarves.

Frigg's favourite son Balder evokes her motherly cares. Once she finds out that something bad is about to happen to him, she does everything in her power to protect him. In my opinion, she applies the pentagram glyph to shield Balder. In folk customs, this symbol is used to ward off nightmares.

Runes related to Frigg are Berkana and Pertho. Berkana is a Mother Rune associated with protection and healing. Frigg is called upon in labour. Pertho stands for seeing wyrd.

Runes:	Pertho, Berkana
Animal:	Falcon, wagtail
Plant:	Birch, mandrake, chamomile
Colour:	White
Planet:	Venus, Orion
Attributes:	Distaff, keys, linen, pentagram

THOR

This son of Odin and Mother Earth drives his thundering chariot through the sky and dangerously swings his sparkling hammer crushing the skulls of wicked giants. His hammer Mjollnir is made by dwarves.

As a Storm God he bestows fertility on all levels. He is also summoned to calm storms, especially at sea. Therefore, anger and other emotional outbursts can be calmed by invoking Thor. He takes the pressure off.

Thor is regarded as the strongest among the Aesir. His might is used to safeguard the world of men and the world of Gods against the disrupting giant forces. He is a man of action and once invoked immediately appears. Snorri compares him to Hercules. The Ancient Germanic people linked him to Zeus/Jupiter, the storm God of the oak.

Runes associated with Thor are Thurisaz, Raido and Sowulo. Thurisaz refers to lightning and Raido to thunder. Sowulo represents Thor's weapon.

The most famous figurine of all the Gods is undoubtedly that of Thor, found at Eyrarlandi, Iceland. He is shown seated. His hands clutch a weapon, resting on his lap. His chin rests on the top. Presumably, Mjollnir is shown, although the weapon does not match contemporary hammer amulets, nor is it reminiscent of the swastika. The weapon looks more like a cudgel, the handle of which has the shape of an animal's head touching the God's chin.

One possible way to assume this position is with the arms hooked. The elbows are supported on your body with your forearms level. The hands extend forward as if grasping a large object. If power is raised in this position, it rises up from your lap on the inside of your arms to about shoulder height. The energy field above the lap is a sacred space ruled by Thor. It obviously refers to fertility, as the hammer was put into the bride's lap to invoke the Gods' blessing at a wedding.

A similar posture is found among the Lewis Chessmen. The king pieces are depicted seated with their swords on their knees. Their hands rest on the knees, as in the usual God posture. The king forms fists with his hands, since he holds the sheathed sword. The weapon is a sign of authority. The figurine is given context by *Havamal* 3. The stanza mentions how a wandering guest enters a hall to get warm by the fire. Now, the Old Norse word for hearth is *brandr* which is also a kenning for sword (Kenaz). The guest recognizes who is in charge by the weapon on the king's lap. By the same weapon, an individual was ritually bound into kingly service (Gebo).

Runes:	Thurisaz, Raido, Sowulo
Animal:	Bear, goat
Plant:	Oak, rowan, leek
Mineral:	Flint
Colour:	Red
Element:	Fire
Planet:	Jupiter, Great Bear
Attributes:	Hammer, wain, the swastika, club

SIF

Thor is married to Sif. Their daughter is Thrud. Sif had a son called Ull from an earlier marriage. The Goddess symbolizes the family as a unit and she portrays the qualities of brotherhood and kinship. Her name means clan.

Her golden hair represents ripe wheat. Hence her Greco-Roman equivalent being Demeter/Ceres. Jera would be an appropriate Rune. The clan symbolism relates to Wunjo.

Runes:	Wunjo, Jera
Plant:	Cornflower
Colour:	Gold and green
Element:	Earth
Attributes:	Ear of corn

BALDER

The archetypal child of Odin and Frigg is Balder. He symbolizes integrity, boldness, innocence and immortality. His name reveals his nature. Balder means bold. The name of his twin brother, Hoder, means combat.

The myth of Balder and Hoder is one of the core mysteries of the Northern tradition. One day, Balder wakes up sweating heavily, because he had nightmares foretelling his doom. Instantly, Frigg wants to save him from any possible harm. However, she disregards the mistletoe as a possible killer, but through Loki's doing, Hoder slays his brother with this very plant. Afterwards, dead Balder fares to the Underworld and abides his time. Once the world of living creatures is demolished at Ragnarok, a new world arises. Then, Balder will rise again.

Sowulo is the most appropriate Rune to associate with Balder. He is seen as an aspect of the Sun and corresponds to Apollo.

Runes:	Sowulo, Berkana
Plant:	Oak, mistletoe, chamomile
Colour:	Gold, white
Element:	Fire
Planet:	Sun
Attributes:	Ring

NANNA

Balder's wife is Nanna. Their son is Forseti. Only one thing is known about Nanna: she follows her husband in death. Overcome with grief she casts herself in the burning pyre. That is why she represents faithfulness and devotion. Her father's name Nep means sorrow. Clearly, Nanna is a Goddess of grief and sadness. Nauthiz reflects her state of mind. The Rune also refers to Balder's cremation.

Runes:	Gebo, Nauthiz
Element:	Water
Planet:	Moon
Attributes:	Ring, linen

BRAGI

The union of Odin and Gunnlod results in the birth of Bragi, God of poetry and eloquence. Together with Hermod, Bragi is given the task of guarding the gates of Valhalla. The two Gods complement each other. What Bragi lacks in bravery Hermod has in abundance. What Hermod lacks in wisdom is found in Bragi. The key is to unite the introverted with the extroverted and so become whole.

Bragi is married to Idun whose job it is to open up Bragi's heart and teach him to enjoy life.

His Runes are Ansuz and Uruz. Ansuz links him with inspiration, communication, wisdom and ecstasy. Uruz refers to Bragi's drinking horn. A *symbel* toast was named after him, the *bragafull*, and was drunk to swear oaths or make a boast.

Runes:	Uruz, Ansuz, Pertho
Plant:	Willow, hops
Mineral:	Amethyst
Element:	Air
Attributes:	Harp, drinking horn

IDUN

Idun presides over youthfulness and springtime. Her name would mean rejuvenation and is linked to the mythical place Idavöll. Her quality is found in the apples she tends. These she feeds the Gods to keep them young. She is given a great responsibility. The life of the Gods is at stake.

She carries her golden apples in a maple basket, the wood of which was used for hygienic reasons. Idun is therefore a Goddess of health. She may be Hestia/Vesta.

Her image recalls the Matrones cult, where a young maiden sits among two mothers and carries a basket filled with fruit. Frigg would be one of the elder Mothers. In *Hrafnagaldr Odins*, Idun is classified as an elf. This is confirmed by the *Haustlong* poem where Idun is said to come from the south, i.e. Alfheim, when she arrives in Jotunheim.

If Pertho means apple, it is Idun's Rune. The Rune shape alludes to her basket. Berkana emphasizes her spring aspect. Her power animal is the swallow.

Runes:	Pertho, Berkana
Plant:	Apple, maple, ash
Animal:	Swallow
Mineral:	Emerald
Colour:	Gold, green
Attributes:	Apples, basket, the pentagram

TYR

It is said of Tyr that he headed the Germanic pantheon before dear Odin did. This claim must be true, since the Teiwaz Rune comes first in the celestial *aett*. The God also headed the Germanic folk assembly. Not only matters of war were discussed there, but all kinds of social matters too. Tyr corresponds to Ares/Mars. He presided over holy places.

Tyr is a sky father and a God of war. He is known as the One-handed Áss. The myths tell us that he lost his hand in binding the big bad wolf. His sacrifice represents the willingness to give up all that may hinder spiritual growth. Therefore, he symbolizes daring and selflessness. The wolf, Fenrir, represents greed and self-centredness.

A Danish bronze figurine dating back to 200 BCE shows Tyr, or rather Teiwaz, on his knees, with his left hand on his heart and his right hand missing from the elbow down. His right arm hangs passively alongside his body. It refers to the myth of binding the Wolf. The posture reminds the magician of the meaning of the myth.

Tyr has his left hand rested on the heart area. It emphasizes qualities of truth, integrity, gratitude, mercy and innocence. He wears a horned helmet, relating Tyr to the higher realms of the mind. The horns are an expression of divinity.

The God is shown sitting in a very particular way. He kneels in a praying position. This kind of sitting is still much used in Japanese martial arts schools. It signifies dedication, piety, respect and vigilance.

He has his right hand chopped off at the elbow indicating the loss of expressing himself. Left-handed people may choose to put their right hand on their chest while temporarily disconnecting their power hand. Presumably, a young Tyr would have both his hands resting on his chest in an expression of deep compassion. Tyr was not born with one hand only, so that this alternative posture is appropriate to use. It is symmetrical like that of Odin and resembles the Teiwaz Rune made by the forearms. Note that sometimes the younger Tyr Rune is written with one stroke only.

Runes:	Teiwaz
Animal:	Wolf, dog
Plant:	Oak, lime tree, aconite
Planet:	Mars, Pole Star
Attributes:	Sword, horned helmet, Irminsul

JORD

A sky father needs an Earth Mother. Among the Germanic people, the Earth was regarded as a primordial giantess. Her name is Jord. She is considered to be Odin's first wife, mighty Thor being their son. Frigg is either a daughter of Jord or identical with her. Jord is a Goddess of fertility. Furthermore, her name is cognate with Gerd, the giant maiden wooed by Lord Frey.

Runes:	Raido, Jera, Berkana, Inguz
Animals:	Snakes, dragons
Plants:	Leek, garlic
Colour:	Green, brown
Element:	Earth
Planet:	Earth

Attribute: Trees

NJORD

The king of the Vanir is called Njord. He is the proud father of Frey and Freyja. In Ancient Germanic times, he was called Nerthus and Tacitus defined him as *Terra Mater*.

It is difficult to say whether Njord is a sea deity or an earth deity. He was invoked to secure a good catch at sea, which, metaphorically, may allude to love magic. He also bestows riches, in which he resembles Hades/Pluto. Njord's reserved attitude corresponds to theirs. Yet his energy feels more related to that of the planet Saturn, whose power resonates with both Thurisaz and Nauthiz. The deep sea is Aegir's realm corresponding to Poseidon/Neptunus.

Possibly, the name Njord is related to Jord. That would make him a sea deity as opposed to the Earth Goddess Jord. The same linguistic play is found in the names of the mythical plains Idavöll and Nidavöll, as also in the dwarven names Váli and Náli in *Voluspa*.

The I-Rune is Njord's Rune. Laguz refers to his water aspect, whereas Laukaz reflects his earth aspect. Other Runes associated with Njord are Jera and Uruz. Jera signifies riches. They are the result of his blessing. Uruz refers to Njord's oxen pulling the plough.

Runes: Uruz, Thurisaz, Nauthiz, Jera, Laguz
Plant: Willow, wheat
Animal: Ox, seagull, fish
Element: Water, earth
Planet: Saturn
Attributes: Pair of feet, wain, ship

SKADI

As one of the giants, Skadi incidentally enters Asgard. When her father is killed by the Gods, she cries for vengeance. To soothe her, the Aesir propose to let her choose a husband among the Gods. However, she is allowed only to see their feet. She intends to marry beautiful Balder, so she chooses the man with the most beautiful feet, but this happens to be Njord.

This Goddess of vengeance is a well-trained skier and archer. She lives in the snowy mountains and hunts for a living. In that respect, she resembles Artemis/Diana, although Diana was equated with the Valkyric Gefjon in medieval Iceland. Skadi means destruction and symbolizes loss. Contrary to Nanna, she does not give in, but fights. She represents our fighting instincts.

Her qualities match those of Ull, who is known to have had a twin called Ullin. Maybe s/he is Skadi. This would support the comparison between Skadi and Diana, since Artemis/Diana has a twin brother, Apollo. Even more so because there is a myth in which a certain Skjold is married to Gefjon. Skjold means shield, which is Ull's sacred emblem.

The Runes of winter belong to Skadi. They are Hagalaz, Nauthiz and Isa. Thurisaz reflects her retaliating nature and recalls her giant ancestry.

Runes:	Thurisaz, Raido, Hagalaz, Nauthiz, Isa, Eihwaz
Animal:	Wolf, snake
Element:	Ice
Planet:	Moon
Attributes:	Rackets, skis

FREY

The Vanic God Frey is praised by the Aesir as an excellent warrior. He leads the pack and fights at the front line. All the same, most people only know his gentle side. But even in battle Frey is a real gentleman. Generally, Frey symbolizes masculine power, which is represented by his solar sword.

As a fertility God, he brings spring rains and makes the crops grow. Vikings had a special toast to invoke him for peace and prosperity. The same formula, *til árs og friðr*, was used to address Njord. Odin's blessing was procured with a similar but more warlike *til sigrs ok ríkis* ('to victory and power').

Frey rides a magical boar, but horses, too, are sacred to him. Both animals are symbols of the priestly class. Frey possesses a ship called Skidbladnir. Its sails always catch a favourable wind. For this reason, he may be invoked for astral travelling.

The Runes of Frey are Fehu, Jera and Inguz. Frey's main Rune is Inguz, since it really is his ancient name. Jera refers to a good summer. Runes indicating his peaceful aspect are Gebo and Wunjo. Both Runes belong to the Vanir in general. Fehu symbolizes Frey's bravery. It also symbolizes the fire of his sword and the fire of his desire to see Gerd.

A small statue of Frey is found at Rällinge, Sweden. It dates from the 11th century. The God is shown seated in a cross-legged position. I suspect that this stance has shamanic roots, as Frey is a Lord of Wisdom and his blood sister Freyja is a Goddess of sorcery. The horse, too, ties Frey to shamanism.

Frey holds his hands in a way that seems to reflect contemplation. He strokes his beard with his right hand, while his left hand supports his elbow. Lacking a beard, you can touch the chin to mimic this pensive state of mind. The stance can also be practiced standing.

People naturally adopt this posture when they ponder a question before answering. Sometimes it becomes a listening posture, as one carefully takes in new information, contemplating its use and meaning. But it always expresses a reflective mood. The posture symbolizes the integration of information.

Runes:	Fehu, Gebo, Wunjo, Jera, Sowulo, Inguz
Animal:	Horse, boar
Plant:	Barley
Planet:	Earth, Venus
Attributes:	Sword, ship, Sun Wheel

FREYJA

The Goddess of love is called Freyja. Snorri says that she is fond of love songs.

Her husband is Od. The Goddess Freyja is strongly connected with wealth and creativity. To this, her myths attest. Her children are Jewel and Treasure. She wears a golden necklace, obtained in a creative way. And she weeps gold as an expression of creativity.

After Od left her, Freyja wept tears of gold and amber. Her husband's name means inspiration (óðr), and it is this that she is hunting. After his leaving, she is devastated and travels the Nine Worlds looking for him. In her process of acquiescence, a new source of inspiration wells up from within herself. Gradually, deeper parts of her Self are contacted and new ideas surface. These materialize as golden tears of good ideas and self-expression. As a love story, the myth describes a woman's search for her *animus*.

Freyja rules the realms of sexuality and sensual love, but esoterically, she demonstrates the power of attraction on all levels. The Goddess corresponds to Aphrodite/Venus. She is also a sorceress, which means that she trusts her inner power. Freyja possesses a falcon dress. Wearing this, she is able to fly through the air and travel the Worlds. Her darker side she shares with Odin. Whenever Odin claims the honourable dead, Freyja is present. She has first pick.

Runes associated with Freyja are Fehu, Kenaz, Gebo, Wunjo, Laguz and Inguz. Her witching aspect is represented by Hagalaz. Many of these Runes are shared with Frey. Typical love Runes are Gebo and Inguz. Note how well they are constructed symmetrically. Gebo symbolizes a kiss. Laguz represents the power of attraction, falling in love, seduction and the manipulation of emotion. Kenaz refers to lust. Wunjo stands for the Vanir family.

There are almost no representations of any of the Goddesses. However, the posture of Freyja is reflected in the image of the queen pieces of the Lewis Chessmen. The queen is shown seated with one hand on her cheek while the other supports it. The posture resembles that of Frey. Additionally, the Goddess name Freyja is translated as 'lady' referring to a queen. This way, it seems plausible to explain the Lewis queen piece as a female version of the Frey statuette. Obviously, they go back to a common posture practiced in ancient Scandinavia. The Lewis queens are throned.

Freyja's posture seems to reflect emotions of worry, grief or care. It reminds us of the motherly concerns of Lady Frigg. Freyja might well have been one of the Mothers (*Oddrunargratr*).

One of the Lewis queens carries a drinking horn in the hand usually supporting the right elbow. This too relates the pieces to Freyja. In myth, Freyja and the Valkyries are said to carry around the drinking horn. As *Sigrdrifumal* explains, this hornful of sacred mead contains immense powers and serves as a medium to obtain wisdom and to enter the Inner Planes. The archetypal Valkyrie is Gunnlod, who may be recognized as Freyja veiled.

As it happens, Valkyrie iconography is well known in the Northern tradition. Images are based on a votive grave find dating from the 6th century, found in Birka, Sweden. They are shown standing presenting a mead filled horn with both their hands. This simply implies an act of giving and refers to the mysteries of the Gebo Rune. The Tjängvide stone from Sweden, among others, also shows a Valkyrie offering a drink.

Runes:	Fehu, Kenaz, Gebo, Wunjo, Hagalaz, Laguz, Inguz
Animal:	Cat, sow, goat, falcon, butterfly
Mineral:	Amber, gold
Plant:	Birch, daisy
Colour:	Gold and white, green
Planet:	Venus
Attributes:	Necklace, flax

HEIMDAL

The Northern God of light is Heimdal. He does neither belong to the Aesir nor to the Vanir. He was created by an occult ceremony at a place that is not a place in a time before time. Nine waves, of giant ancestry, bore him by the blood of a sacrificial boar, much in the same way as Pegasos was born, or

Kvasir, many years later. Mankind, too, was created in a similar way, on the borders of earth and water.

In the beginning of time, Heimdal was appointed the task of guarding Asgard. He keeps watch at Bifrost Bridge. At the same time, the God leans with his back against the age-old tree to prevent the giants from entering Asgard. Heimdal's abode is Himinbjorg, the Celestial Fortress, pictured at the end of Heaven – at the borders of Asgard where Bifrost Bridge enters the deep states of mind.

The way up on Bifrost is for man to take. Only through an unwavering act of intention will Heimdal grant access to the deepest parts of the mind. The way down is that of the Gods. Their descending represents deep concentration, meditation and flashes of insight. It is clear from the myths surrounding Heimdal that he interconnects different states of consciousness.

As a guardian God, Heimdal owns some peculiar abilities. He is able to hear grass growing as well as wool on a sheep's back. He needs less sleep than any bird. All this makes Heimdal a watchful, sensitive, observant deity. He represents awareness and through awareness is he contacted. The Algiz Rune has much in common with Heimdal's abilities and mental qualities. The Rune symbolizes Bifrost Bridge and the bridging of mind states.

Often, Heimdal is associated with Mannaz. Dagaz is the Rune of light. It symbolizes Heimdal's vigilance. He Is also a Sun God, since he is called the White Áss. Heimdal is Eternal Blue Heaven.

Runes:	Algiz, Sowulo, Mannaz, Dagaz
Animals:	Ram, seal, boar
Mineral:	Lapis lazuli
Colour:	White, rainbow colours
Planet:	Sun, Milky Way
Attributes:	Lur, horn, rainbow, aurora borealis

LOKI

Originally, Loki was a giant, but Odin adopted him into the Aesir society. As a result, Odin added a playful, unpredictable touch to the otherwise conservative world of Asgard. Loki's main job is to test the established order. But at the end of times, he will bring about the destruction of the Gods.

Loki is famous for his unruly children. He fathered Fenrir, Jormungand and Hella. Hella is presented the world of the dead. Jormungand is a dragon banned to the vast sea. He encircles the Nine Worlds, thus representing the Ring Pass Not of esoteric thinking. At Ragnarok, Jormungand will cause a flood that will engulf the Earth. Fenrir is a wolf who will devour the Sun and the sky. He symbolizes greed and fear and all those petty emotions that bind a man to his ego. Loki himself symbolizes astral illusion. He designs a fishing net that represents *maya*, which is the net of illusion that people get caught in.

As a dynamic God, Loki is able to produce many creative treasures for the Gods. Through him, Mjollnir, Gungnir, Skidbladnir and Sleipnir, among many other things, were created. Loki rules comedy.

His principal Rune is Thurisaz as a Jotun ambassador among the Aesir. Dagaz symbolizes the dynamics of yin and yang, initiated by Loki's rebellious character. The Rune is in fact a double Thurisaz. Dagaz explains Loki's relation with Heimdal. Whereas Heimdal represents dawn, Loki symbolizes nightfall. Dagaz also indicates the end phase of an era. Kenaz is Loki's inner fire; just like Thor's, his appetite is insatiable. Hunger is definitively a Loki sensation. Metaphorically, this translates as a thirst for power.

Runes:	Thurisaz, Kenaz, Dagaz
Animal:	Fox, seal, salmon, falcon, fly, flea
Element:	Fire
Planet:	Sirius
Attributes:	Fishing net, torch

HELLA

Loki's daughter is called Hella. She rules the dead. Snorri says that only those who die of old age and sickness go to her. In my opinion, she rules all things dead and forgotten. Why else would she harbour Balder, who was slain by a weapon! Moreover, when Hermod travels to her realm, a host of fallen heroes had just marched over that same bridge.

Death is associated with time standing still. In Hella's realm, time slows down to a rate that it almost freezes. She has two servants moving so slowly that you can barely see them move. In her world, space and time freeze over. She is the absolute zero.

Hella represents the dark aspect of the Goddess, hidden in Berkana. More specifically, Hagalaz is associated with Hella's nature and qualities. Hagalaz also refers to snow, relating Hella with the Continental Goddess Holda. Dagaz represents the two halves manifesting in Hella. She is portrayed as half dead and half alive. Dagaz may also refer to the timelessness of her realm, death in general, and in particular the transcending of time and space. Timelessness is an aspect of Isa as well as Eihwaz.

Runes:	Hagalaz, Berkana, Dagaz
Plant:	Elder
Animal:	Dog
Colour:	Black and white
Planet:	Moon
Attributes:	Snow

6

THE
NINE
WORLDS

One more ingredient has to be added to the system of the Northern tradition: the Nine Worlds. It is exactly in these mythic worlds that the different powers of the Gods find expression. And the powers they express are represented by the Runes.

The system is therefore built around three components: the worlds, the Gods and the Runes. Metaphorically speaking, all of these refer to aspects of the mind. The worlds symbolize different levels of the mind, whereas the Gods represent archetypes playing within these areas of action. The Runes are energies present. In daily life, the worlds refer to different contexts a situation takes place in. The Gods represent our response patterns, and the Runes symbolize conscious decisions throughout life.

The system resembles that of astrology. Naturally, the worlds correspond to the houses. The planets, and other celestial bodies, correspond to the Gods, although their divine expression may relate to the energy of the Runes. The Runes themselves would compare to the astrological aspects.

Each world is inhabited by a race akin to that region. Each race expresses a particular quality of character and a particular level of consciousness. Each world represents a door of consciousness.

Boundaries keep these worlds apart. Sometimes this makes it difficult to pass from one world to another, but the Gods guide us. They travel throughout the Nine Worlds and interact wherever possible to connect the many layers of reality.

Three Main Worlds

Both in a temporal as in a spatial sense, the number 9 symbolizes a large amount. In Eddic myth the number recurrently indicates a long period of time. In Ancient Greek myth and ritual the number has exactly the same meaning. As related to space, the number may signify any multitude of worlds.

The motif of nine worlds is found in almost every traditional culture. For example, nine heavens are found in Siberian, Chinese and Aztec traditions as well as in Buddhism. There are nine Angelic choirs. Most of the old cultures also record a nine-fold Underworld. And this, too, is found in the Northern tradition, where it is said that Hel contains nine worlds of its own.

Although the number of these worlds may be purely symbolic and may have no meaning beyond there being a great many, it is possible to offer at least two alternative interpretations. Firstly, nine is the sum of 1 and 8, the latter referring to the eight horizontal directions. And secondly, nine is three times three, the number 3 symbolizing the standard vertical division of the cosmos.

In the Northern tradition, 9 is based on the number 3. There are three main worlds in Northern cosmography. They are Asgard, Midgard and Utgard. The latter is the first world, and it is inhabited by giants. It represents the subconscious. Out of the Utgardian chaos Midgard was created, which is the world of man. Midgard represents the conscious world of rational thought and decision. But the highest world is known as Asgard, which is inhabited by Gods. It therefore represents higher consciousness. This world houses ideas, inspiration and intuition. In effect, these three worlds respectively represent instinct, intelligence and intuition. Their order also indicates the natural process of evolution, from raw and primitive to highly refined.

The natural order of these three basic worlds falls into two distinct arrangements. A distinction must be made between the races and the worlds. Giants are the first race to emerge. Next, the Gods appear, and the Gods create mankind. But the Gods also create Midgard, which is the Earth raised from the primal sea. Then, on Midgard, the Gods slice up the territory in three and finally build Asgard in the centre of it all. As stated above, the creation of the worlds represents the evolution of consciousness. The succession of the races represents the materialization of subtle energies.

On a symbolic level, Utgard is regarded as the world of emotions and our animal nature. In this world, our drive to act is found. From this perspective, and as a world of primal chaos, the element of Water is associated with this realm. In dividing the territory, the Gods banned the giant race to the outer rims of Midgard, towards the sea. Utgard is a realm of potential. In the body, Utgard corresponds to the area of the lower abdomen and the gonads, known as Dan Tien in the Chinese tradition and as Hara in the Japanese tradition.

Midgard is the physical Earth emerging from the primal waters of creation. It symbolizes the crystallization of potential. Midgard is essentially a world of matter and of sensory registration. The element of Earth is connected to this world.

Asgard is situated in the heavens. The wind element of Air is strongly associated with it, that being the element of Odin. This world also holds the promise of the Fire element. Through the skies of Asgard the Sun Goddess rides her wain with a spark of Muspel-fire enlightening the day. The Aesir lend the quality of soul to the gross physical world.

Asgard	Gods	Higher consciousness	Intuition	Air
Midgard	Humans	Everyday consciousness	Intelligence	Earth
Utgard	Giants	Subconscious	Instinct	Water

The three main worlds of Northern myth relate to each other in a three-dimensional way. On the horizontal plane, the forces of Midgard and Utgard meet each other. They wage their eternal battle until the raw and upsetting power of the lower self is fully refined and assimilated in the personality. In the body, Utgard corresponds to the first three chakras whereas Midgard corresponds to the heart centre. The horizontal plane represents physical experience. It explains a man's suffering, his desires and wish life, and the resulting inner and outer conflicts.

The vertical plane links Midgard and Asgard. Their relation is visualized as a tree and represents spiritual aspiration, vision. Similarly, the process of spiritual ambition inherent in the vertical axis is embodied in the Bifrost glyph and the Algiz Rune. To man, Bifrost Bridge offers the opportunity to reach out for higher ideals and the realization of immanent divinity. To Gods, this bridge is a means to inspire the minds of men. Every day, the Gods ride out over that bridge to moot over the meaning of life at the Well of Wyrd in a person's meditation. Therefore, this vertical duality does not signify struggle but rather the wish to transcend the earthly bounds towards a higher purpose.

In conclusion, these three basic worlds express the integration of the horizontal and the vertical plane. The horizontal plane is characterized by the great world serpent Jormungand (Jera). The vertical plane is symbolized by the great World Tree Yggdrasil (Eihwaz), whose physical representation is known as Jormunsul. And the totality may be given the name Jormungrund (Pertho).

Gunnungagap

Before the creation of the three basic worlds, there already existed a world thick with forces. This world is called Ginnungagap and it is characterized by two main energies, corresponding to the archetypal elements of Fire and Water. The World of Fire was first among all and is known as Muspelheim. The World of Water comes second and is called Niflheim. Through them, all energy forms and differentiates. They are Spirit and Matter. These first two realms personify the first polarity and are impersonal.

Niflheim	Muspelheim
Water	Fire
NORTH	SOUTH
Matter	Spirit

Death   Life

Yin   Yang

The polarity of the two most ancient worlds created a field of tension that is termed Ginnungagap in the Northern tradition. This field is usually defined as a magically loaded void. Its nature is analogous to the electromagnetic field.

Muspelheim	Ginnungagap	Niflheim
Fire	Air	Water
South	Centre	North
Positive	Neutral	Negative
Proton	Neutron	Elektron
Spirit	Mind	Body
Monad	Soul	Ego
Surt	Ymir	Audumla
Chokmah	Daath	Binah
Pillar of Mercy	Pillar of Equilibrium	Pillar of Strength
Expansion	Balance	Contraction
Ring Cosmos	Ring Pass Not	Ring Chaos
Movement	Light	Sound
Future	Present	Past

These are the ingredients of the Viking myth of creation. As a metaphor, the myth is true to the insights of esoteric tradition. In her book *The Cosmic Doctrine*, Dion Fortune schematically describes how the creation of the cosmos may have come about. It corresponds nicely to what is known from Ancient Scandinavian mythology.

According to esoteric thinking, the creative power of Muspelheim (Ring Cosmos) instigates a checking force in order to obtain balance. This second force corresponds to Niflheim (Ring Chaos). The combination of both results in a third aspect that roughly matches the concept of Ginnungagap, which is nothing else but space (Ring Pass Not). Then, the interaction of these three primal forces creates movements of power within the sphere of Ginnungagap. This results in twelve individual currents of energy, corresponding to the Aesir, the evolution of which only reflects the differentiation of energy. And last but not least, the movement of these twelve powers creates a segmentation, which divides Ginnungagap into seven planes. These correspond to the remaining Worlds of Northern mythology: Jotunheim, Asgard, Midgard, Svartalfheim, Vanaheim, Ljosalfheim and Helheim.

3x3

As Ginnungagap marks the sphere in which the entire evolution of the universe is played, it is in this force field that the three main worlds eventually emerge. And from these three, the nine evolve. In my opinion, the Nine Worlds are not necessarily divided up equally among the three basic ones.

Utgard harbours four worlds. These are the netherworlds. They are Niflheim, Jotunheim, Svartalfheim and Helheim. Asgard rules the heavenly abodes; four worlds also. They are Asgard, Vanaheim, Alfheim and Muspelheim. In between these lies Midgard. Of the heavens, Vanaheim and Asgard lie closest to the world of Midgard. The world of elves is the highest place. It is the realm of the soul. Beyond these, Muspelheim is situated. It is from this deep place that monads descend into incarnation. Of the chthonic worlds, Jotunheim is closest to Midgard. Next is the dwarven realm. Deepest lies Helheim. Beyond these Niflheim is situated. From this realm matter is gathered.

5.	ASGARD	**Muspelheim**	Surt	⋈	ᚠ
4.		**Alfheim**	Frey	ᛊ	ᚹ
3.		**Vanaheim**	Njord	◇	ᚷ
2.		**Asgard**	Odin	ᚷ	ᚾ
1.	MIDGARD	**Midgard**	Thor	ᛜ	ᚱ
2.		**Jotunheim**		ᛁ	ᚦ
3.	UTGARD	**Svartalfheim**		ᛇ	ᚲ

| 4. | **Helheim** | Loki | ᚾ | ᚾ |
| 5. | **Niflheim** | | ᚴ | ᚻ |

333

The Nine Worlds appear in a specific order. Much of this is related in the myths and has already been discussed earlier. In short, there was firstly the world in the south called Muspelheim (1). Then, the cool force of Niflheim (2) countered its blazing fire. A race of giants came into existence as a result of their interactivity (3). From that race the Gods developed (4). They created mankind (5).

Of the next three worlds, the order is uncertain. Next to no stories of creation exist about Svartalfheim, Vanaheim and Alfheim. However, *Voluspa* reveals that the war of Aesir and Vanir only takes place after the creation of the dwarves (6), so that the myth of the First Battle pins down the position of the Vanir World (7). In addition, 7 is the number of the planet Venus, who rules the Vanic House. Next, the elf world is linked to the Vanir world. Frey of the Vanir is made Lord of Alfheim (8) as a child. This would naturally place Alfheim after Vanaheim.

The ninth world is last because it is the realm where everything ends. It is presided over by Hella, and created much later in the history of the Gods (9). The position is aptly that of the Moon.

The mythological sequence of the Nine Worlds coincides with the symbolism of the first nine Runes. Their relation is easily established. (1) Fehu has a quality of fire about it. Its energy drives all creation. (2) Uruz is related to water and supplies the form to contain the energy of Muspelheim. Of Niflheim is said *inn í frá úr ok gustr*, which means 'from it [Niflheim] drizzle and a gust (fill Ginnungagap)'. The next Rune, (3) Thurisaz, evidently corresponds to Jotunheim. The same straightforward correspondence is found in (4) Ansuz. Interestingly, this Rune is glossed Jupiter in the Rune Poems. (5) Raido refers to Thor, warder of Midgard and friend of Man.

Likewise, the symbolism of (6) Kenaz and (7) Gebo fits well the World it is ascribed to. Gebo refers to the war of Aesir and Vanir. (8) Wunjo symbolizes the state of bliss found in Alfheim. And finally, (9) Hagalaz is in effect Hella's Rune.

Nine Nymphs guide the Way

MUSPELHEIM

The first world is Muspelheim. It is situated in the far south of the void preceding any substantial creation. Its Master is Surt, who is a fire giant known to be the catalyst of cataclysm. At the end of time, it is he who disintegrates creation by the purging qualities of fire. His name refers to the torch blackened by fire. His fire represents Will and acts both as the fire of creation and as the fire of destruction. This is the world of the Lords of Flame.

According to the creation myth, the Aesir seize a spark from this world and shape it into the Sun. Subsequently, the Stars and Moon were made from similar embers. These particles represent divine sparks, the monads of esoteric tradition. The monad is our real connection with the spiritual world. It is the Sun in the heart of every being.

As a fire world, Muspelheim stands for expansion, dynamics and energy. It symbolizes pure life. Psychologically, Muspelheim is the world in which intentions are formed. The state of mind that is most likely coherent with its vibration is the deep trance of theta brain waves. Initiatives and ideas emerge from this world, fire providing the necessary drive and motivation to venture forth. Intention is the keyword of this World.

Runes:	Fehu, Sowulo, Dagaz
Colour:	White
Planet:	Sun
Element:	Fire
Attribute:	Torch, sword

NIFLHEIM

The world balancing Muspelheim is Niflheim. It lies in the far north of Ginnungagap. Niflheim means 'world of mist'. In the centre of this world, there is a spring called the Well of Hvergelmir. From this rise the Elivagar; a complex of twelve rivers that run through Niflheim until they cross the empty space of Ginnungagap for such a long way that they congeal and finally freeze over. The Well is guarded by the dragon Nidhogg. Niflheim is home to the *Hrímþursar*.

The element of water is known for its capability of taking any desired shape. Once water has been imprinted with information, it carries that information with it forever. In the same way does the Well of Mimir work. Water does not only flow out of the well, but information is added. In other words, the water becomes charged.

As the polar opposite of Muspelheim, Niflheim stands for contraction and the cooling down of fire. After the Aesir shaped the Sun from a spark they needed something to cool it down. If not it would singe the mountains and boil the oceans. However, without the influence of Muspelheim's warmth, too much of this quality would cause depression, melancholy and what alchemists call phlegm. In this respect, Niflheim's energy can have a restricting, habituating or impeding effect.

Psychologically, this world stands for thoughts, memories and mind dust (*chitta*) needed to give ideas and inspiration a concrete form. Ideas are given form in the subconscious world of Niflheim. The world of Niflheim bears a relationship to the etheric body. In Niflheim are seated the Lords of Form.

Runes:	Uruz, Nauthiz
Animals:	Otter, dragon
Colour:	Indigo
Planet:	Moon
Element:	Water, ice
Attribute:	Salt, drinking horn

JOTUNHEIM

The polarity of Muspelheim and Niflheim results in the conception of a primordial being Ymir. He represents the framework of creation. His life marks the first crystallization of the potential that is present in Ginnungagap. The raw mixture of life and matter that makes up this Ancient Giant is only later refined by the Aesir. That second stage heralded the emergence of consciousness and the creation of Asgard and Midgard. The Age of Ymir, however, corresponds to the preconscious world of the giants.

Jotunheim is peopled by Jotuns, Thurses, Trolls, and Wargs, and *Bergrísar*, and *Gýgjur*. The land is named after one of the giant races and is consistently situated in the east. These beings represent a low grade of consciousness in the human evolution and personify our emotional concerns and our wish life. The world of giants is in effect an image of the astral plane. Another name for Jotunheim is Utgard, which is ruled by Loki. Two other rulers of Jotunheim's are Geirrod and Thrym.

The myths repeatedly state that giants possess the power of illusion, deception and manipulation. Giants are known as shapeshifters. They either take the shape of eagles, symbolizing astral projection, or wolves, symbolizing dreaming. In the Northern tradition, the astral body is called *hamr*. Shaping the *hamr* at will (*hugr*), however, is an aspect connected with the world of the Aesir. The deeper part of the mind is able to control the deeper part of the body.

Psychologically, Jotunheim relates to the dream state and the deep sleep. It stands for both the subconscious and the body mind. As embodiments of emotions, giants habitually express themselves as anger, passion and fear. Jotunheim is a world of raw power and alludes to the concept of libido and the Freudian id. Jotunheim is a world of instincts, needs, desires, compulsions and inner conflicts. This is the world we face when straying off the path or acting against our better judgement. In the woods of this land the wolf lurks.

Runes: Thurisaz, Isa, Ehwaz

Animals:	Horses, wolves, eagles
Colour:	Red
Planet:	Saturn
Element:	Water
Attribute:	Iron

ASGARD

Ymir was nursed by the primordial cow Audumla. In her turn she fed on the ice of the Elivagar rivers. When she licked the ice, a man appeared from it who was to become the ancestor of the Gods. From him, Odin and his brothers stem. One day, these primordial Gods, who lived among the giants then, revolted against the established chaos and killed Ymir. Or rather, they sacrificed him for the greater good. From his body, they shaped the world.

The process of creation instigated by the Aesir took place by defining the unknown. Names were given to everything they met and so they called manifestation into existence. The technique of naming is powerful indeed. It makes an abstract thought concrete. Asgard is readily linked to the bridging of abstract thought to concrete thought.

In the myths, the Aesir come together in assemblies to discuss weighty matters. Metaphorically, the image evokes the exercise of meditation: the gathering of the Gods symbolizes the concentration of mental forces. Their drawing together results in decision. And decision making is one of the great virtues of Asgard's powers. Another of its virtues is the power to organize.

The Aesir world represents the mental world on all levels. Asgard embodies the archetypal heaven. It is the world of vision and ideals, truth, beauty and good-will. In this world are also found those psychic faculties that come with the development of mind, such as telepathy, clairvoyance and intuition. Asgard symbolizes mind, and the capacity to think, contemplate and meditate. Esoterically, this world is ruled by the Lords of Mind. An alternative name for Asgard is Asaheim.

The Great Life ruling this world is Odin. In his ranks the initiates are taken up to drink the mead of wisdom and to train for the Last Battle. Asgard is home to both Valkyries and Einherjar.

It is possible to reach Asgard by crossing the rainbow bridge in meditation. From this world, man takes down into his physical life all the deepest that he is able to contact. From this world, too, the artist is blessed with inspiration.

Runes:	Ansuz, Gebo, Algiz
Animals:	Horses
Plants:	Oak, ash
Colour:	Blue
Planet:	Mercury
Element:	Air
Attribute:	Throne

MIDGARD

In the centre of the universe lies Midgard, the world of man. Its prominent position implies that the myths apply to the psychology and soul life of man. We ourselves are at the centre of the mythological world. Additionally, the number 5 symbolizes life and humanity. It is in Midgard that the World Tree Yggdrasil grows. Here it connects the Nine Worlds as one big whole. Every one of these Worlds feeds into Midgard, making it a world of synthesis and transition. The World is warded and looked after by Thor, who is likened to the Archangel Michael.

Midgard represents everyday life and the superficial state of mind that comes with it. The outer senses, like sight, hearing and touch, are associated with this world. Especially the sense of touch is linked to Midgard, since this is the world of the physical body. The Gods raised the Earth from out of the waters. In the same way, the physical body is a manifestation of subtler energies, such as the astral and etheric. At the same time, the myth explains the evolution from the subconscious mind to the typical human conscious mind. The power of Midgard is that of individuality.

Being mankind's world, it embodies the level of logical thinking and reasoning, yet the rational mind has the upper hand. Its state of mind is that of beta brain waves. However, as a world of physical plane experience, it is the plane of material manifestation and social activity.

This world is sometimes called Ljodheim.

Runes: Raido, Jera, Mannaz

Colour: Green, brown

Planet: Earth

Element: Earth

Attribute: House

SVARTALFHEIM

The race of dwarves is juxtaposed to that of the elves by name. Dwarves are called Svartalfar and Dokkalfar, while the elves are called Ljosalfar. Their common ancestor is Ivaldi. The dwarven names mean Black Elves and Dark Elves. They have this name because of their profession. They are blacksmiths. Their faces are black from soot. The race of dwarves lives in the mountains where ore and minerals are extracted and precious jewels mined. The echo heard in the mountains is said to be their speech. As guardians of the Earth's resources, we keep them close to our hearts!

As smiths, dwarves represent the, mostly subconscious, creative processes in the mind. In their realm, raw material is transformed and resynthesized into new and purer shapes. The precious treasures and trinkets they conceive are the results of much time and effort. In the hidden forges of the mind is constantly remodeled that material and information that is taken in during the day, either consciously through study or unconsciously through experience. By the process of time, these experiences are transformed into insights and these lessons into wisdom. The summit of their work must be the inner alchemical process of turning the karmic lead of Saturn into the solar gold of inner life.

Through the creative process, Svartalfheim corresponds to the alpha state of mind in which associative thinking takes the upper hand. This view is strengthened by the fact that dwarves have access to non-existent materials representing the illogical stuff that dreams are made of, and by the fact that they turn to stone by the Sun's first rays. The power and function of dreams can be traced back to the dwarves' work.

The king of the dwarves is said to be Modsognir and second in command is Durin. However, the name that appears most often in poetry and legend is Dvalin. Incidentally, these three names all refer to sleep, which confirms their work with dreams.

Runes:	Kenaz, Eihwaz, Dagaz
Animals:	Deer, swan
Colour:	Red, gold, black, orange
Planet:	Saturn, Pluto
Element:	Fire
Attribute:	Hammer and anvil

VANAHEIM

The Vanir are Gods of good fortune and plenty. They bestow riches and procure peace. Their credo is goodwill and their dealings compassion. Everything they do is accompanied by a real sense of respect and love. Many connect the world of feeling with Vanaheim.

More esoterically, I would ascribe such qualities as empathy and sympathy to the beings of this world, their key being devotion. Although devotion is present in the world of Asgard, too, the difference lies in the approach. Whereas the Vanic personality is more mystically inclined, the Aesic personality will be more occultly oriented. Someone who works under the auspices of Asgard will work with ceremony and know the tools of discipline and order to be of great significance. Someone who is in contact with the Vanic powers dispenses with the paraphernalia of the magician but rather enjoys the miracles of a nature walk.

From Vanaheim flows a feeling of trust and confidence. The Witches' saying 'in perfect trust and perfect love' comes right from sensing the ideals of this world. It is a world of beauty and perfection. It is linked with the dream world through the faculty of imagination. Their world relates to lucid dreaming. Psychologically, Vanaheim represents our gut feeling, our intuition. The power of its light sends a wave of harmonizing energy into the world. In Vanaheim, individuality is respected, but transcended.

Runes:	Gebo, Wunjo, Inguz
Animals:	Cattle
Plants:	Wheat
Colour:	Green, yellow
Planet:	Venus
Element	Earth, water
Attribute:	Wain

ALFHEIM

Ljosalfheim or Alfheim is the realm of the Light Elves (*Ljósálfar/Álfar*). Possibly, the Disir belong to this world too. Elves are renowned for their beauty, which is said to be more brilliant than that of the Sun. Their world lies above and south of Asgard, symbolizing a higher state of consciousness and a higher grade of evolution. It corresponds to the realm of angelic beings known from Judaeo-Christian myth. It is home to the Solar Angels.

Alfheim is in particular associated with the concept of Light. It is consequently a world of spiritual truth, devoid of any misinterpretation. No feeling of separation exists on this level. It is pure, like fire, situated close to Muspelheim, and functions as an unfathomable reservoir of universal life energy.

Esoterically, Alfheim represents the realm of the soul. In my opinion, this world symbolizes resting quietly in the deep state of mind. The language of this world transcends that of symbols. It speaks in terms of intuition only. According to Northern myth, Frey of the Vanir has been made Lord of this world from the earliest of times. From this world, contact can be made with what lies beyond our solar system, beyond our own petty psychology and mythology. Achieving this state of mind implies a life in permanent meditation.

Runes:	Wunjo, Sowulo, Laguz
Animals:	Swan
Plant:	Garlic
Colour:	White, violet
Planet:	Sun, Venus, Uranus
Element:	Fire
Attribute:	Wheel

HELHEIM

The world of the dead is known as Hel, Niflhel or Helheim in Northern cosmology. According to *Gylfaginning*, Hel is a domain in Niflheim. Snorri also gives away that Hel is composed of nine worlds in itself implying that the dead of every world eventually end up in this place. The Underworld is a part of every world.

Metaphorically, the dead represent everything that has been forgotten or suppressed. Lost memories can be regained and past lives recalled by regressing into Helheim. It is a boundless world.

Psychologically, Hel represents the collective subconscious. The contents of this world transcend the personal. As a result, it is a great storehouse of information that can be accessed through divination. The *völva* that Odin consults in the poem of Balder's Dreams is buried in Hel. In the Northern world, the dead were often consulted in an act of divination.

Runes:	Hagalaz, Nauthiz
Animals:	Horse, rooster
Colour:	Black, white

Planet: Moon

Element: Earth

Attribute: Ship, memorial stone

JORMUNGRUND

For lack of a better term, the whole universe of Northern myth might be called Jormungrund. It contains the Nine Worlds, their inhabitants and rulers.

The table presented provides basic information on the Nine Worlds: their order, their Runes, their names, their spirit family, their male ruler, their female ruler, their planet and their non-invertable Rune. In regard to their rulers, the information given is only a suggestion.

1.	ᚠ	**Muspelheim**	Fire	Surt	Sunna			ᛗ
2.	ᚢ	**Niflheim**	Water	Tyr	Skadi			ᛉ
3.	ᚦ	**Jotunheim**	Giants	Loki	Gerd	Saturn	ᛁ
4.	ᚨ	**Asaheim**	Aesir	Odin	Frigg	Jupiter	ᚷ
5.	ᚱ	**Ljodheim**	Mankind	Thor	Sif	Mars	ᛇ
6.	ᚲ	**Svartalfheim**	Dwarves	Dvalin	Thrud	Sun	ᛃ
7.	ᚷ	**Vanaheim**	Vanir	Njord	Jord	Venus	ᛜ
8.	ᚹ	**Ljosalfheim**	Elves	Frey	Freyja	Mercury	ᛊ
9.	ᚺ	**Helheim**	Dead	Balder	Hella	Moon	ᚺ

2	9	4	ᚢ	ᚺ	ᚨ
7	5	3	ᚷ	ᚱ	ᚦ
6	1	8	ᚲ	ᚠ	ᚹ

ᚺ	ᚻ	ᚠ
2. Niflheim	9. Helheim	4. Asaheim
MIMIR	HELLA	ODIN
ᚷ	ᚱ	ᛃ
7. Vanaheim	5. Ljodheim	3. Jotunheim
NJORD	THOR	THRYM
ᚲ	ᚠ	ᚦ
6. Svartalfheim	1. Muspelheim	8. Ljosalfheim
MODSOGNIR	SURT	FREY

The Nine of Saturn

Northern mythology does not only give us the order of the manifesting worlds, it also grants us a glimpse as to their mutual position. Muspelheim is in the south. Niflheim is in the north. Jotunheim is in the east. Midgard is in the centre. What remains are the worlds of the Gods. They would consequently be situated in the west. According to Ellis-Davidson, Valhalla originally referred to the burial mound, and being ancestral Gods, the Aesir have a bearing on the concept of death and afterlife. These concepts are associated with the west. Vanaheim might be close to Asgard. In the same way, Svartalfheim might be close to Jotunheim. Alfheim is south of Asgard according to *Gylfaginning*. And last but not least, Hella's abode is a part of Niflheim.

Although the above is a good start, there is a more solid way of arranging the Nine Worlds. The alternative diagram I am about to suggest has its roots in *seiðr* practice. *Mariusaga* mentions that an ox hide is inscribed with nine squares. This hide is designed for a *seiðr* ceremony. I believe the nine squares represent the Nine Worlds. Their orientation has not been preserved, but this can easily be reconstructed when the squares are correlated to the Magic Square of Saturn.

When the first nine Runes of the Futhark are arranged according to the numerical arrangement of the Magic Square of Saturn, then a pattern for the Nine Worlds is created. The diagram looks like this:

The diagram is rotated in such a way that the north side faces up and Jotunheim faces east. Not surprisingly, the orientation of the worlds in the Saturn Square fits well their mythological background. Niflheim and Muspelheim are opposite each other. Jothunheim is in the east. The world of the Gods is in the east as well, emphasizing the element Air. Vanaheim is in the west, the element Water ruling the Vanic nature. The worlds of the Light Elves and Dark Elves are opposite each other. Helheim lies next to Niflheim. And last but not least, Midgard is in the centre.

The *seiðr* ceremony of sitting-out on an animal skin in order to make contact with the spirit world is a well-founded practice in Europe, by Greeks, Romans, and Druids, alongside the Scandinavian shamans. In the Celtic tradition, the *Dream of Rhonabwy* mentions this motif. In the Northern tradition, the elf smith Völund is also said to sit on a bearskin. In *Brennu-Njalssaga*, goatskin is used to work *seiðr*. A passage from *Kormakssaga* describes how an ox hide marks the sacred space for a *hólmganga*. The saga of Eirik the Red gives even more information. Both this saga and *Mariusaga* instruct chanting to get a trance going. A number of sagas confirm the use of a high seat, reminiscent of the *völusessi*.

Clearly, animal skins create a link between man's world and the Gods' world. In his works, Bertiaux hints that primitive methods support access to the spirit world. According to Ellis-Davidson, alongside cow, the hides of sheep and walrus were also used for sitting-out. In *Eirikssaga rauda*, the seeress sits on a cushion of hen feathers. But it could as well be a flying carpet. In my opinion, magic carpets have exactly the same ceremonial function as animal skins. For example, the Quran describes how King Solomon travels on a carpet that was driven by the wind.

It is possible to visit the Nine Worlds and enter these dimensions and contact the beings that live there. Set up your work space. Either have a cloth or skin to sit on or draw the diagram on the floor. Open the rite as you are used to. Sit in the middle square and face either North or East, as it feels right. Go under the cloak. You might want to have a spear or distaff or magic wand about, as the sagas have it. Induce a firm trance state. Traditionally, this is obtained by singing, although silence works just as well. When you are there, invoke Thor and be aware of the fact that you have entered Midgard, for that is where you are. Hail the spirits of the different worlds and connect. Then, guide yourself through an effort of will. From the central square you can move about the different zones in time and space by moving the mind and/or body in any of the eight directions. When you are done, recall the world of Midgard and listen for Thor's presence. Thank the spirits of the different worlds and disconnect.

> From his weapon shall a person on the planes
>
> Not go one foot
>
> Because unknowable it is to know when on the out-ways
>
> The spear be needful to the youth

7

EK
FAHI
RUNOZ

Although Runes function wholly on a symbolic level, they do have a physical representation. This is their letter shape. And exactly this is used in writing, sigil magick and the casting of lots.

From ancient texts, it is deduced that the physical representation of the Runes involved ritual. Rune crafting always possessed an energy component. Some of the ritual techniques have already been talked about in the chapter on mythical origins. The symbols were conceived, scored and painted, and the names were sung. Another Eddic stanza is even more enigmatic. *Havamal* 144 mentions eight different techniques on working with Runes. They explain how a set of Runes is made for ritual purposes.

Once the Runes are created on the physical plane, they are consecrated by the power of the Gods. In particular, Thor was invoked. A Viking Age inscription on a stone monument from Glavendrup contains the words *Þórr wígi þæssi rúnar*. The Velanda Rune stone says *Þórr wígi*. Thor's name and hammer repeatedly appear on memorial stones and have a consecrating purpose. It may be the equivalent of the earlier Ancient Germanic *alu*-formula. For that reason, a crafting ritual would include the blessing of Thor.

Do you know how to carve?

A Rune set is created in many stages. Firstly, material has to be selected. Then, the individual pieces have to be inscribed. Next, the signs have to be stained. And once the set is finished, the whole is to be consecrated. Only then will the Runes be useful for any given purpose.

One particular stanza in the *Havamal* poem gives extant information on the different stages of creating Runes. According to stanza 144, Runes are carved, read, coloured, tried, entreated, worshipped, sent and sacrificed. An overview of the eight different actions may be enlightening.

rísta	ráða
fáa	freista
biðja	blóta
senda	sóa

RISTA

Do you know how to carve the Runes? The verb *rísta* means to carve. Runes were carved in wood, bone, metal and stone. In a magical sense, they can be drawn into the ether. Ancient Germanic inscriptions use terms like 'to make, to write and to wright'. Old Norse synonyms are 'to score, to mark'.

RADA

Do you know how to read the Runes? *Ráða* has many meanings, but in relation to Runes it stands for reading. The word can be interpreted literally and metaphorically. It may refer to a text if the Runes are silently read. It may refer to a charm if the Runes are read out loud. It may refer to divination if the Runes are consulted as oracular symbols. *Ráða draum* means to explain a dream. One other meaning of *ráða* may shed light on the stanza. The word has connotations of employing or commanding. This makes sense if the powers of the Runes are considered to be numinous beings.

FAA

Do you know how to colour the Runes? The word *fáa* means to stain and was already used in runic context by the Ancient Germanic people. Traditionally, the Runes were stained with sacrificial blood. As a substitute, red ochre and spit will do. According to passages in *Havamal* and

Sigrdrifumal, the staining was accompanied by chanting. That is why this action means to load the Runes.

FREISTA

Do you know how to try the Runes? The verb *freista* means to try one's strength, which is why it is often translated as 'to test'. However, the verb usually implies a competitor. For example, it is said of horses running a race – to test their strength. But it is also used for mental competition. Of this *Vafthrudnismal* is an example. The poem describes how the giant Vafthrudnir is challenged by Odin on an intellectual level. First, Vafthrudnir asks Odin certain questions, which the Áss is able to answer. Then, Odin tests the knowledge of the giant. However, in *Voluspa* and *Hyndluljod* the word *freista* means to conjure up a *völva*; the scene compares to *Baldrs draumar*. Then, the *völur* are questioned as to their hidden knowledge. In the same way, the Runes are questioned as to their might and meaning. Metaphorically, this means contemplating their symbolism. What it would have meant traditionally is difficult to say. In an act of divination, it might have referred to the selecting of Runes, the drawn lots being the most powerful.

BIDJA

Do you know how to entreat the Runes? *Biðja* means to beseech. The original Germanic word means both to ask and to pray. The Rune Spirits are prayed to so that they will run your magical errands. The first Rune charm of *Havamal* (146) may well refer to this technique. The half line may also be translated as 'do you know how to pray to the Runes'.

BLOTA

Do you know how to worship the Runes? The verb *blóta* means to worship and refers to a sacrificial ceremony known as *blót*. In the ritual a dedicated animal is sacrificed, so that its blood and meat be offered to the spirits and the Gods. Afterwards, the meat was shared in celebration. The animal's blood was food for the Gods; according to Simek, *blóta* originally probably meant to strengthen. In return for the offerings, favours were asked (*biðja*) or expected, which was the whole point of sacrifice and worship. Likewise, the *blót* was especially carried out to hallow Runes for divination (*blótspánn*). The sacrificial blood (*hlaut*) was considered sacred and it made sacred what it was sprinkled on. The *blót* celebration was followed by a *symbel*. A more correct translation of the half line would be 'do you know how to worship the Runes with sacrifice'.

SENDA

Do you know how to send the Runes? The verb *senda* simply means to send. The act implies a target much as sending a message implies a person to receive it. The technique therefore includes the statement of intent. Runes are 'sent' on their way to fulfill a task. Whether the subtle information of the Runes was meant to be received by the Gods or by the target person is irrelevant. The verb's secondary meaning is to cast, to throw, which possibly refers to the heathen custom of offering at a lake. Votive offerings were cast into the water as if sending a message to the Gods.

SOA

Do you know how to sacrifice the Runes? *Sóa* means to sacrifice. Its secondary meaning is to waste, to destroy. The verb refers to a ritual in which a sacrificial animal, usually a boar, was bled. In other words, the blood was spilt. In this case, the sacrificial blood was called *dreyri*, indicating that the animal was not necessarily killed. The Old Norse phrase *dreyr-fáðr* means that something was ritually stained with blood. The word *dreyr-stafir* denotes blood stained Runes. The whole act was supposed to transfer the life force of the Godhead to whatever was stained. If, however, it was the Runes that were sacrificed, then their power was transferred. Indeed, it must refer to the act of scraping off a cut inscription. *Sigrdrifumal* contains a passage where it is said that 'all [the Runes] were scraped off that were written on'. This is done to 'send them on the wide ways'. The Runes are sent to the Elves, Aesir, Vanir and Mankind. Sagas, too, allude to this technique of activating magic. A real example of this would be the wooden stick of the Roskilde 6 ship. The stick shows how certain Runes of the inscription were scraped off to activate the amulet. The stick was fastened to the longship, reminiscent of spells of safeguarding a sailing ship (*brimrúnar*). The ritual to which *sóa* refers is also known from myth. Through this ritual both Kvasir and Heimdal were caused to be born. In the story of the Mead of Poetry, Kvasir is killed by two dwarves who collect his blood in three vessels. One of these vessels is Són. The very word is based on the verb *sóa*. It means reconciliation and refers to the truce between Aesir and Vanir. In general, a *són* might refer to a ritual of peace; it was performed as a part of a *blót*. In the poem *Voluspa hin skamma*, Heimdal is said to be born from 'mighty Earth, very cold Sea and *sónar-dreyri'*. Moreover, he was born on the foam of Nine Waves. Interestingly, this tale much resembles the birth of Pegasus and that of Aphrodite of Greek myth. When these myths are read closely, they state that blood, spit and sperm are equally sacred.

From the above, two things come to the fore. Firstly, the interpretation of the verbs makes it clear that the actions are interconnected. Secondly, the Runes must be regarded as numinous beings.

As to the interrelation of these eight actions, our basic assumption is that the Runes were made to consult the Gods. In order to do so, a *blót* was organized (6), which included a *són* (8). Runes were carved (1) and then stained with the sacrificial blood (3). Then, Runes were selected (4) and interpreted (2). Finally, the Runes were prayed to for help (5) and sent directly to the Gods (7). Hagiographies testify that animals were sacrificed in order to stain Runes.

As to regarding the Runes as spirits, verbs as *freista, biðja, blóta,* and *sóa* testify. Runes were prayed to and worshipped. They themselves were sacrificed and challenged. To a lesser degree, *ráða* and *senda* might imply the Runes as spirits as a direct object. Runes may have been commanded and may have been sent on errands. Even the verbs *rísta* and *fáa* may refer to spirits since idols of the Gods were carven and coloured.

Of these actions, reading, trying, entreating and sending seem to relate to applications. Carving and colouring relate to the making of Runes. Worshipping and sacrificing relate to ritual. Therefore, it seems that the actions are paired up, one verb relating to ritual and the other to magical applications. If this is true, then we are dealing with four different techniques.

The idea is supported by the next *Havamal* stanza. In *Havamal* 145, the verbs are read in pairs. To ask and to worship are related, and to send and to sacrifice are also connected. Imitating this model, the following verse is obtained:

> Better not to carve than to read too much
>
> Better not to stain than to challenge too much
>
> Better not to ask than to worship too much
>
> Better not to send than to sacrifice too much

The first technique consists of carving and reading the Runes. Both actions are evidently related. One can only read what has been written. More specifically, reading refers to consulting the Runes in divination.

The second technique consists of colouring and testing. It is known from other passages that the colouring was accompanied by chanting; the colouring also involved staining with blood. On the other hand, testing means that as much information as possible is distilled from the source you are addressing. The relationship is obscure. If referring to divination, *freista* would imply that a Rune reading would be tested by additional divinatory techniques. If independent of the first technique, *freista* would involve a more direct way of consulting the spirit world and be plain *seiðr*.

Biðja and *blóta* form another pair. In this context, *biðja* means to ask a favour. Through the Runes, help is sought from above. That is why a ritual is performed. It is meant to honour the Gods and would include prayer and libation. Essentially, the Rune in question is given energy, so that it can work your will.

Finally, sending and sacrificing form a last pair. Runes were destroyed in order to either release or neutralize their power. The technique reminds us of the lake offerings. Before shields and swords were 'sent' into the water they were first bent and broken and destroyed. As a matter of fact, they were also inscribed first.

On the whole, it seems that the first two techniques deal with divination and the last two deal with magic. Additionally, the stanza contains hints both to heathen worship and the construction of amulets.

From a modern occult perspective regarding Rune magic, the above might be summarized as follows. Firstly, the Runes are physically crafted. This is the first stage. Then, they are named, maybe through singing. That is the second stage. Then, they are loaded with power. This is done by staining the Runes. It implies feeding them and consists of the third stage. Then, a meditation follows, which is the fourth stage. Next, the Rune Spirits are prayed to. The intention is stated. This is the fifth stage. After that the Rune Spirits are worshipped with sacrifice, involving bodily fluids and alcoholic drinks. This is the sixth stage. Then, the Runes are sent away to do their job, which is the releasing of power. This is the seventh stage. Finally, the Runes are destroyed, because they no longer serve their purpose. This is the eighth stage. These procedures can be followed in making any talisman.

Ok Rúnar váru Nafn Gefit

In my opinion, a runic consecration ritual can be based on the Viking name-giving ceremony. After all, the naming of the Runes is a vital part in the process of their creation. Not very much is known about the ceremony, but a ritual can still be built reconstructed.

The name-giving ceremony of pagan Scandinavia consisted of a baptism, a name-giving and a blessing. Afterwards, the child was given a present. In the sagas, the ritual is often referred to as *sá var vatni ausinn ok nafn gefit*.

Correspondingly, the Runes may be 'sprinkled with water and named'. To each of the Runes, a separate ritual must be dedicated; and an appropriate gift given.

To carry out the consecration ritual, the Rune in question is laid on the altar. Take it up. Present it to the Gods. Then, hold it in the palm of your hand. With your power hand, draw the sign of the Hammer/Swastika, and say 'Thor, bless this Rune'. Then, sprinkle water over the Rune and say 'I give you the name [Rune name]'. Blow on the Rune or sing its name. Put it back. In completing the ritual, a drink should be offered to the Spirit of the Rune that has just been named. If more power is wanted, chant the Rune's name over the scored piece of wood for two weeks to three months before performing the name-giving ceremony.

Drawing down the Might

Traditionally, Runes were made of wood. However, bone would also have been common since the ceremony of making Runes involved animal sacrifice. The animal's bones were used to score the Runes on and the blood was used to bless them. Different material was also used. For ritual purposes, metal objects were inscribed. But more importantly, Runes were written in stone. Some of these monumental stones marked the presence of holy sites. Nonetheless, Runes can as easily be made of clay, paper or cardboard.

Wood as the original medium to carry runic power dictated the Rune staves to be cut in a certain way. This is why all the strokes are made from top to bottom. Runes that have two vertical lines will have those cut first; then the diagonals are added.

On a subtle level, energy follows thought. Accordingly, it becomes highly important how to trace the Runes to express an intention. The way a symbol is drawn establishes its energy flow. By definition, symbols form an abstract representation of a configuration of energy. It is therefore important to study the individual strokes of every Rune.

Runes as a Writing System

When a writing system is first adopted by a formerly illiterate society, there are no rules whatsoever in regards to orthography. Primitive epigraphy in about every ancient culture shows that writing initially is not bound to linear prescripts. It does not matter whether an inscription is written from left to right, vice versa, or both ways. In runic epigraphy, one inscription sometimes included both ways of writing.

Similarly, letter shapes were volatile according to the scribe's interpretation. As long as a letter resembled the archetypal form, everyone would be able to discern its meaning. This freedom allowed for evolution and poetic license.

Conditions such as these have their advantage. They are typical of non-linear thinking and reflect the active presence of the subconscious. By the same poetic state of mind, myths are understood. Through this state of mind, too, children perceive the world. When children first learn to write, their letter shapes often differ from convention. Their subconscious takes over. And so it was when writing was first introduced to civilization. Gradually, orthographic rules developed and were firmly applied. Consequently, writing increasingly became an expression of linear language instead of the more magically inclined and original non-linear expression of thought.

All in all, you should feel free to use the Runes in any visual way you like.

8
OBJECTS
OF
POWER

In reality, every Rune you craft becomes an amulet. But in specific, power objects can be made to serve one particular purpose. Just as with Runes, these are usually made of wood, although Western Mysteries magicians often prefer metal. Impromptu situations may call for paper. In spite of all this, power can as easily be downloaded in the imagination.

If power is stored in an object, it becomes spirit possessed. And henceforth the thing is called a power object, be this a wooden slip, a chair or a house. The technique primarily consists of inviting a spirit to inhabit the object. However, more elaborate methods and procedures do embellish this simple rite.

The runic design you use will represent the energies you want to attract. Sometimes one Rune suffices. Sometimes a combination is more apt, sometimes a drawing. Inspiration can be found in the Galdrabok manuscripts and the grimoires of old. A modern approach on sigil magick is found in Jan Fries' book *Visual Magick*.

If two or more Runes are combined into one symbol, this is a bind Rune. In Ancient Germanic inscriptions bind Runes occur to save space, yet in magical contexts they gather the powers of different Runes into one sigil. The Rune shapes naturally lend themselves to create monograms. Feel free to use runic variants or change the writing direction to arrive at an aesthetic whole.

Ristnar á Gulli

A talisman can be made according to the process described in *Havamal* 144. The procedure is quite straightforward and can be summarized as follows. The medium is first inscribed with the desired design. Then, it is loaded. Then, the intention is stated, and finally the magic is sent on its way.

The eight stage process:

1. draw the Rune
2. chant the Rune
3. colour the Rune
4. meditate on the purpose of the Rune
5. formulate the purpose of the Rune
6. feed the Rune
7. activate the Rune
8. use the Rune

Chanting the Rune has a twofold purpose. It helps you to make contact with the desired energy, but it also helps you to get into a trance. Colouring/staining the Rune gives life to the amulet. During the process of chanting and staining the Rune, see the life force in your amulet grow and glow before your mind's eye.

Once the amulet is alive, you tell it what to do. First of all, you visualize the desired effect, and then you formulate the intention verbally. Particularly make use of alliteration, that being typical of the Germanic magical mind. After that, you give it power to do its job. You feed it energy.

Eventually, the energies are sent on their ways. This can be done by saying a few words; again, use alliterative verse. But there are other techniques, too. The Runes can be scraped off. The amulet can be burned to release the power. Sometimes it is appropriate to bury it. At other times, the amulet is meant to be carried.

Paper

To create a paper power object, get a piece of paper the size of your choice, a pencil and a red marker. Instead of actually carving the Rune, the shape is drawn and coloured.

Light a candle if you like (*blóta*). Lift your hands and summon each of the Runes (*biðja*). Then, draw the circumference of the Rune or bind Rune on the paper slip (*rísta*). Now, hold out your arms horizontally besides you. Keep the palms cupped upwards and three times chant the Rune's name (*ráða*) steadily holding the power (*freista*). Finally, mark the paper Rune in red (*fáa*). Activate the amulet with a *galdr* verse that states your intention (*senda*). Use, carry, burn or bury the amulet as you see fit according to its purpose (*sóa*).

When a bind Rune is made, follow the same procedure for each of the Runes. Close with a *galdr* to tie up the whole.

A talisman like this is excellent to put a glass of water on, much like a beer mat. The drink then continually charges with the Rune's energy. Every time you drink the water, you take in its power. Similarly, a candle can be put on top of these paper amulets. As long as the candle burns, it feeds the wish expressed by the Rune. If you create a paper amulet for each of the Runes, this may build up a powerful magical circle.

Mind Matter

Although talismans are usually made of material media, the technique can be done wholly internally. It is perfectly acceptable to visualize the technique without being worried about any supply of blood.

Imagine sitting quietly in a natural environment with a knife in one hand and a piece of wood in the other. Carve the Runes in the wood. Next, imagine before your mind's eye how you cut your arm using the blood to stain the Rune. Chant the Rune in your mind and make the charm light up. Make it glow as bright as possible so that it fills your whole awareness. At a certain point when the power saturates the amulet glows brightly and the Rune is activated.

9

I AM ODIN

Literary and archaeological sources prove the magical use of Runes. In saga and myth, many instances are found, but the main Old Norse poems containing Rune lore are *Havamal*, *Sigrdrifumal* and *Rigsthula*. Besides them, a few traditional Rune Poems are known, such as the Old Norwegian, the Old Icelandic, the Old English Rune Poem and the Abecedarium. Runic inscriptions, too, help to gain a better understanding. And lastly, there is the Galdrabok tradition of medieval Scandinavia.

In particular, *Havamal*, *Sigrdrifumal*, *Rigsthula*, *Grogaldr* and *Ynglingasaga* make reference to Rune charm lists. For example, *Sigrdrifumal* mentions Victory-Runes for success, Brim-Runes for a safe journey, and Limb-Runes for healing. These charms are also mentioned in the other sources, albeit not by name. Set lists such as these would have been part of a mystery tradition.

Maybe certain Runes were associated with certain of these charms. However, I think, a more flexible approach would in fact be the case, because each of the Runes is able to work on different levels at the same time. All Runes possess a warding aspect. All Runes have a healing quality. Any Rune can be used in matters of love and relationships. All Runes have an aspect of self development, and so on.

Practical Magic

In order to make contact and harness the powers of the Runes, two main methods exist. These are meditation (*seiðr*) and ritual (*galdr*). From a modern perspective, both include visualization. Often, visualization in itself is not powerful enough, but it makes an excellent focus in practicing *seiðr* or *galdr*. Even then, it is not strictly necessary to focus on say the shape of the Rune. Sometimes it is better to visualize the concept of the Rune.

Seidr

Meditating on the Runes teaches to experience and recognize the energy of these symbols. It is worth the effort to devote a longer period of time contemplating the Runes.

In these exercises, the Runes are only the object of focus. In reality, the mind is trained. And regular practice will easily show after a short while. Meditation is of all means the best way through which humankind is able to tune in to the grandness of the universe.

You may want to close your eyes for meditation. Become aware of your body and focus on the breathing or heart beat. Inhale deeply. Exhale slowly. When you inhale, visualize breathing in Light. When you exhale, relax the mind. This will take you deeper.

Galdr

Rune magic centres on the voice. One of Odin's nicknames as a Rune Mage is Hroptr, which is based on a word meaning to shout. The word is cognate with Dutch *roepen*. In a similar fashion, the Old Norse word *galdr* literally means to yell. The word *runa* etymologically refers to whispering. Secrets were whispered.

Whenever you sing the Runes, the mind attempts to tune in to the vibes of that Rune's energies from a deep knowing. You sub/consciously contact the Rune and internally attune to its power. The *galdr*-technique includes magic spells, but then again, spells are sung as well. Galdr is mainly about intoning the Rune sounds.

The most straightforward way to chant the Runes is to sound their names in a long drawn-out breath. For instance 'iiingngnguuuzzz' or 'inguz inguz inguz'. By contrast, the vowel Runes can easily be sung in a full way by chanting the sound they represent. An Othila-*galdr* would sound like 'ooooo'.

Consonant Runes are combined with the five runic vowels. An example would be 'du-da-di-de-do'. The vowels may be sounded somewhat prolonged but will always follow the order of the Futhark alphabet.

The latter practice still echoes in a Belgian nursery rhyme that starts with *moe ma mi mee*. It also recalls the 'fee fi fo fum'-tune of the giant in the story of *Jack and the Beanstalk*, originally a British folktale. Moreover, many Scandinavian runic charms contain this kind of repetitive consonant-vowel magic, such as the Kragehul spear shaft.

Celtic and Greek tradition use vowels in particular to accompany ritual processions. In the same way, runic vowels may be chanted during ritual; Eihwaz included. Incidentally, the runic vowels correspond to the five sounds of Hebrew mysticism. At least some Kabbalistic traditions use the same order as is found in the runic alphabet. In his book on the *Sefer Yetzirah*, the Book of Creation, Kaplan explains the system of Rabbi Rokeach. The system is based on combining the five vowels with each of the Hebrew characters. The same is done in runic chanting. Rabbi Rokeach's exercise intends to create a golem. The five runic sounds also relate to the five Chinese elements. In the Hindu tradition and in Gnosticism, too, sound has a creative value. Correspondingly, the workings of a *galdr* are analogous to the mantras of Hindu tradition. Rune names and magical formulas are essentially seed mantras.

When chanting Runes, their sound causes a subtle change in the intangible world. The sound resonates with the energy field of a specific type. Not just the body, but the mind too resonates in harmony with the vibes of the song. This way, a *galdr* possesses an almost massaging effect. As a matter of fact, every spoken word has this deep, non-visible power. True *galdr* is speech. It is every word you say.

Connected with a specific intention, the technique of song becomes quite powerful. Simultaneously, the act of chanting or humming helps to deepen the mind and attune it to more subtle realities. On this, the might of a magician depends, who knows and wields the Laws of Cause and Effect reverberating throughout the various layers of reality.

What is more, a Rune chant has an immediate effect on the world. The subconscious recognizes the performance of a *galdr* as ritual behaviour and will respond accordingly with activating the appropriate archetypes. Purely psychologically you will evoke the personal and collective associations of the Rune chanted. It urgently bids the subconscious mind to haul the power out of the Rune's reservoir of energy.

I challenge You

Galdr constitutes one of the main charms of runic practice. That is why I encourage everyone to start practicing it. Choose a Rune that appeals to you; a Rune whose power you want to invite in your life, and start singing, humming, calling the Rune for a while.

Chant your *galdr* once or twice a day over a period of at least nine nights. Keep a diary of your practice. Every time you start chanting, begin by quietening the mind. Reserve a time and space to practice undisturbed for about fifteen minutes to half an hour.

Maybe you want to adopt a particular posture while you chant. The God postures can be assumed or the Rune shapes imitated. For instance, you can lift your arms towards the sky or keep your arms level to the floor having the palms of your hands facing either up or down.

Note your experiences in a diary. Check your dreams. Once you become more skilled, you will more easily trust the support of runic energies.

Εν Αρχη ην ο Λογος

When working with a charm, the words can be used over and over. Once an amulet is made or visualized, it can be recalled. Once more, visualize the Runes glowing brightly and repeat the charm. The words will work as a kind of mantra; one that gains more strength every time. Remember, every thought is a spell, every image a ritual.

Blithe Frey – free me from fear
Break the bonds – and bring me frith

10
ANCIENT GERMANIC MAGICAL FORMULAE

Under Roman influence, the Ancient Germanic people began to make amulets. These small discs of gold are now called bracteates. Amulets as these were made sacred, dedicated and given an intention through inscriptions, images and symbols. An inscription typically contained a reference to the item, a reference to the owner, bearer or maker, and a reference to the item's function.

A small corpus of formulaic words has been reconstructed. Exactly because these words of power were frequently used, they must have formed part of the magical tradition at that time. The core of these magical formulae and symbols are discussed below. The majority is divisible into two categories. One part centres on the mysteries of the sacred mead, wisdom and initiation. The other part centres on the Tree of Life.

ALU ᚨᛚᚢ

The most renowned Ancient Germanic magical formula is **alu**. It appears in many different contexts, with variations stretching from **al** to **lau**. Its Old Norse equivalent *öl* is repeatedly found in correlation to Rune magic. Alu is mainly a formula of blessing.

Old Norse *öl* means ale. However, *Alvissmal* sums up many synonyms for *öl*, among which ale, mead, *sumbl* and *veig*. The Old Norse *veig* is found in the name Gullveig, which makes her a personification of the sacred mead. The *symbel* was an Ancient Germanic social rite. A horn was passed around and oaths were sworn and the Gods honoured. The rite formed part of the *blót*.

In the main, Alu has a twofold ritual meaning. On the one hand it refers to an offering of beer. On the other hand, it refers to the mysteries of drinking the holy mead.

The Alu-formula is most frequently attested and appears on bracteates and other material, such as monoliths, where it refers to a ritual of dedication. An object or place was made sacred by an offer of mead or beer. According to MacLeod and Mees, the formula signifies a dedication, but has originally been borrowed from the Reitia cult of Northern Italy. Alu refers to a ritual libation or a ritual of thanksgiving associating the *alu*-formula with *biðja* and *blóta*. In inscriptions, **alu** always comes at the end.

In the Viking Age Edda, mead or beer is related to the passing of wisdom. The wisdom is always represented by the contents of a drinking horn and always presented by a Valkyrie. Specifically *Sigrdrifumal* describes how a Valkyrie, Sigrdrifa, offers the hero a hornful of mead. The drink is filled with power, spells, *galdr* and Runes. The text is a vestige of an initiation rite.

Later in the *Sigrdrifumal* poem, Sigrdrifa reveals another custom. Runes are engraved on certain objects and body parts to endow them with magical power, representing different skills. Afterwards, the symbols are shaven off and mixed in the mead. Thus the drink is charged with the power of the Runes and the respective objects. The poem explains that Sigrdrifa hallows the horn with Runes and that she sings incantations over it. Next, the loaded drink is offered to the Gods. This means that the twofold function of dedication and initiation is indeed one and the same metaphysical process.

In practical work, ALU can be sung at the end of a working to close a rite. In that respect it resembles chanting AUM at the end of Hindu mantras.

LATHU   ᛚᚨᚦᚢ

Like **alu, laþu** refers to a ceremony. The formula is sometimes abbreviated to **laþ** or **lþu**. Other variants are **laþo** and **laþodu**. It literally means invitation, request, and is cognate with Old Norse *löð*. Ritually, this formula is used to summon the Gods. Perhaps Lodurr is connected to this concept.

The morpheme *löd* is found in mythological names like Gunnlöd and Menglad. Both act as wisdom dispensing Valkyries. Gunnlöd presents Odin the mead of poetry, whereas *meng* in Menglad refers to the mixture of mead and magic. The formula therefore belongs to the mysteries of the holy mead. In relation to Alu, Lathu is used to open a ceremony. The forces, the Runes and the Gods are made welcome. Lathu comes in the beginning of a working, Alu comes at the end.

LAUKAZ   ᛚᚨᚢᚲᚨᛉ

In the Germanic culture, **laukaz** represents growth, virility, purification and detoxification. Inscriptions also show the shorter forms **lkaz, lkz, lk** or **lauz, luz, lz**. The word means leek or garlic, but *laukaz* can denote any plant of the *allium* family. Garlic literally means spear-leek. Leek or garlic was a symbol of royalty, authority and power. The plant was sacred to Thor.

Sometimes, the I-Rune is named after the Ancient Germanic formula Laukaz. Two main reasons lead to this interpretation. First of all, the formula **laukaz** occurs rather frequently on Ancient Germanic inscriptions. And secondly, the *Codex Leidensis* has *laukr* for the I-Rune.

The onion family has an overall warding and healing power. On the continent, garlic was used to protect against witchcraft and sorcery; three cloves were put in the cradles of new born babies. In Germany, stable doors were smeared with garlic on Walpurgis Night. Onion was even added to fodder to protect cattle against witchcraft. Sailors wore garlic to secure a safe journey, linking Laukaz to Laguz. According to Pliny the Elder, garlic dispels snakes, a belief that is also found in other cultures. Strings of garlic were hung or onions laid in the four corners of a room specifically to neutralize airborne disease. The occurrence of **laukaz** on bracteates suggests protective qualities seen in the leek-plant.

In the Northern tradition, garlic is specifically used against poison (*Sigrdrifumal* 8). Therefore, the *laukaz*-formula is associated with the mysteries of the holy mead. It cleansed the drink.

The concept is sometimes paired with Lina. A secondary formula of 'leek and linen' comes to the fore. This complex is concerned with fertility magic. 'Leek' is a kenning for sword and refers to men, while linen is associated with women. A kenning for woman is 'Goddess of linen'. In my opinion, this second formula is seen in the inscription from Telemark, Norway, which has five I-Runes followed by five i-Runes. These represent five times **Ii**, which might be short for **lina**. Another inscription, the Gjersvik knife, Norway, has ten I-Runes, possibly representing five times Lina and five times Laukaz. Similar 'love' inscriptions have been documented by Flowers. The original context of *lina laukaz* has been lost, although reference to it is made in the *Volsungasaga*.

GAUKAZ   ᚷᚨᚢᚲᚨᛉ

Gaukaz, sometimes **gakaz**, means cuckoo. The bird is typically associated with springtime. It is therefore a formula of new beginnings and growth. Folklore associates the cuckoo with money, prosperity and longevity. To Siberian shamans, the cuckoo heralds the awakening of nature, aiding the magician in raising power. In the same tradition, the bird is linked with the dead and life after death, much as the rooster in the Northern tradition. Possibly, Rune formulas such as **gagaga** and **kkkiiiikkk** refer to Gaukaz.

EHWAZ   ᛖᚺᚹᚨᛉ

The Rune name Ehwaz is sometimes found as a magical formula, sometimes abbreviated to **eh**. Runologists connect the occurrence to the frequent appearance of horses on bracteates. The shown horse is interpreted as Balder's mount. Ehwaz then becomes a formula of resurrection and healing.

Like the garlic plant, the horse too was a symbol of leadership and status. The animal is associated with the supreme deities Odin and Frey.

The use of this word on amulets and the survival of this word in the Old English Rune Poem is remarkable, since this word has not come down to us in any Germanic language save modern Icelandic, Old Norse *jór*. Other words for 'horse' were more readily used. This means that *ehwaz* had a special meaning. First of all, it is etymologically connected with the Celtic horse Goddess name Epona. Secondly, the term seems to be reserved for sacred horses. In all likelihood, it refers to the ability to communicate with the Gods.

OTA   ᛟᛏᚨ

The runic formula **ota** appears on a handful of Migration Period bracteates. Presumably, it means wealth, being related to Old Norse *auðr*. However, considering the individual Runes as concepts, the formula can be read as a powerful basis to strengthen one's *hamingja*, or soul power. Othila represents the physical body and the associated personality. This first Rune of three symbolizes your present physical incarnation. Teiwaz connects you with your soul and through the soul with your previous forms of existence. Invoking this Rune's power will enable you to tune in to these capabilities waiting deep within yourself. Skills may surface that you acquired in lives past. Ansuz, on the other hand, connects you with your ancestors. They will open to you their treasure house of talents slumbering deep within your DNA. Along the symbolism of these Runes, a short rite can be constructed to enjoy the full range of your *hamingja*. The triad Othila-Teiwaz-Ansuz creates a triangle of force.

FUTHARK   ᚠᚢᚦᚨᚱᚲ

The **futhark** represents the entire runic alphabet and thus symbolizes the sum total of laws and forces in the universe. It is because of its abstract quality that a system of symbols, like the Rune alphabet, becomes a trustworthy image of the universe. The mathematical configuration of the Futhark symbolizes perfection, as much macrocosmically as microcosmically.

In a mythological way, the Runes are the source on which the Tree of Life feeds. A harmony of powers plays through the complex of the Rune alphabet. As a whole, the Futhark is used as an amulet against evil (*Havamal* 137).

Yggdrasil

Tree symbols appear from the Scandinavian Bronze Age onwards. In inscriptions, these symbols appear at the end of a **futhark** formula. In later times, the walls inside a house were decorated with tree symbols, whereas real trees were planted outside when a child was born. Scandinavian villages each had their own sacred tree until very recent times.

The tree symbolizes life. One form looks like a bind Rune of Teiwaz Runes (**ttt**), the other consists of Algiz Runes (**zzz**). They stand for respectively the archetypal conifer and deciduous tree representing winter and summer. The Germanic people regarded the Tree of Life as a lime tree, an ash, a birch or a yew.

In Northern cosmology, all trees relate to Yggdrasil, the World Tree. Symbolically, Yggdrasil links all the different worlds with one another meaning that Yggdrasil connects the different layers of reality, the so-called dimensions. It is the only means by which one can travel from one layer of existence to the next. Yggdrasil is central to the cosmos (Eihwaz).

As a closing symbol, the tree stands for the synthesis of different powers. That is why Yggdrasil symbolizes unity, more precisely unity in multiplicity, a theme also found in the Assyrian Tree of Life.

Hrungnir's Heart

Hrungnir's Heart is a symbol that is made up of three I-Runes and is known in other traditions as *triskelion*. In the Northern tradition, the symbol is known as *trefot*. The symbol is found on the Snoldelev stone, where it is associated with the mysteries of the sacred mead. Another triskele symbol appears on the Snake-witch stone from Gotland, Sweden, where the symbol is made up of snakes.

It is easy to recognize the symbolism of all the existing symbols of trinity in this sigil. However, in my opinion, it seems more accurate to connect the three 'legs' only with the three cosmic wells of Northern mythology. The three I-Runes each stand for one of Yggdrasil's roots, at which end the wells are situated.

The symbol can be linked to the *antahkarana*, so that it refers to the integrated relationship of body and soul. And on a higher level, it attunes the soul to the cosmos. The symbol stands for a person's relationship to life, to creation and to the ageless wisdom. These three aspects correspond to the three cosmic wells of Urd, Hvergelmir and Mimir.

Mjollnir

The name of Thor's weapon is Mjollnir. In medieval Scandinavia, this weapon was conceived of as a hammer, though in earlier epochs it might have been an axe or a club. The weapon was originally portrayed as a swastika. In later times, a hammer-like form evolved.

The swastika symbol is continually present in Scandinavia since the beginning of the Bronze Age. Nonetheless, it is known as a universal symbol and makes its first appearance in Neolithic India. In ancient China, the glyph is associated with the magic square of Lo Shu. It is found in many cultures and time periods and the Sanskrit name *swastika* literally means wellbeing.

Principally, the swastika is a Sun glyph, known as *sólarhvél* in Old Norse. In the Hindu tradition, the Sun disc is called *cakra* and refers to Vishnu's weapon. The God corresponds to Thor. The swastika pertains in particular to the heart centre. As the weapon of Thor, it symbolizes protection and blessing.

Magically, the symbol is used to attract universal life energy. Readers familiar with Reiki will see a semblance with the CKR symbol. The swastika can be used with the same intention. Evidently, all Rune signs can be applied in the same way as Reiki symbols.

The practice of Reiki is entirely compatible with Rune magic. This straightforward modern Japanese system deals with life energy, healing and the use of symbols. The first aspect falls nothing short of being the basis of every magical work. Secondly, healing is one of many practical applications of magical powers; an objective that can be supported by the use of Runes. Lastly, Runes are symbols and can be taught and applied in the same way as any Reiki symbol.

The Pentagram

Although the pentagram may not be an indigenous Germanic symbol, it has unquestionably been incorporated in the runic system by our very ancestors. In German speaking parts of Europe, the symbol is known as *Drudenfuss* or *Drudenkreuz*, Dutch *drudenvoet*. The name derives from Old Norse *þrúðr*, which means strength. It is the name of Thor's daughter. Yet, a whole class of supernatural beings is called after her. These *Druden* were believed to be witches or elves and were famous for the Harz Mountains. In Dutch speaking parts of the Continent, the same symbol is frequently called *marevoet*, relating it to the Mare or Nightmare. The Mare was a much feared night demon comparable to the succubus. The pentagram was used to ward off nightmares.

It is interesting to note that the German word for nightmare is *Alpdrücken*. It means that the Mare is of an elfish nature. Presumably, the Thrudar are a subfamily of Dark Elves. The Mare was always regarded as a female spirit who attacked people in their sleep. Apart from the pentagram, mistletoe, too, was used to protect against it. That is why mistletoe is called *maretak* in Dutch. It also explains the awkward appearance of mistletoe in the tale of Balder's death. I therefore associate the pentagram with Frigg. She uses the symbol to protect Balder from nightmare and harm.

11

SUMMONING THE SEERESS

About the historical practice of Rune casting, there is only scanty information. Notwithstanding, the practice has become popular nowadays and has been fully integrated in the modern Northern mysteries.

Literary passages refer to the casting of lots, although these are almost never specified as Runes. Such passages are found in hagiographies (*Vita Ansgari*, *Vita Willibrordi*) and in accounts from Roman historians (*Germania*). Only once, lots are explicitly termed *rhuna*. This occurs in a letter by Fortunatus. Old Norse itself frequently uses another word than 'Rune' to denote lots which is *hlutr*. The word also denotes a talisman.

In modern times, Runes are used as an instrument of soothsaying. Because the signs are rich in symbolism, Runes naturally apply for this kind of work. Their meaning is very precise on the one hand and on the other hand quite flexible. They can be explained on many different levels, in the same way as dreams.

Various patterns of reading are suggested in the Northern tradition, grafted on the Tarot tradition. To begin with, any spread rooted in the Tarot tradition can be adopted in its entirety. It binds the new to the old, the unfamiliar to the known. However, within the Northern tradition specific spreads have developed as well. The basic spread uses three Runes. But often, nine Runes are drawn, because of the significance of this number in the Northern belief system. Thirdly, the arrangement of the Futhark itself also chances to be a nice basis for a lay-out. All these spreads offer a mental compass to consider a question. On top of that, they offer a handy procedure of interpretation.

Three Norns

The simplest method to cast the Runes is to draw three staves. The drawn lots are associated with the Norns and their particular influence. In myth, the three Goddesses of fate, Urd, Verdandi and Skuld, determine the lives of all beings. Urd represents the past. Verdandi represents the present. And Skuld represents the future. This last Rune gives a clue as to what power is gaining weight in your current life situation. It also shows a guiding influence.

Urd	Verdandi	Skuld
Past	*Present*	*Prospect*
passive power	active power	increasing power

A ritual of divination can be constructed along the lines of Systemic Constellations. The querent is guided by Frigg to the Well of Wyrd. There, three Norns reflect the person's different aspects, translated by the use of Runes.

Nine Worlds

Based on the number nine is the Nine World spread. As the magic square of Saturn represents the arrangement of the Nine Worlds, it can be used in divination too. Runes are interpreted according to the mythical world they appear in. On top of that, the diagram has the advantage of combining the threefold divisions of past, present and future with the subconscious mind, the waking conscious and the higher conscious. The upper realms may also denote external influences, such as the impact of friends and family upon your pattern of deciding.

	Past	**Present**	**Future**
anima	ᚢ	ᚺ	ᚨ
persona	ᚷ	ᚱ	ᚦ
shadow	ᚲ	ᚠ	ᚹ

Utgard – Present ᚠ

A Rune that makes its appearance in Muspelheim indicates your subconscious drive. Picking up on this force will feel like going with the flow. This Rune represents projects you would rather work on as well as desires, sometimes deep-rooted and suppressed, sometimes the recognized and more obvious ones.

Asgard – Past ᚢ

In the mists of Niflheim, ideas and insights are found that have been forced to the back of your mind meaning to meet them in due time. This world holds everything you put in the fridge. Niflheim signifies Asgard's past, which means that you keep certain wishes alive but are presently unable to work even in their general direction. It also stands for achievements.

Midgard – Future ᚦ

The Jotunheim position indicates the most likely physical outcome of the current amalgam of circumstances. As a realm symbolic of the unknown and the ungovernable, Jotunheim's Rune shows potential influences entering your life. There is nothing hard and fast in this world yet. Forces are forming, dangers are possible, but so are opportunities. Shape these powers like the Aesir created the Nine Worlds from the body of old Ymir.

Asgard – Future ᚨ

Asgard indicates what you are aiming for. It shows your real ambitions, and in combination with Jotunheim it shows whether these are backed by the Gods or not. It stands for the promise of fulfilling one's higher aspirations.

Midgard – Present   ᚱ

The centre square represents the current situation. The Rune that turns up in this square shows the energy to which the querent is subject. It may reveal a person's attitude towards his own question.

Utgard – Past   ᚲ

Svartalfheim indicates skills and insights gained in the past that are now assimilated in the mind. Past experiences may greatly support the querent in his undertakings. Runes therefore show psychological patterns, but also indicate what internal power the querent may wield in his existing quest.

Midgard – Past   ᚷ

Vanaheim gives a clear indication of the external or known past conditions that have led to or still have impact on the situation.

Utgard – Future   ᚦ

Muspelheim kindles the lights of Alfheim. This position indicates helpful powers or inner drives not yet realized but faintly sensed. The energy of this Rune is always a source of help. It can usually be found within, or through friends and family. The subconscious mind knows how to respond. Alfheim represents Utgard's future, that which will happen unconsciously.

Asgard – Present   ᚺ

Helheim represents the present from the Gods' perspective, hidden in the clouds of the subconscious. It shows how you can learn from the current situation. It stands for issues that need to be dealt with. Runes appearing in this position help to elucidate your karma.

Twenty-four Runes

A very elaborate method of casting Runes involves laying out all the staves in the order of the Futhark. Each drawn Rune is explained according to the symbolism of its position in the Futhark diagram. A Rune drawn in the position of Fehu shows a financial aspect. A Rune in the position of Uruz reveals health issues, and so on. The pattern is discussed by both Thorsson and Aswynn.

ᚠ	finance	ᚺ	deep-seated issues, enemies' attitude	ᛏ	constructive actions, direction
ᚢ	health	ᚾ	needs, disinclinations	ᛒ	others looking out for you
ᚦ	conflicts, obstacles, small fears	ᛁ	suppresions	ᛗ	relationship, work
ᚨ	expression, communication	ᛇ	improvement, hope	ᛘ	realization, social situation
ᚱ	deciding, advice	ᛁ	challenge	ᛚ	emotions, desires
ᚲ	skills, opportunities	ᛈ	fate	◇	what is promised
ᚷ	relations, talents	ᛦ	support, protection	ᛉ	ideals, how you feel
ᚹ	rune of luck, friends' attitude	ᛋ	higher will, goal	ᛗ	vision

Unloading the Lots in your Lap

Last but not least, according to the Ancient Germanic tradition, Runes were literally cast. Tacitus observes that lots were thrown on a white cloth. Then, the priest gazed up at the heavens and three Runes were selected.

The procedure has been preserved in the Old Norse phrase *bera hluti í skaut*, which means 'to throw lots onto a piece of cloth' (*hlutfall*). The word *skaut* is of interest. It literally denotes the hem of a robe or the corner of a square cloth. With time, the term began to refer to a person's lap, the word being cognate with German *Schoß* and Dutch *schoot*. Moreover, the English word 'lap' originally meant cloth. Possibly, the priest held up the front of his robe to collect the Runes. Or, he might have been sitting.

The method is therefore simple. You toss the Runes onto a cloth or in your lap; you pray to your Gods, pick three Runes and interpret them.

In modern practice, the technique of throwing Runes is somewhat different. Firstly, you decide the number of Runes you will read. Then, you toss them onto a cloth and interpret the Runes according to the way they fall. You may decide to read only those Runes that end up face-up, or you might interpret closed Runes as subconscious powers. If Runes end up in a pile, this is a 'crux'. It usually indicates difficulties. It definitely denotes a set of crucial circumstances.

A Reading

Before embarking on a Rune session, it is recommended to come in a good state of mind first. In this way, the Rune caster will more easily contact the divine powers, his intuition and clues from the subconscious mind.

There are primarily three aspects in reading any Rune. These are the Rune's symbolism, the querent's question and the pattern's position.

Always explain the Runes in a general way first, getting more specific as you go along. Use the three primary aspects of reading a Rune to get

```
        ┌─────────────────┐
        │                 │
        │    Question     │
        │                 │
        └─────────────────┘

              Rune
             Reading

┌───────────────┐                    ┌───────────────┐
│               │                    │               │
│  Symbolism    │                    │   Position    │
│               │                    │               │
└───────────────┘                    └───────────────┘
```

specific. The impact of a Rune mainly appears from its position. You also examine the Runes' mutual meanings and compatibility. Do their meanings complement or do they signify conflict?

Runes can always be examined from different angles. Accordingly, they may indicate external conditions as well as individuals or objects. At the same time, Runes convey a more abstract symbolism. They refer to forces and metaphors. Sometimes a Rune refers to the querent, his psychological or emotional condition. Sometimes it refers to others; their counsel and attitude. Sometimes Runes represent the interference of your own patterns of behaviour or outside stimuli, which has naught to do with the reading.

Lastly, Runes do not always particularly communicate a future event, but rather give advice or forewarnings.

```
┌─────────────────┐
│                 │
│    1/Other      │
│                 │
└─────────────────┘
```

Symbolism

```
┌─────────────────┐       ┌─────────────────┐
│   Situation/    │       │    Positive/    │
│    Object       │       │    Negative     │
└─────────────────┘       └─────────────────┘
```

When the Runes are cast, matters are slightly different. Runes are spread randomly in all directions. Attempt to find meaning in this.

If you habitually draw a daily Rune, you may want to keep a separate diary for that. At the end of each day you ponder on which events and conversations correspond to the selected Rune. Briefly jot them down. Soon enough you build up a rich source of associations. If you consult these on a regular basis, your understanding will steadily grow.

Poetry of the Soul

From a divinatory point of view, Runes have much in common with dream symbols. Quite easily, dream symbols are associated with runic concepts. Not only is their literal meaning considered, but their metaphorical meaning too. In this way, Fehu does not only appear as money in dreams, but also as teeth. Othila often manifests as a house. Pertho corresponds to books and computers. Cars, bikes and boats are Ehwaz, while trains and buses refer to

Raido. Raido particularly designates transport and roads. Eyes correspond to Laguz.

Dreamwork was practiced in the Viking Era (*draum-heill*) and was probably associated with Tyr. His name is hidden in the *draumstafur* sigil of Old Icelandic grimoires. However, much of what is found about dream lore in sagas is based on the common medieval dream books. It is true that Northern magicians also invoked Morpheus.

From experience, I know that dreams do foretell the future. I try not to anticipate on the prophetic meaning of dreams, because, as the oracle of Delphi shows, you never avoid your doom. Nonetheless, through regular dream analysis it is fairly easy to connect events in the waking world to dream imagery.

If a dream has prophetic value or refers to the past, it does not mean that it has no other symbolic layer. Dreams typically have a way of condensing many ideas into one image or scene. Freudians term this Verdichtung. The construction of bind Runes is similar to this. Different energies are bound in one sigil; as opposed to different layers of meaning in dreamscape and of single Runes.

Often, dreams reflect what others think of you. At night, when the surface mind goes to sleep, you experience the astral impressions of others upon you, created by their mental expression of you. One of the dream's functions is to assimilate telepathic communication and information that did not sink in during the day. This information is absorbed once you fall asleep.

Runes work in much the same way. When you regularly contemplate the Runes, their meaning will become apparent in divinatory exercises. This is why it is useful to pull a Rune every day. In the same way as with dreams, an event during the day will tie in with the drawn Rune. Sometimes nothing of notice will have happened, and in those cases it is not absolutely necessary to force an interpretation. Although I believe that a foretelling dream is produced every single night, events during the day do not always allow finding the connection. Life is full of dull days. For the mind to strongly refer back to a dream or Rune, one must rather experience something out of the ordinary. Although such experiences might still look ordinary, they will be meaningful to you. A meaningful event is easier to trace back to a Rune or a dream or an omen.

Auto-galdr

Consciously working with dreams means to consciously use the processes of dreaming. When a difficult matter is on your mind, especially emotionally, it will show in your dreams, which illustrates the power of the mind. And the best way to consciously develop this mental faculty latent in every one of us is through autosuggestion, which is a form of *galdr* because it makes use of a formula. Dreams are a rewarding medium to experiment with this technique, since results appear straightaway.

Autosuggestion is a technique by which the subconscious mind is addressed. This deeper part of the self thinks in puns and metaphors, archetypes and symbols, just like dreams do. In fact, it feels spoken to when addressed in a language that you do not (fully) understand, because it tries to make sense of it through the instinct of association. That is why Runes are most fit for this practice. The language that our deeper mind understands best is that of poetry and symbols.

In ancient times, mystics and priests addressed the Gods through a body of water, be it a lake, well or river. They symbolize the Underworld and correspond to the subconscious. What bubbles up from the deep is the answer to your input, taking on the form of ideas and insights. And that corresponds to the Runes that turn up in divination.

Water is strongly connected with divination and with the Underworld. In the saga of Thorstein Mansion-Might, a boy leaps into a river that leads him right into the Underworld. The myth of Holda is much the same. In a broader sense, the seeress of *Voluspa* is a Lady of the Water that is consulted for her wisdom. Through the water, she is connected with the cosmic wells of wisdom. Using Runes, tuning in to the energy of Laguz will help communicating with your own subconscious mind. The subconscious mind is susceptible to suggestions – with Laguz on your side all the more so.

Different ways of addressing your subconscious mind are possible. Ritual is one. A more straightforward way would be to write a letter in Runes addressed to either you or the Gods. If you know a second language, you may even want to write in that language. Wielding a second language will wake up a different part of your brain than your everyday awareness. Using a language that you are acquainted with but don't use as your native tongue can be like surfing the waves of your subconscious. The third option would be autosuggestion. This technique makes use of a spoken formula.

The art of autosuggestion easily fits in with the Northern mysteries system and a small rite may give body to the formula of suggestion. Begin the rite with a small invocation, address your patron deity. As it is your subconscious you are working with, you might as well plead directly with Hella. At the same time, use Laguz to make a connection with a deeper part of the mind. Then, count from Fehu to Dagaz. This will guide you somewhat deeper. After the mental preparation, say your *galdr* three times. The *galdr* formula consists of a verbal suggestion and the runic translation thereof. Have three Runes represent your wish. After each time you recite your mantra, chant those Runes. Afterwards, count back from Dagaz to Fehu and wake up with the formula taking root in the shadows of your mind. The sky is the limit!

12
THE
ART
OF
WISHING

The laws of magic apply to the Northern tradition as much as in any other tradition. Magic is wrought on the inner planes. It is given shape by energy. And energy is given direction by intention. Every working includes these necessary steps.

In order to enter the inner realms, it is customary to invoke the Gods and say a prayer. Conscious discarnate beings, such as the heathen Gods, dwell in the spiritual dimension and are interlinked with the grid of universal life energy. When contacted, these beings pull you deeper onto the inner planes. Praying also pulls the mind deeper because the mind is focused to a higher reality. On the other hand, simple meditation is at least as effective and does not initially rely on a response from a discarnate being.

As a rule, any magical act is programmed by an intention. Once the mental temple is entered and the link is established between the magician and the Gods, it is useful to state the intention verbally.

The body of the ritual then consists of giving form to the intention. Firstly, energy is raised to power the working. Then, it is shaped according to your wish. A specific power is summoned; and this force is asked to activate and guide the realization of your wish. Again, seeking out this specific power is done by a tuning in to the desired energy form within the sensed sphere of the inner dimensions. This time, you do not align with a God but with a

Rune. When you trace a Rune in the air in front of you, you draw the symbol into existence. If a living link exists between the individual and the Runes, results can be expected.

Look for the Rune you wish to work with. Make it real. Pretend carving the Rune into the thick of the Earth's etheric energy field. After the Rune is drawn you give it life by intoning its name. The symbol's name acts as a magical formula. This runic alignment seeks to contact the specialized power that the magician so sorely needs. The whole thing can be done entirely mentally, and meditating regularly will enhance your ability to mentally align.

Drawing a Rune is an act of creation by which you clone the essential power of the Rune from the higher realms into a denser sphere of energy. For this reason, it is useful to view the Runes as archetypal symbols. A drawn Rune is a temporary and single expression of the eternal, archetypal power that the symbol represents. Every time a Rune is used or expressed by an individual and underpinned with a certain intent, this information is recorded in Mimir's well. It adds to the entirety of that Rune's powers, according to the laws of evolution.

In short, a formal rite consists of an opening, a summoning and a releasing. To open a ritual, a candle is lit and a prayer said. Then, the intention is stated. Now, power is summoned, shaped and released.

It is customary to embellish the hardcore technique of ritual science with imagery from myth and mind. Images help to stay tuned subconsciously with a current of energy that you cannot as yet enter consciously. Yet repeated contact with the spirit world makes one realize that myth is based on a true reality. The Gods are not mere fantasy. Nor are they just metaphors. They are intelligent beings.

Colours, too, may support your magic. Usually, the Runes are visualized in a red hue. Blue more readily channels energy from the spiritual realms, whereas red draws from the Earth planes. Red and blue may also stand for the outer and inner world, yang and yin, fire and water or reason and intuition, and so forth. Instead of blue, golden light or white light can be visualized to activate the Rune. Gold represents the pure, uncorrupted energy of the material plane. It is connected with the Earth's etheric dimension. Brilliant white is more connected to the higher, subtler dimensions. Green has a healing quality and represents the worlds of nature.

Charms may be included in the ritual. They verbalize your intention, but they can also serve as a solemn affirmation at the end of a small rite. Charms lend themselves to formally close a session and release the power. Solemn words send the energy of your intention efficiently away. Words can also open a ritual. The remainder of the rite then becomes a charging of your worded intention.

The Northern tradition makes extensive use of poetry in magic and ceremony. Viking initiates depend heavily on the use of alliteration and kennings. The latter refers to poetic circumlocutions usually built on mythological lore. From the Viking Era, many different metres are known, two of which served mystical and occult purposes. These were *Fornyrdislag* and *Galdralag*.

And last but not least, most ritual work is performed alone, but rituals and ceremonies can always be performed with partner or in group. These three different modes all have their own dynamics and value, but solitary practice leads to the greatest development in the long run. Most rituals can be adapted to group work, keeping in mind that every person should actively participate.

Shaping your Wyrd

The power of the magician primarily lies in the ability to create his own circumstances. Although this can be done on a purely intuitive basis, a wish is usually expressed formally through ritual. The following working specifically invites the Norns, the Northern Goddesses of fate, to help you consciously create your own wyrd. The rite is inspired on hints from the works of Michael Bertiaux and David Beth and has been downloaded through magical means.

Have three candles and a bowl of water ready. The candles represent the Norns, Urd, Verdandi and Skuld. The water represents the Well of Wyrd. It is recommended to prepare a sigil for each of the Norns; the candles are placed on top. Appropriate colours can be taken into account.

The bowl of water occupies the centre. Urd is placed in the west, Verdandi in the north and Skuld in the east. You stand in the south, naked.

In this short rite, three Eddic stanzas are incorporated. They are *Voluspa* 20, *Fafnismal* 13 and *Helgakvida Hundingsbana in fyrri* 4.

Voluspa

Thence come maidens of much wisdom

Three out of that foam, under which the young fir stands

Urd is named one, another Verdandi

They score the lots – Skuld is the third

They lay the laws, they choose the lives

Of time's children, they tell örlög

Fafnismal

Of special birth many

I say – of the Norns are

They are not of the same family

Some are kin to the Aesir

Some are kin to the Elves

Some are daughters of Dvalin

Helgakvida Hundingsbana in fyrri

They in east and west the ends conceal

There has the hero his home in the centre

Ties the sister of Neri on northern ways

A bond that ever she bids to hold

1. Light the left candle and say: "Hail Urd of the Norns, I invite you. I welcome you to weave my wyrd."

2. Light the middle candle and say: "Hail Verdandi of the Norns, I invite you. I welcome you to weave my wyrd."

3. Light the right candle and say: "Hail Skuld of the Norns (Valkyries), I invite you. I welcome you to weave my wyrd."

4. Touch the bowl and say stanza 20 of *Voluspa*.

5. Recite stanza 13 of *Fafnismal*.

6. Drop wax of the left candle in your left palm and say: "Good Urd shaped good fate."

7. Drop wax of the right candle in your right palm and say: "Good Skuld will shape good fate."

8. Present the palms of your hands to the Norns and verbally formulate your intention.

9. Visualize your intention.

10. Rub your hands together above the bowl until some of the wax drops in the water and say: "Good Verdandi shapes good fate."

11. Bless your hands with the water from the bowl and say: "Good Norns, come in my hands. I make my own luck."

12. Bless your eyes with the water and say: "Good Norns, come in my eyes. I see every opportunity."

13. Bless the soles of your feet with the water and say: "Good Norns, come in my feet. I walk the path of success!"

14. Say: "Good Norns and those of noble birth shape good fate!"

15. Sprinkle water over the northern candle and say stanza 4 of *Helgakvida Hundingsbana in fyrri*.

16. Chant ALU three times to finish.

17. Leave an offering to the Norns.

The core of the ritual is the visualization. However, it should not be a mere imagining of events. Through the phrased intention emotions should be stirred and spirits roused. And these personal and impersonal contacts must form the basis of your working. Through these you draw in the powers that you want to attract in your life. It is even fitting to make fists in a gesture to mentally and emotionally draw those wanted circumstances into your field of experience. Power is drawn in.

The core of the working can be done at any time of day by just pulling in the powers you want to attract. The mantras of the hands, eyes and feet can also be said at any time. Sometimes, however, it will feel better to send out power in which case that is what should be done. In ritual, the creating of circumstances can be accompanied by gestures, mimicking the drawing or releasing of power.

A similar but more specific rite is available if a greater need is upon you. This working of 'turning your wyrd', be it a disease, discomfort or dissatisfaction, is built around the poem of *Grimnismal*. The magician sits between two candles every night for eight days contemplating the problem at hand. The ninth night the magician turns his wyrd by saying words from the poem. He will then have a cup of mead ready to drink at the end.

DDDD

The following is a small ritual for solitary use, although it can be expanded on to accommodate for more people. The ritual is based on the Lesser Banishing Ritual of Crowley's work but adapted to suit the Northern tradition. It is fundamentally an exercise of empowering and making yourself familiar with the spirit world. If performed regularly, it will increase your energy at the beginning of any magical operation, it will assimilate left-over energy at the end of a working, and it will generally act as a window to help you communicate with the world beyond matter.

1. Face north. Lift your arms and say: "Hail Aesir, hail Asynjur; hail Earth our Mother."
2. Then trace Dagaz in front of you and intone the name of Tyr. Turn to the east. Again trace Dagaz. Intone the name of Thor. Turn south, trace Dagaz

and intone "Frey". Turn west, trace Dagaz and intone "Odin".

3.   Then you turn north again. Stretch out your arms in the form of the cross. Say: "Before me Niflheim, behind me Muspelheim. Asgard on my left and Utgard on my right."

4.   Continue: "All the Runes ray around me. In Midgard rises Yggdrasil, ruled over by the Sun."

5.   Close with the opening prayer, and

6.   Chant ALU three times to finish.

Three of the four quarters are associated with the sacred wells of Northern mythology. In the north, Hvergelmir's well is situated, from which the Elivagar spring – the birth place of Tyr according to *Hymiskvida*. In Jotunheim, Mimir's Well is found. In the west, Urd's Well is situated, where the Aesir assemble. The southern quarter has no well, but balances the threefold element of Water by a source of warmth and light. This is the Sun's quarter.

The realm of Muspelheim can be substituted by the realm of Alfheim which also lies in the south and is related to the fiery world of Surt. Likewise, the deities can be replaced by the names of Goddesses, e.g. Hella, Idun, Freyja and Frigg. Colours can be added to liven up the rite.

In combination with intoning the God names, Runes can be used. Tyr combines with Teiwaz, Thor with Sowulo, Frey with Inguz and Odin with Ansuz. Yggdrasil is combined with the Rune Eihwaz. The Sun overhead is visualized as a whirling swastika. Using these Runes to accompany the ritual, you can establish a larger rite for group workings. In this rite, God postures should be adopted. I would also suggest incorporating the *Voluspa* stanzas on Yggdrasil.

> Once came three from that host
>
> They found ashore with little might
>
> An ash and an elm without doom

Breath gave Odin, soul gave Hoenir

Life gave Lodurr and good looks

The ash (elm) I know, his (her) name is Yggdrasil

Ever it stands green over Urd's Well

⋈	N	Niflheim	Elivagar	Tyr	↑	TEIWAZ	Hvergelmir
⋈	E	Utgard	Jotunheim	Thor	⟨	SOWULO	Mimir
⋈	S	Muspelheim	Alfheim	Frey	◇	INGUZ	Sunna
⋈	W	Asgard	Valhalla	Odin	ᚨ	ANSUZ	Urd

SSS SSS SSS

Inspired by Gundarsson's Rite of Wheels, I will next outline a meditation to work on the energy centres of the body. The exercise is dedicated to Heimdal, guardian of Bifrost and warder of the holy places of the Gods symbolizing chakras or point chauds (vé).

In this working, the Nine Worlds correspond to the seven major chakras, including the centre above the crown and the centre below the feet. The topmost centre is associated with the primordial world Muspelheim and is situated at the point above the head when reaching up with both hands. This centre symbolizes your higher self or soul. The bottommost centre is associated with Niflheim. In Daoist tradition, the centre at the soles of the feet is known as the 'bubbling well'. Muspelheim symbolizes the power of spirit whereas Niflheim identifies with the power of matter.

Aswynn associates the nine non-invertible Runes with the Nine Worlds. In accordance with her work, these worlds and Runes are best suited for the purpose of this rite. It is essentially a working of harmonizing, aligning and cultivating the body's energies. Through the invocations, the mind will more easily tune in to the subtle layers of reality. The rite is open to variations. The table is as follows:

9.	ᛊ	Higher self	Muspelheim	ᛞ	DAGAZ
8.	ᛊ	Crown centre	Ljosalfheim	ᛊ	SOWULO
7.	ᛊ	Third eye	Vanaheim	◇	INGUZ
6.	ᛊ	Throat centre	Asgard	ᚷ	GEBO
5.	ᛊ	Heart centre	Midgard	ᛃ	JERA
4.	ᛊ	Solar plexus	Jotunheim	ᛁ	ISA
3.	ᛊ	Sacred centre	Svartalfheim	ᛇ	EIHWAZ
2.	ᛊ	Root centre	Helheim	ᚺ	HAGALAZ
1.	ᛊ	Feet centre	Niflheim	ᚾ	NAUTHIZ

Have a cup of mead ready. After invoking a chakra/Rune, you will hallow your cup and say a formula of intent. The formulas are as follows:

- I drink from the well of Muspelheim. The power of Fire awakens within me.
- I drink from the well of Ljosalfheim. The power of the Elves awakens within me.
- I drink from the well of Vanaheim. The power of the Vanir awakens within me.
- I drink from the well of Asgard. The power of the Aesir awakens within me.
- I drink from the well of Midgard. The power of Men awakens within me.
- I drink from the well of Jotunheim. The power of the Giants awakens within me.
- I drink from the well of Svartalfheim. The power of the Dwarves awakens within me.
- I drink from the well of Helheim. The power of the Dead awakens within me.

- I drink from the well of Niflheim. The power of Water awakens within me.

1. Start with an opening prayer: "Heimdal. Warder of the Gods, watcher of the tree. Walk us over the bridge!"

2. Draw a large brilliantly white swastika in front of you, intoning the Rune name Sowulo.

3. Activate each of the chakras by visualizing a small white swastika at that centre and hissing the Sowulo-*galdr*, either sssss or susasiseso seeing the swastika spinning. Start at the topmost centre and end at the feet.

4. Name the Runes associated with the centres from bottom to top while focussing on each centre in turn.

5. Integrate the energies by intoning iiiii three times visualizing the Eihwaz Rune along your vertical axis connecting the nine steads of power.

6. Now, each of the chakras is addressed and its energy roused. You do this by intoning the Runes at each of the stations. Begin at the topmost centre. Focus with all your intent in that particular centre and chant the Rune's name three times. Then bless your cup, utter the appropriate formula and sip your mead. When you are ready, focus on the next chakra and do the same. Either the colour gold or the traditional chakra colour will do.

7. Once at the feet, the whole is integrated again. Chant "Eihwaz" three times.

8. Close with a prayer: "Heimdal. Warder of the Gods, watcher of the tree. Wield the shrines!"

9. Chant ALU three times to finish and reconnect.

13

DO

UT

DES

The whole idea of magic and divination is based on the premise that there exists a reality beyond ordinary perception. In the days of our ancestors, the demarcation line between the material and the invisible world did not exist. The mythical world was fully integrated in everyday life. Each family served their own local spirits.

To our ancestors, magic without the agency of the Gods was unthinkable. It is therefore fundamentally important to connect with the spirit world. And to bridge those worlds, mages use a medium.

Who

Northern myth is full of supernatural beings, some of which are close to mankind and some of which are not. But all of them are real and ready to be of assistance. Practitioners dedicate themselves to one of the Aesir or Vanir. However, interaction with all classes of spirits is encouraged.

By and large, our forebears venerated three classes of spirits: the Gods, the ancestors and the house wights. Of course, these three classes are related through time and space and no clear distinction is absolutely necessary. Furthermore, it somewhat depends on your upbringing who of these you contact more easily. For most people, however, interaction with wights is by far the commonest.

The word 'wight' is rooted in the verb to be. Although it can denote any living being, it relates in particular to nature spirits and spirits that associate with human society. The latter kind is who we invite in our home and care for as a member of family. In the English language, terms for these beings have been mainly adopted from the Celtic tradition. However, in Dutch speaking parts of Europe they are called *kabouter* and in German speaking parts *Kobold*; the English cognate would be 'goblin'. In Anglo-Saxon times, the English knew these house wights as *cofGodas* or 'cove Gods'. These words are all based on the Ancient Germanic word *kubo* which describes a small room. They correspond to the Roman *penates*.

What

The principal method of making contact with the spirits is to concentrate on their existence. The mind must be taken down to their level. Then, it is a matter of becoming aware of their presence. You can provoke a response from them, which can then be perceived and recognized as intelligent interaction. This method is technically called invocation, although it is only prayer.

Prayer and sacrifice are the two main ways of interacting with the spirit world; dreaming would be a third method. The habit of leaving milk or beer survives in contemporary Western European folktales. It was left outside to give thanks to the little people for the work they have done for the family the night before. Similarly, our forebears left out food and drink for the wights, albeit on a regular basis. In Scandinavia, drinks were offered on Thursdays, but it was especially done on holidays, such as Yule.

Central to the act of worship is the idea of giving. In the runic system, this notion is represented by the Rune Gebo. The Old Norse cognate *gefa* describes the act of sacrifice. Gebo symbolizes an offer but also implies 'return on investment'. Quite correctly, the mystery of this Rune suspends on entering into a contract with the Gods.

Where

Although the spirits are everywhere, a tangible focus makes it easier to contact them. To our ancestors, the immediate landscape served as the main focus for worship. People made their offerings especially to trees, stones and wells, and prayed there. This is where they met their Gods. But they also made altars and idols and amulets to serve as a civilized focus.

Having a material focus helps to make your prayers and offerings more meaningful and it helps to make your relationship with the wights and the spirit world more physical. On top of that, the object of focus will gradually accumulate power and magical substance. As a result, you will be better able to tune in to their world and to communicate with them. Touch the object when you say your prayers and leave your offerings.

An outdoor focus can consist of a pile of stones, which is called a *hörgr*. But an indoor focus can consist of an altar (*stalli*) and/or a wooden effigy (*blœti*). A portable focus would be a talisman (*hlutr*). Outdoor offerings mainly consist of bread and beer, whereas indoor offerings mostly consist of candles lit in the Gods' honour. Offerings made to trees and wells were directly related to the indwelling nature spirits, whereas those of a *hörgr* were invited to live there. In my opinion, the best way of giving home to the spirits is to build an outdoor *hörgr*.

The Vikings and Ancient Germanic people had different names for places of worship. Most of these were directly connected to the land and the veneration of both local spirits and national Gods. Places of worship included *lundr* '(sacred) grove', *haugr* '(sacred) mound', *fors* '(sacred) waterfall' and *hólmr* '(sacred) islet'. Man made sacred spaces included *hof* and *vé*. A Hof is a permanent place of worship and consists of a building. A Vé is a temporary place of worship and is made of a ring of hazel poles and rope to mark the area. According to Ancient Scandinavian mythographers, Midgard, Asgard and Utgard were considered sacred places institutionalized by the Gods. As such, Midgard is called *alda-vé*, Asgard is called *ginnunga-vé* and Utgard is called *út-vé*.

Blót

A ritual of worship traditionally consisted of a sacrificial meal. An animal was sacrificed and its blood used to bless the sacred space, the wooden effigies and the participants. The meat was boiled and shared among Gods and humans alike. Afterwards, a *symbel* was organized to praise the Gods and ancestors, and sacred oaths were sworn.

In myth, the ultimate sacrifice is an act of creation. According to Northern mythology, our very universe is the result of a sacrificial rite. Three priestly Gods, commanded by Odin, sacrificed the primal giant Ymir. His blood was spilled and filled Ginnungagap that was thus transformed into the sea. The giant was then dismantled and reconstructed as a physical reality. At the same time, the sacrificial blood of Ymir drowned as good as all of the giants, which, taken as a metaphor, reveals its sanctifying power.

To invite the Gods in a ritual setting, candles can be lit and the quarters called. In the Northern tradition, the spirits of the elements are well defined. Three of the elements are the sons of Fornjot, who himself might be the same as Ymir. They are Aegir, Logi and Kari. The fourth element is created by the priestly Gods from the blood of the giant and is identical with Earth herself, Jord.

N	**Jord**	Land	*Aesir*
E	**Kari**	Wind	*Jotnar*
S	**Logi**	Fire	*Alfar*
W	**Aegir**	Sea	*Vanir*

A central candle either invokes Ymir, Odin, Heimdal or a specific God that you want to speak to. A glass of water or a horn of mead is used to have the power of the Gods manifest. The mead is dedicated to Kvasir and drunk at the end.

Opening prayers to invite the Gods at your table have barely come down to us. But a formula is known from *Sigrdrifumal*, and, as a matter of fact, is paralleled in *Lokasenna* 11 and a stanza from *Örvar-Oddssaga* 29. Additionally, MacLeod and Mees indicate that spirits were welcomed with the usual greeting phrase *heil sé þu ok í hugum góðum* "hail to you and in good spirits", which is also found in *Hymiskvida* 11. Compare also *Vafthrudnismal* 4 and *Havamal* 156.

> Long live the Aesir
>
> Long live the Asynjur
>
> Long live the Earth – Mother of us all!
>
> Help me, Aesir
>
> Help me, Asynjur
>
> Regin of Creation - help your humble servant!
>
> Ginn-holy Gods - help your humble servant!

14
BEYOND
THE
RUNES

This weird collection of Ancient Germanic signs constitutes a mysterious language through which the magician interacts with the invisible side of reality. Instinctively, symbols are the means through which the human mind communicates with the subconscious/the collective consciousness. As a set of symbols, the Futhark maps the different energies and forces that play through that medium.

As bearers of universal powers, symbols serve as a point of contact between the physical and the immaterial realities. As guidelines towards spiritual development, they become rituals. As living symbols they find expression in the names of deities. Each Rune is indeed equal to a God. The sum of these powers forms the breathing complex that we call cosmos.

In the Northern tradition, the layers of reality are conceptualized as *örlög*. The morpheme *lögr* refers to 'layer; law', associated with Laguz. *Ör* means ancient and is associated with Uruz. Consequently, *örlög* stands for the sum total of cosmic laws expressing themselves in our tangible reality as a set of circumstances experienced as destiny. *Örlög* is the cosmic constitution. Our freedom within those bounds is *wyrd*.

In Northern mythology, the Norns preside over this concept of fate. Onto Yggdrasil's roots, they carve the Runes symbolizing inner and outer events. The well over which they rule marks the boundary with the invisible, eternal world. Functioning as a mirror, this leads one into the subtle realities of meditation. The myths speak about how the Norns rub layers of silt onto the World Tree. This mud comes from Urd's Well and feeds the cosmos. It brings life into the events created by the Norns.

From the foregoing principles it follows that the study of the Runes yields numerous insights into the laws of cause and effect, the layers of reality and the harmony of man and world. Exactly understanding and wielding these different layers of reality comprises the study of the occultist. 'Know thyself' and slowly but surely you will learn which patterns work when and why in your emotional as well as in your mental body as in every other aspect of your life – and what it means to be a human being.

Seek

And ye shall find

ALU ALU ALU

BIBLIOGRAPHY

- Paul L. Acker & Carolyne Larrington, *The Poetic Edda. Essays on old Norse Mythology*, Routledge, New York 2001.

- Freya Aswynn, *Northern Mysteries and Magick*, Llewellyn, St. Paul, Minnesota 2002.

- Alice A. Bailey, *Education in the New Age*, Lucis, New York 1954.

- Alice A. Bailey, *Esoteric Astrology*, Lucis, New York 1951.

- Alfred Bammesberger, *Old English Runes and their Continental Background*, Carl Winter Universitätsverlag, Heidelberg 1991.

- Paul C. Bauschatz, *The Well and the Tree*, The University of Massachusetts Press, Amherst 1982.

- Michael Bertiaux, *The Voudon Gnostic Workbook*, Red Wheel/Weiser, San Francisco 2007.

- David Beth, *Voudon Gnosis*, Fulgur, London 2010.

- Richard Ceasby & Gudbrand Vigfusson, *An Icelandic-English Dictionary*, Clarendon Press, Oxford 1874.

- Jean Chevalier & Alain Gheerbrant, *The Penguin Dictionary of Symbols*, Blackwell Publishers, London 1994.

- Marcel De Cleene & Marie Claire Lejeune, *Compendium of symbolic and ritual plants in Europe,* Man and Culture Publ., 2003 Ghent.

- Aleister Crowley, *Magick (ABA)*, Weiser Books, Boston, MA/York Beach ME 2002.

- Scott Cunningham, *Cunningham's encyclopedia of magical herbs*, Llewellyn, St. Paul 1998.

- Georges Dumézil, *Gods of the Ancient Northmen*, University of California Press, Berkely 1946.

- Ralph W.V. Elliot, *Runes*, Manchester University Press, Manchester 1971.

- Hilda Roderick Ellis-Davidson, *The Road to Hel*, Greenwood Press Reprint, 1968.

- Thor Ewing, *Gods and worshippers in the Viking and Germanic world*, The History Press, 2008.

- Stephen Flowers, *Runes and magic: magical formulaic elements in the Elder Runic tradition*, Peter Lang Publishing, New York 1987.

- Stephen Flowers, *Galdrabok, an Icelandic Grimoire*, Red Wheel/ Weiser, Maine 1989.

- Dion Fortune, *The Training & Work of an Initiate*, Weiser Books, Boston MA/York Beach, ME 2000.
- James George Frazer, *The Golden Bough*, Penguin Books, Middlesex 1996.
- Jan Fries, *Visual Magick. A Manual of Freestyle Shamanism*, Mandrake, Oxford, 1992.
- Jan Fries, *Helrunar. A Manual of Rune Magick*, Mandrake, Oxford 1993.
- Alan Gardiner, Egyptian Grammar: Being an Introduction to the Studies of Hieroglyphs, Oxford University Press, London 1957.
- Peter Gelling & Hilda Roderick Ellis-Davidson, *The Chariot of the Sun and Other Rites and Symbols of the Northern Bronze Age*, J.M. Dent and Sons, London 1969.
- Jane Gifford, *The Celtic Wisdom of Trees. Mysteries, Magic, and Medicine*, Godsfield Press, New Alresford 2000.
- Jacob Grimm, *Teutonic Mythology*, Vol. 1-4, Dover Publications, Dover 2004.
- Kveldulfr Gundarsson, *Teutonic Magic*, Thoth Publications, Loughborough 2007.
- Aryeh Kaplan, *Sefer Yetzirah. The Book of Creation: in theory and practice*, Weiser Books, York Beach, ME 1997.
- Gerhard Köbler, *Germanisches Wörterbuch*, Arbeiten zur Rechts- und Sprachwissenschaft Verlag, Giessen-Lahn 2003.
- Yves Kodratoff, *Nordic Magic Healing 1: Healing Galdr, Healing Runes*, Universal Publishers, 2003.
- Pim Van Lommel, *Consciousness beyond Life*, HarperCollins, 2010.
- Tineke Looijenga, *Runes around the North Sea and on the Continent AD. 150-700*, SSG Uitgeverij, Groningen 1997.
- James MacKillop, *Oxford Dictionary of Celtic Mythology*, Oxford University Press, Oxford 2004.
- Mindy MacLeod and Bernard Mees, *Runic Amulets and Magic Objects*, The Boydell Press, Woodbridge 2006.
- Sean Nowak, *Schrift auf den Goldbrakteaten der Völkerwanderungszeit*, Georg-August-Universität, Göttingen 2003.
- Kaedrich Olsen, *Runes for Transformation*, Weiser Books, San Francisco 2008.
- Vincent Ongkowidjojo, *Runen in de Noordse Traditie*, Uitgeverij Ankh-Hermes, Deventer 2007.

- Marcel Otten, *Edda*, Ambo, Amsterdam 1998.
- Nigel Pennick, *Practical Magic in the Northern Tradition*, Thoth Publications, 2005
- Nigel Pennick, *The Complete Illustrated Guide to Runes*, Element Books Ltd., Shaftesbury, Dorset 1999.
- Stephen Pollington, *Leechcraft*, Anglo-Saxon Book, Norfolk 2000.
- James Robinson, *The Lewis Chessmen*, The British Museum Press, London 2004.
- Rudolf Simek, *Dictionary of Northern Mythology*, D.S. Brewer, Cambridge 1993.
- Ch. Sutherland, *Transformed by the Light. Life after near-death experiences*, Bantam Books, Australia, London, New York, Toronto 1992.
- Edred Thorsson, *Futhark. A Handbook of Rune Magic*, Samuel Weiser, York Beach, Maine 1984.
- Edred Thorsson, *Runecaster's Handbook*, Weiser Books, York Beach, Maine 1999.
- P.A.F. Van Veen & Nicoline van der Sijs, *Etymologisch Woordenboek: de herkomst van onze woorden*, Van Dale Lexicografie, Utrecht 1997.
- Jan de Vries, *Edda*, Uitgeverij Ankh-Hermes, Deventer 1999.

Appendix:
Cabinet de Curiosités

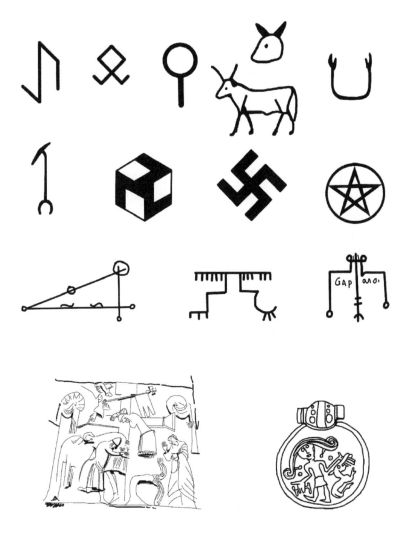

*From Top Left: Ull; Erda; Sól; Ka (k3); Was sceptre; Antahkarana; Swastika
(Fylfot); Pentagram; Draumstafur; Gapaldur; Gapandi; Externsteine, early 9th
century CE, Teutoberger Wald, Germany; Tyr and Fenrir, Trollhättan bracteates,
5th century CE, Sweden.*

From Top Left: Odin, Lindby, 7th century CE, Sweden; Thor, Eyrlandi, 10th century CE, Iceland; Wolf's Cross, 10th century CE, Iceland; Thor's Hammer, Rømersdal, Bornholm, 10th century CE, Denmark; Tyr, Zealand, 2nd century BCE, Denmark; Frey, Rällinge, 11th century CE, Sweden.

From Top left: Valkyrie, Birka, 10th century CE, Sweden; 1. Bishop piece, Lewis Chessmen, 12th century CE, Scotland; 2. Queen piece, Lewis chessmen, 12th century CE, Scotland; 3. King piece, Lewis Chessmen, 12th century CE, Scotland; Hrungnir's Heart; Snoldelev rune stone, 9th century CE, Denmark; Triskelion, Snake-witch stone, Gotland, 5th-6th century CE, Sweden; Rock carvings from Tanum and Bohuslän, Bronze Age, Sweden.

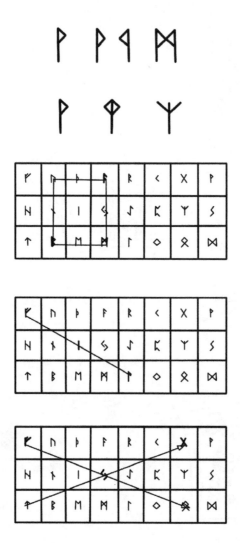

Starting at top: Mannaz; Maðr; Anthropogenesis; Ymir; Material gain & spiritual gain

Index

Symbols

Visual Magick: - A Manual of Freestyle Shamanism

By Jan Fries, ISBN 978-1869928-575 / £10.99/$20/ 196pp

A new edition of the highly acclaimed manual of freestyle shamanism, Suitable for all those inspired by such figures as Austin Spare and Aleister Crowley, and who feel the imperative to develop one's own unique magick way. Visual Magick aims to build vision, imagination, and creative magick. It shows how magicians, witches, artists and therapists can improve visionary abilities, enhance imagination, activate the inner senses, and discover new modes of Trance awareness. The emphasis is on direct experience and the reader is asked to think, act, do, and enjoy as s/he wills.

Seidways Shaking, Swaying & Serpent Mysteries

By Jan Fries ISBN 978-1869928-360/ £12.99/$23/ 350pp

The definative study of magical trance and possession techniques. The author is inspired by the Nordic tradition of Seidr, said to have been taught to the human race by Odin. The book provides an extensive survey of the manifestation of this powerful technique through several related magical traditions - shamanisn, mesmerism, draconian cults and the nightside of European paganism.

'Mandrake should be applauded for producing yet another fine book of modern magical practice and thought. Buy it, you won't be disappointed!' - Phil Hine

Bright From the Well By Dave Lee

ISBN **978-1869928-841 £11.99/paperback**

'Bright From the Well' consists of five stories plus five essays and a rune-poem. The stories revolve around themes from Norse myth - the marriage of Frey and Gerd, the story of how Gullveig-Heidh reveals her powers to the gods, a modern take on the social-origins myth Rig's Tale, Loki attending a pagan pub moot and the Ragnarok seen through the eyes of an ancient shaman. The essays include examination of the Norse creation or origins story, of the magician in or against the world and a chaoist's magical experiences looked at from the standpoint of Northern magic.'

Helrunar - a manual of rune magick

3rd enlarged edition By Jan Fries

ISBN 978-1869928-902 / £19.99 450pp / crown octavo / 200 illus

Contents: Meaning /Urda /Origins /Futhorc /Magical inscriptions / Memorial stones /Fascism / Titles / Cosmology / Nature / Qabala / Vision / Werdandi / Rune stance / Breathing/ Vowel song / Problems / Tune in / Health? / Divination / Alignments / Sigil sorcery / Seiðr and Seething / Energy /lda / Rune companion / Sources

'...*eminently practical and certainly breaks new ground.*' *- Professor Ronald Hutton (author Pagan Religions of the Ancient British Isles)*

CPSIA information can be obtained
at www.ICGtesting.com
Printed in the USA
FFHW01n1518060718
47268835-50178FF